# Scooped!

# Scooped

**Media Miss Real Story on Crime**

**While Chasing Sex, Sleaze, and Celebrities**

David J. Krajicek

columbia

university

press

**new york**

Columbia University Press
*Publishers Since 1893*
New York   Chichester, West Sussex
Copyright © 1998 David J. Krajicek
All rights reserved
Library of Congress Cataloging-in-Publication Data
Krajicek, David J.
    Scooped! : media miss real story on crime while
chasing sex, sleaze, and celebrities / David J. Krajicek.
        p.   cm.
    Includes index.
    ISBN 0–231–10292–5
    1. Crime and the press—United States.  2. Investigative
reporting—United States.   3. Television broadcasting of news—
United States. 4. Sensationalism in journalism—United States.
5. Sensationalism in television—United States. I. Title.
PN4888.C8K73   1998
070.4'49364973—dc21
                                            97–39538

∞

Casebound editions of Columbia University Press books are
printed on permanent and durable acid-free paper.
Printed in the United States of America
c 10 9 8 7 6 5 4 3 2 1

For Edward L. and Helen M. Krajicek

# contents

# preface

It first occurred to me that the conventions of journalism were changing about a decade ago as I watched a colleague hunched over a portable radio at his desk in the newsroom at the *New York Daily News*. He was listening to the Howard Stern show and gleefully scribbling notes for a story as Jessica Hahn giggled and gossiped about the ungodly sexual acts allegedly committed against her by a TV preacher—and about whether she had had a boob job.

This was a new type of news and a novel form of news-gathering. These and other tabloid techniques quickly became a trend that took root, and the American media seemed to transform itself into a hybridized combination of *Police Gazette* and *Confidential* magazine. *Scooped!* explores that transformation and its impact by looking into crime, crime news, and crime policy, three things that often have less to do with one another than one might expect.

Of course, a journalist undertakes a critical analysis of his own profession at some peril. Some of my best friends, as the saying goes, are journalists. Most of the reporters, editors, and producers who work in the trenches of the business are earnest people who are concerned about journalism's occupational drift. They are as confused as anyone about what has happened to the profession and why.

Journalism is like a team sport in many ways, and I have been proud and humbled to work beside a number of inspiring people over the years. A bit of each of them is in this book. In Omaha, I learned from Mike Hendricks, Jim Fogarty, Larry King, Marty Connolly, and Fred Thomas, among many others. I am especially grateful to Carl Keith, whose humor and human touch brought out the best in his people. In New York, I was lucky to work with Bill Boyle, Jerry Capeci, Larry Celona, Jim Duddy, Bill Farrell, Mary Ann Giordano, Vinnie Lee, Jim Peters, Patrice O'Shaughnessy, Gil Spencer, and Carlos Velez.

I wish to thank three particularly inspiring journalism teachers, Warren Francke, Bob Reilly, and Judy Serrin. Marian Davis and Ruth Schubert provided valuable research help on this book. Thanks also for the encouragement of my colleagues at Columbia University, especially Barbara Belford, Helen Benedict, Sam Freedman, Ken Goldstein, and Donald Shanor. Special thanks to Richard J. Blood, an uncompromising newspaperman, incisive editor, and obliging mentor. Most important, thanks to my wife, Julie, for her enduring support and discerning eye and ear.

# Scooped!

One night in the fall of 1988 I was roused from sleep at nearly midnight by a telephone call from an editor at the *New York Daily News,* where I worked as a crime reporter.

"Sorry to bother you at home," he began, "but there's a story in another paper about the Mike Tyson divorce, and I think we'll have to chase it. It's about Reuben Givens."

A couple of weeks earlier I had been summoned from my desk at One Police Plaza in lower Manhattan for a meeting at the newspaper's main office on East 42d Street. My boss told me that I had been selected to join a group of five or six reporters that would probe a pressing story: the breakup of the marriage of boxer Mike Tyson and actress Robin Givens. Our Tyson team, which also included Jack Newfield, the eminent investigative reporter, and Bill Gallo, the paper's revered sports cartoonist and resident boxing buff, set out to dig up dirt about the divorce.

With the help of Newfield's sources I had tracked down Reuben Givens, Robin's down-and-out father, in the Bronx. We were hoping that he could provide inside details on the breakup, but he turned out to be of little help. My photographer and I woke him at eleven one sunny September morning by banging on the door of the row house where he was staying in the Sound-view section. A former star athlete, Givens looked weak and thin, and he acknowledged that he had had bouts with booze and drugs. He told me that he had split with Robin's mother when their daughter was just five years old, and he said with unmistakable bitterness that he had not been a part of her life, particularly since she had found fame as a TV celebrity.

I spent about an hour with Givens. As I was leaving, he followed me outside and awkwardly asked whether I could pay him for his time. When I told him that I could not—that paying for information is a breach of journalism ethics—he rephrased his question: "Then can I borrow five bucks for some cigarettes?"

I wrote a four-hundred-word account of the interview and filed the story with the editor who woke me that night. The piece reported that Reuben Givens had been estranged from his daughter for some time. It gave his opinions about the marriage and breakup, but the story noted that he had not spoken with his daughter for more than a year and had never met Tyson. The story was to have been a small part of a package of Tyson-Givens stories that would be published after we had collected all the gossip.

But that changed when a competitor scooped me.

"I'm looking at a story that says Givens called his daughter last week and told her to dump Tyson," the editor told me. "It says he loves his daughter dearly, talks to her all the time, that they're real tight, that he's met Tyson many times and was not impressed by him."

"That's impossible," I said. "It contradicts everything he told me. Who's got it?"

There was a nervous titter on the other end of the line.

"Well," he said, "it's in the *Enquirer*."

"The *Philadelphia Inquirer?*" I asked.

"No," the editor said, "the *National Enquirer*."

As I sat there on the edge of my bed, I wondered whether I was dreaming. Had I really been called at home at midnight by an editor trying to gauge the veracity and accuracy of my reporting against that of the *National Enquirer?* Yes, I had been, and it turned out that the editor was ahead of his time in chasing a supermarket tabloid. Within a few years nearly everyone in journalism was doing it.

Flirting with insubordination, I told my boss that I was certain that my account of Givens's tenuous relationship with his daughter was dead-on accurate and that I would not stoop to pursue a paper filled with stories about Martians and two-headed cows. I told him it was obvious that one of two things had happened: either Givens had lied to make his story more valuable to a tabloid that paid for information, or the *Enquirer* had fabricated details to get more for its money. Unconvinced, the editor asked me to call Reuben Givens to confirm that what he had told me was true. When I refused, he asked for Givens's phone number, which, conveniently, I did not have. He settled for the Bronx address where Givens was staying.

I don't know whether he sent another reporter out into the night to find Reuben Givens. I do know that the *Enquirer*'s version of his comments did not make it into the *Daily News.* But neither did mine, except for a couple of quotations that an editor lifted from my story and added to another piece produced by our Tyson team. By default the *Enquirer*'s false account prevailed.

I seethed over this incident, but I chose not to confront the editor. We never once spoke about that late-night phone call, nor did he offer to explain why my Givens story was spiked. This is the nature of daily journalism. There is no time today to resolve yesterday's conflicts because we are consumed by the production of tomorrow's news. Over time, I convinced myself that it was better for my mental health and professional standing to pretend that the incident had not happened.

But I was wrong to acquiesce. That phone call has come to mind frequently in the decade since, each time I have heard or read a reference to *tabloidization,* or the burgeoning tabloid influence on mainstream American media—daily newspapers and local and network television news broadcasts. During the late 1980s trashy stories came to dominate our news and popular culture as newspapers and news broadcasts chased the *National Enquirer* and its broadcast playmate, tabloid television, to the margins of legitimacy. Initially, tabloidization occurred not by conscious decision but by collective assent among reporters and editors. It happened because too many journalists like me were willing to acquiesce to a series of breaches of the traditional values of our occupation.

When critics accuse journalists of sensationalism, the evidence they cite typically comes from the police and court beats, where lowest-common-denominator journalism has proliferated. Today, reading a newspaper or watching a news telecast can be like looking at the country's reflection in a fun-house mirror. The society we see presented in the news is a warped place, often morbid and alarming. An information conveyor heaped with deviance, death, moral decay, adulterous ministers, pedophilic priests, and Texas cheerleader moms feeds a gaping media maw that has proved to have an insatiable appetite for the violent, the sexy, and the salacious. These stories come to us daily in the form of crime news that shocks and titillates but rarely informs. Murder and sexual indiscretions are the marquee offenses, of course, and certain cases, generally based upon nubility or celebrity, are anointed for extravagant coverage.

Instead of rational tempered stories that might help explain the vexing crime problem in the United States, we find raw dispatches about the crime of the moment, the frightening—and often false—trend of the week, the prurient murder of the month, the sensational trial of the year. If local mayhem suffers a lull, our hometown media borrow violence from afar to flesh out the day's blood and gore—a murder-suicide in California, a factory murder in Michigan, a post office shooting in Texas. On many days the ubiquitous "national news" roundup in most newspapers might more accurately be titled CRIME ACROSS AMERICA. Newspapers laden with these stink-bomb stories are then lobbed onto America's front porches each day.

Most television news broadcasts carry a similar, numbing cavalcade of celebrity crime, warehouse fires, and body-bag video clips. TV news helicopters equipped with remote-control cameras buzz about the cities, shadowing freeway chases, sniffing out smoke, and beaming down images from yellow-taped crime scenes. For news consumers the United States must seem to be a hopelessly savage place that stands teetering on the lip of the Apocalypse.

The timing of this rebirth of crime sensationalism—it is not a new phenomenon—could not have been worse. The over-the-top coverage coincided precisely with an era in which Congress and legislatures across the country were making costly and misguided crime policy decisions. Often, the politicians based important policy decisions upon sensational crimes that clearly were ghastly aberrations, not trends. The United States will be paying for these decisions well into the next century, and the media must bear part of the blame. As journalists chased irrelevant, misleading, or trivial crime news, more important stories about crime and criminal justice policy were subjugated, vanquished. Collectively, journalists were scooped on the biggest crime story of the last quarter of this century by neglecting to adequately inform a puzzled public that our system of law enforcement and punishment, cobbled together with razor wire and prison bars, has been an expensive folly. As important, they neglected to hold policy makers and politicians accountable for their kindergarten criminology. This is not to say that reporters deserve particular blame—least of all the underpaid, overworked, often young reporters on the police and courts beats. Most of the time they simply follow the orders and directives of their bosses. No, the blame must be spread throughout the media institution, from the moguls, stockholders, owners, and publishers down through the editors, reporters, and photographers.

During the 1990s, while crime was declining steeply in the United States, the media presented an image of a crime bogeyman, a menace growing ever more malignant. Not coincidentally, during this same period the country was stricken by a moral panic, as sociologists call it, about crime. The nation galvanized against this menace because it aroused the basic instinct to keep one's family safe. Whether the hysteria was based upon fact or myth became irrelevant; the politicians wanted expedient answers, not information.

Police officers were rushed from one crisis to the next—crack cocaine or methamphetamines, the proliferation of handguns, gangs, career felons, carjackings, the ascending murder rate, youth violence. School programs, social policies, and societal values failed, so the problems landed in the law enforcement in-box. Police, judges, and prison wardens became toy soldiers in a war on crime fought by venal politicians who rattled plastic sabers and recited hollow platitudes and slogans: TAKE BACK THE STREETS, STOP THE VIOLENCE, JUST SAY NO, THREE STRIKES AND YOU'RE OUT.

The media covered this war in caricature, helping to perpetrate the myths. First, they provided crime-anxious Americans with excited accounts of a horrible crime—the kidnapping, sexual assault, and murder of a young girl, for example. Next, they presented tenuous evidence that the crime, however anomalous, could happen to each of us. Third, they sought out an accountable individual—a judge, a probation officer—and devised a snappy slogan to neatly package the problem: JUNK JUSTICE. Finally, the media served up images of scowling politicians and their podium thumping about the latest legislation that surely would stop such an atrocity from ever happening again: We're finally getting tough on crime. We're no longer coddling criminals. We're making America's streets safe again.

Since the mid-1970s most politicians across the country have bellowed *aye* with each new proposal for more arrests, more prisons, and longer sentences, votes that furnish the campaign-season illusion that officials are doing something about crime. Buried beneath the bombast is a catacomb filled with empirical evidence that the lock-'em-up delirium has been a costly flop. It fomented the public's confusion by sustaining a false hope that a law can prevent a crime from happening and that politicians can legislate civilized behavior. In most states sentences of mandatory lengths merely served to push dangerous felons out the back door of prisons to make room for the nonviolent offenders being bused to the front door. As a result of the unprecedented increase in the U.S. prison population since 1980, prison spending has increased exponentially, leaving less money for crime prevention, drug treatment, rehabilitation innovations, and reform initiatives to fix the broken policies.

Of course, "treatment" and "reform" are liberal notions that cannot be broached aloud as Democrats and Republicans parry over stewardship of the "crime issue." They hector one another tirelessly, debating the merits of bilge pumps versus buckets while the vessel is sinking. When the Democrats say "rehabilitation," the Republicans say "Willie Horton." They accept or reject ideas according to ideology, not merit. The politicians have borrowed precisely the insinuating rhetoric of Joseph McCarthy from another fabled era of moral panic in American history, tapping our primordial instincts to gather up sticks and stones against a menace, whether real or perceived. Our elected leaders quibble over who is "tough on crime," who is "soft on crime," and who "coddles criminals." In this milieu the mere suggestion that he or she is a crime wimp is enough to put a Horton-sized lump in any politician's throat. The exercise has not solved our crime problem, but it has served to heighten the citizenry's crime angst.

Too many journalists have covered this rhetorical wrestling match as a stenographer might. Too often, reporters quote the political screeds about crime word for word, without supplying analysis or context. This has happened for several reasons. The media have been caught up in the moral panic of the moment and the search for a burglar under every bed. Second, reporters, editors, and producers have become so consumed by the pursuit of sex, celebrity, and snuff journalism that they have been unable or unwilling to cover crime intelligently. Third, crime news is inexpensive to produce, and it attracts readers and viewers, financial motivations that please owners and stockholders as the media business grows ever more oriented toward the bottom line. Last, and perhaps most important, the newsroom culture holds crime reporting to a lower standard than that for other beats.

Not all crime news is poorly done, of course, and a moderate backlash has begun against the tabloid-style excesses. But it is not difficult to argue that the content of the daily newspaper and the story budgets of television news broadcasts offer irrefutable evidence that certain fundamental conventions of journalism have changed. A tabloid sensibility has clouded the judgment of editors and decision makers who drive an ignominious new journalism in which fame and infamy are synonyms. The media trifle away precious space and air time with gossipy, trivial crime stories that would not have been published as recently as the early 1980s. An arrest for a misdemeanor moment of sexual imprudence that should rate two lines of agate type at the back of a local newspaper now may inexplicably appear on the national news agenda. The celebrity screwups and sexy arrests that the news business traditionally regarded as one-day wonders can have legs that may well last a lifetime. And when they are not obsessing on a celebrity crime, the media tend to present crime as a series of atrocities—ice-pick murders, carjacking murders, triple murders, child murders, grandmother murders. They hold back nothing, and the sordid details might appear anywhere in the news media and popular culture.

On a typical day crime news accounts for one-third of the content of a daily newspaper and up to half of many local TV news broadcasts. Despite all this practice, the media present crime with a baffling lack of sophistication, in much the same manner that newspapers presented it 175 years ago when police and court reporting was introduced. Now as then the bulk of crime coverage amounts to drive-by journalism—a ton of anecdote and graphic detail about individual cases drawn from the police blotter but not an ounce of leavening context to help frame and explain crime. Too many of these stories begin and end with who did what to whom, embellished with the moans of a murder victim's mother or the sneer of an unrepentant killer in handcuffs.

These raw images of crime have become tattooed on the national psyche and now help frame our self-image. We have stared at the image in the funhouse mirror for so long that we have begun to believe that it is our true reflection. We have become what we behold, as Marshall McLuhan put it, and we are left with three options: to be disgusted, inured, or alarmed. The disgusted avert their eyes by turning the page, changing the channel. The inured manage to shrug at the unspeakable. The alarmed, the majority, brace for a carjacking with each dash to the 7-Eleven for a gallon of milk.

I have watched this degeneration with particular interest. For nearly fifteen years I threw bales on the conveyor line of police and court news. I entered my first police station carrying a press card in Council Bluffs, Iowa, in the fall of 1977, and my final stop as a newspaper reporter was New York City, where I spent five years at the *Daily News,* primarily as chief of the paper's bureau at police headquarters in Manhattan. My time at the *News* coincided precisely with the explosion of crack cocaine in the city. My colleagues and I spent a good deal of our time quantifying its effects in the late 1980s as the murder rate rose to a peak of nearly six per day. I was no Johnny Deadline; I did not break into a dogtrot at the smell of blood or the clanging of a fire bell. I tried to specialize in crime trend stories and policy pieces—thumbsuckers, as such stories sometimes are derisively called. But the violent times deemed that the murder of the day should take precedence, and I handled hundreds of murder stories during my years on the crime beat.

Of course, I understood when I walked in the door that the tabloid format—"Give me four hundred words on Armageddon"—was not necessarily conducive to deep-thought journalism. The *New York Daily News,* the country's largest daily newspaper for most of this century, is renowned for its streetsmart crime coverage, not navel-gazing stories about the sociology of crime. One author described the *News* as one of the "low, cheap tabloids that emphasized mob hits and dismemberments." It is true enough that we threw blanket coverage on mob hits. But a limb dismemberment wouldn't draw a double take at the *News,* although we did enjoy a good decapitation now and again.

I left daily newspapers as an act of self-preservation in 1990, a couple of years after my turn on the Tyson team. I had become convinced that I was not contributing to the greater good by writing daily accounts of the latest blows against humanity in New York City. I had grown cynical, abandoning the idealism that drew me to journalism, and I had lost my belief in the basic goodness of people. In my daily-journalism-induced myopia I believed that I was witnessing the decline of American civilization. I was shell shocked.

In the years since, I've thought about how the media portray crime. I can be accused of being a reconstructed police reporter, but I am not a snooty elitist. (My populist blue-collar credentials are impeccable; I come from a long line of bartenders and meat packers.) I still believe that the crime and court beats produce some glorious stories, some great parables. Crime news, and perhaps even a certain amount of sensationalism, have a place in the media. Death and lawlessness are news; when inhuman acts fail to raise a public eyebrow, the end of civilization will have begun. My complaint is crime news that crosses the line into necrophilia, crime news that wastes time and space on sex and celebrity trivia, and crime news that perpetrates myths by presenting chaotic, but ultimately false, images of crime.

This book is no apostasy of journalism. Quite the opposite—it is an attempt to deal frankly with a destructive trend in a profession about which I care deeply. *Scooped!* explores the dichotomies of criminal justice coverage and the public understanding of crime in several ways. It takes a look at coverage of violence and crime waves. It tracks the genesis of the new sensationalism, which bestowed undeserved legitimacy upon publications such as the *National Enquirer* and tabloid TV programs such as *A Current Affair*. It surveys the colorful if ignoble history of crime reporting. It looks inside the world of police reporting for clues to the newsroom culture. It reviews the development of U.S. criminal justice policy and the politicization of crime to try to explain how we ended up with so many prisoners and so much crime. Finally, it tracks the changes that have begun to take root in criminal justice reporting and, as any sincere criticism should, offers suggestions for improvement.

Journalism cannot solve the crime problem, of course. But it can provide the forum in which to explore solutions, and it certainly can encourage a more intelligent, honest, national conversation about crime. To begin with, we could use fewer crime *stories* and more crime *reporting*—news that informs rather than alarms.

# chapter 1

# Dancing with Trash in America the Violent

**H**ow do Americans form their opinions about crime? It seems to me there are three primary sources of information: personal anecdotes, the mass media, and politicians.

Everyone knows someone who has been a victim of a crime—a burglary, a car break-in, a mugging. These anecdotes have immense influence in the public's perception of crime. Journalists who have talked with readers and viewers about their impressions of crime are familiar with the phenomenon. "I know the politicians and police tell us the city is safer," they will say, "but we have more crime than ever in my neighborhood. Why, just last week . . ." And they will launch into a story about the crime-related misfortune of a friend, relative, or colleague. In particular, people are troubled by crime that is close to home, whether geographically or figuratively. Crimes that occur in homes or in automobiles—our sanctuaries—have a profound effect. Tales about the abduction of a child from her home or a carjacking in broad daylight may well have deeper resonance for most Americans than, say, a bombing at an office building. News coverage of individual crimes tends to reinforce those impressions, and drum thumping by politicians on the crime issue serves to further buttress public sentiment.

Of course, newspapers and magazines have published many stories that would appear to contradict those anecdotes: stories that quantify declines in crime. Even collectively, though, such stories amount to a dinghy bobbing in a roiling sea of information about crime. The subject of crime is everywhere, from talk radio to prime-time TV to rap videos to films.

If that is so, how can it be that Americans are so misinformed about crime? Why is it that we know so much about Joey Buttafuoco and so little about crucial crime issues? One reason is that the media have done an increasingly poor job of developing a balance between what is interesting and what is important. This is the difference between a crime story and crime coverage, between a story about yet another anecdotal crime and one that identifies the anecdote as either representative of a trend or representative of absolutely nothing.

Some journalists blame the public for the occupational tendency to choose the interesting over the important; people like to read sexy stories, they will argue, and the media merely give them what they demand. Ratings don't lie, they will say. Without question, the public bears significant blame if it protests the salacious diet coming from the mass media kitchen yet consumes it anyway. But it also is true that the public must eat what the media supply, even if the menu amounts to Twinkies, bon-bons, and offal. It is a chicken-and-egg question: Does society define news or does news define society? Do the media condition reality or reflect it? David Brinkley, the broadcast journalist, has dismissed the debate as specious with seven acute syllables: "News is what we say it is."

Journalists, in essence, ask for the public's confidence that they will make responsible decisions in setting the news agenda for the nation. Journalism has no formal process of accountability, as for medicine and law, and most members of the news profession blanch at that notion because accountability to a board or commission evokes outside interference, which equates with censorship. And everyone understands that the American media have a constitutional right to tell us what Joey Buttafuoco was wearing when most recently released from jail and to shout at him, "Hey, Joey, do you still love her?"

Of course, the same journalists who can summon tears as they expound upon the media's critical franchise as caretakers of basic American freedoms will smile and shrug when confronted with such mindless excess. Lighten up, they say. Buttafuoco is a goof, and everyone in the country knows that. We're having a national laugh at his expense.

But there is a cost. Although Buttafuoco-style crime stories have been omnipresent during the 1990s, the stories about criminal justice that attempt to make sense of the national crime morass have been difficult to find. Those that did make it into print or onto TV were overshadowed by the sheer volume of junk-food crime stories and coverage of violence. *Newsday,* the daily newspaper that covers Buttafuoco's home turf of Long Island, has mentioned Buttafuoco or Amy Fisher, his teenaged paramour, in more than a thousand stories. The tally of stories about the O. J. Simpson murder case, as counted by the Lexis/Nexis electronic clipping service using many large and medium-sized U.S. newspapers and magazines, topped 100,000 in 1996. Keep in mind that each space-wasting story that summarizes the plot of the latest porno flick starring John Bobbitt, the famous victim of a penile assault, bumps a more substantive story. Each hour squandered by the police reporter or courts reporter on a Heidi Fleiss stakeout leaves less time to pursue important crime news.

Newspapers and television news departments have finite news space, reporters, and budgets. The process of journalism—collecting, organizing, and disseminating information—happens in a series of priority-setting decisions about how to use those resources. Editors decide which stories are important, then deploy their reporters accordingly. They set priorities when they choose the stories that fill each page of the newspaper, each segment of a newscast. For regional, national, and international news, editors select from a vast menu that arrives either from staff reports (at the largest newspapers and television networks) or via subscription news services, such as the Associated Press and Reuters. They set priorities when they choose a royal scandal story over one about Russian politics, a triple murder in Maine over a story about the aging of America. The big papers typically expect the staff police reporter assigned to cover today's murder, celebrity arrest, or sexy crime to also pay careful attention to crime trends and to audit the effectiveness of police department strategies and initiatives. The smaller papers seldom make even a pretense of expecting their police reporters to do double duty. Likewise, the staff courts reporter, assigned to sit through today's love-triangle divorce trial, typically also is responsible for monitoring the courts and prisons. Sensationalism, or the dumbing down of crime coverage, to use the phrase favored by media critics, has occurred as editors and news directors modified these priorities to reflect a tabloid-style agenda.

Many journalists, including a number of my friends and colleagues on the crime beat, choose to deny the mutation that the business has undergone. Tabloid is nothing new, they say. They point out, correctly, that journalism has a history of the use of purple prose to describe lurid crimes, and human beings always have harbored a macabre curiosity about death and destruction.

It is true that sensationalized coverage of crime occupies a substantial wing in the museum of journalism history. But there are several important differences today, even discounting the notion of progressive evolution. First, the hot media—TV and radio—did not exist during the earlier high tides of sensationalism, so their effect upon U.S. society has vastly increased. For more than 150 years the tabloid sensibility has prevailed in down-market publications. But after an extended era of relatively sedate, serious journalism by the legitimate media, the tabloid scruffs have climbed down from the supermarket checkout racks and elbowed their way into the newsrooms of the country's most respected news organizations.

Thoughtless, salacious crime coverage now might turn up across the full breadth of the media, from the philistine to the highbrow. This dumbing down might be written off as a harmless diversion, as my friends and colleagues have suggested in the case of Buttafuoco. It might be, except that politicians and law enforcement authorities often set crime policy in response to the week's marquee story, whether it is about the latest drug scourge, a child abduction, a workplace murder, or a sex crime.

Consider the tone of what you read about crime in your newspaper and see on TV. As best suits the situation, the media will employ either a Pollyanna naïveté or the carnality of a road-worn biker. Stories are presented as morality plays, which allows the media to occupy the choir loft of moral sanctimony from which it can cheer the good guy and hiss the bad guy.

Journalists feigned shock, for example, that celebrities and wealthy people in Hollywood were paying to have sex with prostitutes employed by Heidi Fleiss, and her case therefore was deemed national news. If the story is sufficiently sexy but the principals fail to qualify as celebrities, the press repackages them. Thus our man Buttafuoco, an addle-brained statutory rapist with the morality of a billy goat, was recast as a dashing rapscallion in the press version of his life. His media nickname, the "Long Island Lothario," connotes a sly seducer, although it is abundantly clear that the impulses driving the man originate in his groin, not his brain. For most of the 1990s Buttafuoco's every belch appeared as news in hundreds of newspapers and on scores of television news programs in the United States, Canada, and abroad. The peer culture that powers the news business conferred upon Buttafuoco the status of media icon; he was covered relentlessly, beyond all reason. A Florida newspaper took to referring to him as "a pseudo-famous person." Yet the paper failed to acknowledge that it had helped make him pseudo-famous, that its stories gave him pseudo-fame. Even as a newspaper's editorial page carries a hand-wringing column about the country's keel-less morality, its news pages might well contain a story celebrating the latest stumble by our world-renowned body-and-paint man.

The mainstream media's "dance with trash," as newsman Bernard Kalb has called this sensibility, commenced in earnest in 1986 when Rupert Murdoch, the Australian-born media magnate, created *A Current Affair,* the syndicated broadcast magazine that functioned as a video version of one of Murdoch's racy London tabloids. The show, a tawdry cousin of the familiar network newsmagazine programs, relished sex and sleaze. It trafficked in stories about love triangles, sex fiends, and naughty girls in lacy pink knickers, the bacon and eggs of the British tabloid breakfast.

*A Current Affair* was a moneymaker, and copycat programs materialized. During the late 1980s and early 1990s these evening tabloid TV programs became agenda setters for both the print and broadcast media through their aggressive pursuit of crime stories with sultry themes. First, the national wire services would validate the tab TV scoops—an exclusive interview with Bible belle Jessica Hahn, let us say—by distributing details of the story to other news organizations. The legitimate media, which might shy from pursuing the gaudy story with their own reporters, would then practice peeping-tom journalism by reporting what *A Current Affair* had reported, even if the program had violated a basic professional tenet by buying its exclusive story.

Soon, prestigious news organizations found themselves taking a seat aboard a tabloid press bus that crisscrossed the country in search of any crime story that smelled of sleaze, celebrity, or sex: Hahn, William Kennedy Smith, the "Florida Nympho," the Menendez brothers, Joey Buttafuoco–Amy Fisher, Woody and Mia, Tonya Harding, Heidi Fleiss, the Bobbitts,

Michael Jackson. The O. J. Simpson murder case was the terminal destination on the tabloid trip.

At the same time, while too few in the media were paying careful attention, the U.S. criminal justice system was undergoing a fundamental transformation. The election of Ronald Reagan to the presidency in 1980 had announced a new era of crime policy in the United States. Crime had been on the national agenda since the law-and-order campaign of Barry Goldwater in 1964, but Reagan raised its profile, prompted by a growing intolerance among citizens for a problem that was widely regarded, even then, as out of control. Taking his cue from a prison-as-punishment movement that flowered in California in the mid-1970s, Reagan preached that criminals were being pampered by judges who subscribed to namby-pamby sociology theories. He said the country needed more arrests, tougher judges, more prisons, and longer sentences to battle the drug scourge and the crime menace. Politicians of both parties have assiduously followed that simple policy ever since. One leading theory about the country's enduring problem with violence holds that the United States is a victim of its own liberty: in essence, U.S. society is too free for its own good and insufficiently fearful of authority. Since Reagan, the popular legislative tack has been to curb those liberties through rules and hardware: prison walls, chain gangs, curfews, ankle bracelets. In exchange for the promise of increased safety, most Americans have gladly acceded to these initiatives.

The United States now has what Reagan wanted: more prisoners, more prisons, longer sentences. We also have only marginally less crime in most places—and more than ever in others. And we have an intensely heightened fear of crime across the country, and a drug supply that is as widely available—and less expensive—than it was in 1980. The primal solution to crime has filled our prisons several times over, and the increase in the inmate population will continue unimpeded into the twenty-first century. America is on its way to an inmate head count of two million, four times the 1980 prison and jail population. The annual cost of maintaining prisoners increased more than sixfold in sixteen years.

The prison population explosion began when the criminal justice system applied mass-arrest strategies and long mandatory sentences against drug offenders during the 1980s. During the 1990s law enforcement used those same tactics against sex offenders, violent felons, juveniles, and, under the popular three-strikes laws, repeat offenders. As a result, California's prison population, which stood at 125,000 in 1995 (up fivefold from 1980) is expected to reach 211,000 by century's end. Florida's inmate count, 68,000 in 1995, is projected to balloon to 150,000 by 2006. By then the national prison and jail population is likely to exceed three million.

It seems absurd that the United States should have a higher percentage of its residents imprisoned than any other industrialized nation—and it does—and yet be among the world's most violent countries—and it is. Those simple facts call into question the effectiveness of the incarceration vogue of the past two decades. In fact, politicians of both major parties understand that mass imprisonment and mandatory sentences have failed as policy, and they have said so, often on the same day that they voted to approve more of the same. Senator Orrin Hatch, the Utah Republican, said, "Mandatory minimums are a political response to violent crime. Let's be honest about it. It's awfully difficult for politicians to vote against them." George Mitchell, the former Democratic senator from Maine, conceded that any crime legislation put forth by Congress has "little to do with reducing crime and everything to do with increasing votes." This cynicism implies that the voting public is not savvy enough to understand that "tough on crime," in the campaign shorthand, does not necessarily mean effective against crime.

Of course, the politicians and the media understand that efficacy means nothing; image is everything. After Congress gave final approval to the 1994 crime bill, which included provisions for sixty new death penalties, allocations of $10 billion for prison construction, and nearly $9 billion to hire 100,000 police officers, Mitchell, then the Senate majority leader, called a victory press conference. "This could be one of those turning points in our history in terms of positions of the parties and their public perceptions," he said. "I think the time is over when in fact or in perception the Republicans are seen as the party that's tougher on crime. It's the Democrats." During debate in 1993 over a proposal to impose mandatory sentences against violent felons, Senator Joseph Biden Jr., the Delaware Democrat who chaired the Senate Judiciary Committee, said, "We are going to show everybody how tough we are. . . . But I want to advertise as the author of the underlying bill, as author of the death penalty amendment, they are not going to have much effect." The bills were approved nonetheless, he said, "because 80 percent of Congress and 85 percent of the public" still believed the "misinformed rhetoric about the effectiveness of mandatory sentences." Biden added, "If someone came to the Senate floor and said we should barbwire the ankles of anyone who jaywalks, I suspect it would pass."

Of course, many individuals, companies, and organizations have a financial investment in crime. And for most of them, more crime is better than less. The list includes police departments; police and prison unions; firms that operate prisons; the National Rifle Association; Gun Control, Inc.; weapons dealers; shooting ranges; criminal justice think tanks; universities with criminal justice programs; and companies that sell anticrime devices, such as the Club and legalized pepper spray. (A classified ad for one such outfit reads, "Crime is on the rise! Order your keychain pepper spray or stun gun and many other safety products.")

In an honest moment most politicians will concede that crime is big business. They might also tick off some basic myth-deflating truths about crime:

- Although the police will accept no blame when crime increases and take all the credit when it declines, many experts believe that police strategies and imprisonment have only a modest effect on the crime rate.
- Contrary to the prevailing dogma, the U.S. rates for most categories of crime (including burglary, robbery, rape, and larceny) generally reflect those of other Western nations. The United States *is* a world leader in violent crimes involving the use of guns, including murder, and that is ascribed to the wide availability of handguns here.
- The vast majority of crime is intraracial, and minorities have borne the disproportionate brunt of the violence. Minority neighborhoods tend to be the most poorly served by the police, even though they need help the most.
- Whether intentional or accidental, law enforcement strategies have singled out racial minorities for the harshest treatment.
- Those most informed about criminal justice—judges, lawyers, criminologists, and prison wardens—have pleaded with politicians for years to reform a system that has been cankered by sentencing mandates.

Many politicians prefer to ignore one other sequence of statistics. About thirty million felonies will be committed in the United States this year.

Nearly half the households in the nation will fall victim to a nonviolent property crime such as car theft, larceny, or burglary. Frustrated by a system that appears unable to prevent or solve lawlessness, half the victims won't bother to file a report with police. Police will solve fewer than two in ten property crimes. They will not catch the perpetrator in more than half of all violent crimes. One-third of the twenty-one thousand homicides will go unsolved. Only three million—10 percent of the thirty million felonies—will be solved by arrest. Based upon those numbers, many prominent criminal justice experts have concluded that law enforcement has no effect whatsoever on 90 percent of all crimes committed.

The public doesn't know these things because it has been inadequately informed by the media. And information has a profound effect upon public opinion. A number of surveys have shown that most Americans favor harsh sentences—until they are informed of the costs and offered alternatives. When given information and options that deflate the myths about crime and punishment, a majority favor alternatives to incarceration for nonviolent felons, such as the tens of thousands of drug offenders imprisoned across the country.

The three primary influences in the national crime consciousness—a horrible anecdote, blood lust in the mass media, and politicians on the stump—combined in 1993 and 1994 to create a tipping point in public opinion. The anecdote was the kidnapping, sexual assault, and strangulation murder of Polly Klaas, the twelve-year-old abducted from her home during a slumber party on October 1, 1993. The perpetrator, Richard Allen Davis, was a repeat offender, a poster boy for the three-strikes legislation that was just then on the national crime policy agenda. A proposal to mandate long prison terms for three-time offenders had languished in legislative committees, but the Klaas case gave the bill new political appeal, not only in California but in many other states, as politicians rushed to vote for the latest get-tough legislation. Three-strikes mandates stand as a memorial, Polly's Law.

But once again politicians had voted for legislation they knew was indefensible on many different levels, from the financial to the ideological. Senator Biden, the Delaware Democrat, called the three-strikes legislation "wacko." Such a law "promises what we know we cannot deliver," said Assemblyman Phil Isenberg, a Sacramento Democrat. "But we so fear the voters that we can't talk honestly and publicly" about rational approaches to crime policy.

Of course, the issue of recidivism among violent felons was not born with Richard Allen Davis or even Willie Horton, the repeat offender from Massachusetts who played the role of crime policy dupe in the 1988 presidential campaign. A fundamental evergreen story in criminal justice journalism explores how society can stop an ex-con from striking again. The simple truth is that it cannot—no matter how many new laws are passed, no matter how many new jail cells are built. Norval Morris, the University of Chicago law professor and commonsense commentator about crime, is perturbed by the myth of junk justice, or the blaming of judges and parole boards who free predatory felons, only to have them strike again. "Mistakes like Willie Horton are not a probability," Morris said. "They are a statistical certainty. Either we must kill them all or never release anyone from jail."

The murder of Polly Klaas was precisely the sort of crime likely to induce panic about safety. Stephen King couldn't create a more a terrifying plot. Davis pulled her from the sanctuary of her home in Petaluma, California, as her slumber-party companions watched in horror and as her mother slept in an adjacent room. Her disappearance was an ongoing national news story during the fall of 1993, and network newscasts frequently featured the case. Network exposure is one primary high-speed route that a crime story can take to transcend limited local interest. Crime already was high on the national agenda following the 1992 presidential campaign, during which both President George Bush and Bill Clinton exercised the issue on the hustings.

The network television coverage of the Klaas disappearance included the requisite protect-your-family sidebar features that purported to show how viewers might stop the same thing from happening in their homes, without adding the important context that the likelihood was minuscule. NBC included the story as part of a series entitled *Society Under Siege*.

Not surprisingly, the Klaas story had a huge influence on national opinions about crime, according to a number of surveys. Polly Klaas was abducted at the end of a year that featured both the World Trade Center bombing by international terrorists in New York City and the long standoff followed by a catastrophic fire at the Branch Davidian compound outside Waco, Texas. Those troubling events had been in the mass media for months, but they did not appear to cause overt concern among most Americans because they occurred at venues that most would consider remote and foreign. In June 1993, about four months before the Klaas kidnapping, an ABC News/Washington Post poll found just 5 percent of respondents named crime as America's most important problem.

But that summer the word *carjacking* had become fixed in the national crime lexicon as strong-arm car thefts spread from Detroit to the rest of the country. In the fall Polly Klaas and the murders of tourists along Florida interstate highways dominated national crime news. Both were stories about invasions of places where people spend most of their time: their homes and their cars. Then, on December 7 a crazed man named Colin Ferguson walked through a car on a commuter train on Long Island, systematically shooting everyone he could. He killed six and wounded nineteen others, and America was treated to another feast of frightening crime coverage.

By January 1994, after the intense focus on Ferguson, Klaas, and murders by highwaymen, 31 percent of respondents named crime as the nation's top problem—a sixfold increase from June 1993. Media Monitor, a watchdog group based in Washington, D.C., that tracks the content of network news broadcasts, would later report that the number of stories about crime on the nightly news programs of ABC, NBC, and CBS doubled during 1993, and coverage of homicides tripled. All this reporting about carnage had an unmentioned catch: national statistics showed that crime had *declined* during 1993.

The national newsmagazines helped drive the spike of crime anxiety a little deeper. *Time, Newsweek,* and *U.S. News & World Report,* along with their financial cousin, *BusinessWeek*—occupy a peculiar perch in the national news hierarchy. Typically, they cover the same news as the daily media, but they are forced to try to do so in a manner that makes readers believe they have a new and deeper perspective. In crime coverage, that often prompts the news-mags to attempt to divine trends that give broader scope to the crime anecdote of the week.

All the newsmagazines covered the Klaas story as it was developing. In the meantime they began doing big thinking about what the case meant. *Business-Week* checked in first, in its December 13, 1993, issue, with a cover story entitled THE ECONOMICS OF CRIME. Its subheadline read, RAMPANT CRIME IS COSTING AMERICA $425 MILLION A YEAR. WHAT CAN BE DONE? PLENTY. The cover illustration included a smoking bullet out of which flowed a rivulet of blood. Here is the first paragraph from the main story in *BusinessWeek's* crime-cost package:

Americans are scared. The fear of crime permeates their lives. They worry about being mugged or raped in a parking lot or while walking home from work. They're afraid of being robbed at a highway rest stop or having their children kidnapped at a suburban mall. They put bars on their windows, alarms in their cars, and cans of tear gas in their pockets. And they should be frightened. All told, some 14 million serious crimes were reported to the police last year, a number that surely understates the actual magnitude of America's No. 1 problem.

Next came *Newsweek*. The headline on its January 10, 1994, cover: GROWING UP SCARED: HOW OUR KIDS ARE ROBBED OF THEIR CHILDHOOD. Inside, under a headline that read, ROBBING OUR CHILDREN OF THEIR CHILDHOOD, the magazine's coverage began with this paragraph: "Something precious is gone from American culture: the chance of an innocent childhood protected from adult pressures and fears. Increasingly kids must fend for themselves in a world of violence, sexual enticements and economic anxiety." Other headlines in the *Newsweek* package included FEARS OF THE UNSPEAKABLE INVADE A TIDY PINK BEDROOM and NEVER TALK TO STRANGERS—AND WATCH OUT FOR NICE GUYS, TOO.

*U.S. News* took its turn a week later. The cover of the January 17, 1994, issue carried the headline THE TRUTH ABOUT VIOLENT CRIME: WHAT YOU REALLY HAVE TO FEAR. The cover was punctured by three bullet holes. Inside, the package began with the two-page headline VIOLENCE IN AMERICA and a subhead that began, A SCARY ORGY OF VIOLENT CRIME IS FUELING ANOTHER PUBLIC CALL TO ACTION.

Finally, *Time* magazine provided its take in the February 7, 1994, issue with a cover line that read, LOCK 'EM UP AND THROW AWAY THE KEY: OUTRAGE OVER CRIME HAS AMERICA TALKING TOUGH.

The national newsmagazine coverage of a crime wave served to confirm the false impressions presented in network television's coverage of crime. To be sure, each magazine mentioned in varying places of prominence that crime trends were down, not up, as some TV stories had. The basic formula in newsmag writing is to note near the beginning of the story that the crime anecdotes defy the facts, then to rush forward unfettered by those facts, unfurling a ribbon of one contradicting anecdote after another. Moreover, the bullet-riddled cover illustrations, blood-red headlines, and photographs of sneering killers in handcuffs and memorials to dead children simply overwhelmed the whiffs of truth and context.

In March 1994, a month after the last of the national newsmag cover stories about crime, the Times Mirror Center for the People and the Press conducted a poll that measured the public's fear of crime. Fifty percent of the respondents said they feared that they would be victims of crime, up from 36 percent in 1988. The survey also found the public embracing a hard line on crime, just as the *Time* cover story had reported. Seven in ten said they believed longer jail terms would reduce crime significantly. A majority favored more police officers and prison construction. Nearly one-third said crime was the nation's number one problem, and 77 percent said the country was losing ground against crime. Sixty-three percent of respondents said the media give an accurate picture of crime in the country, whereas 29 percent said they exaggerate the problem. Just under half said they trust the federal politicians to make policy decisions that will reduce crime.

In a delicious twist the national news media then began focusing increasing attention upon another crime trend story: having conditioned readers to cower in the corner with the shrill pitch of crime news, they periodically produced stories noting that Americans had a fear of crime that verged upon the irrational. The stories asked, in essence, "Where do people get these funny ideas?"

One player in the proliferation of the national crime anxiety was unmistakable: the local broadcast media. It may be impossible to overestimate the role that local TV news plays in disseminating misinformation about crime. Although the tabloid sensibility has had an influence on all forms of American journalism, the influence has been most acute in local TV.

In the 1970s television overtook newspapers as the medium that supplies the majority of Americans with their news. TV, therefore, must be a primary suspect in the perpetration of crime myths. That is no surprise to most broadcast journalists, who know all too well that many local TV news broadcasts have simply given up any pretense of substance in the ratings race. They present viewers with a community self-image straight out of *Road Warrior*—forty-five-second snippets of jackknifed tractor-trailers on the interstate, smoldering fires, flashing police lights. The newscast is likely to lead with a reporter stationed far afield for a "live" stand-up at a place "where just hours ago" some calamity has occurred. This is followed by video showing something burning/bloody/damaged, someone screaming, or someone crying.

Television news is based upon visual images, of course, and crime scenes provide the cliché settings for reporters in great-looking trench coats to stand and deliver. If the pictures aren't sufficiently terrifying, words can enhance them. In many cities TV journalists routinely refer to a house break-in as a "home invasion," and some newspapers have picked up the lingo.

The local gore is mixed with celebrity scandals, sleazy crime stories from afar, and fluff pieces that invariably focus upon the antics of animals. News from public meetings of the city council or the school board simply doesn't pass ratings muster unless a scuffle or shouting breaks out. In the popular parlance, news directors say that the tabloid TV influence has led many stations to introduce a "spicy meatball" story or two to each broadcast. But viewers today are being served so many meatballs that there's no space on the plate for spaghetti.

All journalists are thin skinned when it comes to criticism, but I have found broadcasters to be particularly defensive. First of all, many suffer from an inferiority complex because they know that print journalists, by and large, have little respect for their craft. Second, broadcasters argue that it is impossible for those of us outside their business to understand the difficulty of preparing stories that are image driven. Without good video there is no story, they will say. But that truism is being turned on its ear. Today the possession of any "hot" video means that there *will* be a story, whether it rates a story or not.

Many local broadcasts have been reduced to the daily news version of baseball's plays of the week. But instead of seeing baseball players crashing through the outfield fence or sprawling to make a catch, we see the most pathetic, most horrifying, or most anxiety-inducing video available that day, presented as news. Each day, news broadcasts across the country air video-driven stories that have little value to viewers. One day in early 1997 WNBC in New York aired, in sequence, video stories about flooding in Australia (so moderate that residents were shown standing on their porches watching the water go by), a train wreck in Kent, England (no fatalities), and snowfall of a mere twelve inches in, of all places, Aspen, Colorado. WWOR in New York, part of the Universal Paramount Network, is at least honest about its use of this material. It has aired a nightly newsreel that is introduced as "the most dramatic video from around the country." On a given night it might include a body-bag shot from Detroit, a car wreck on icy roads in Minneapolis, a grain silo fire in Kansas, or the ubiquitous West Coast freeway chase, shot from a helicopter. Since Los Angeles police were captured on videotape beating Rodney King in Los Angeles, video shot by amateurs has become another staple of TV news. On a day of flooding in the New York area in January 1996 WABC repeatedly promoted "home video" that it would air during its 6 P.M. newscast. It turned out to be a jerky ten-second snippet showing fast-moving water shot from behind trees at a distance of more than one hundred feet—tape that no self-respecting professional camera operator would dream of submitting.

For this book I screened scores of local newscasts, samples drawn from across the country. It will come as no surprise that the fare and faces are hardly distinguishable from one city to the next; only the skyline scene behind the anchors changes. On February 8, 1996, a routine news day, the 6 P.M. news broadcast on KNBC in Los Angeles began with a grave introduction by anchor Wendy Tokuda about a "breaking story." A police hazardous materials squad had been called to a federal building where a worker had gotten nauseous *the previous day*. Tokuda threw the story to Bob Pettie, the waxed-mustachioed pilot of "Chopper 4." The entire story amounted to a live picture taken from the helicopter hovering over the building. It showed a police vehicle parked out front. Pettie said nothing was known about the seriousness of the illness or whether police had found anything. The man was never named, and no sources were interviewed. This so-called breaking story, the top news of the day, was whirlybird journalism at its worst.

The second story was about a pool accident in which one child had drowned and another was seriously injured. Before throwing the story back to the studio, the reporter noted with a smile that the injured child's vital signs were stable and that he was expected to recover. "That's great news," said Tokuda. Next came a piece about a repeat sex offender who had been arrested again, and that was followed by a brief report from an appellate court of a case concerning proprietorship of twelve vials of the frozen sperm of a man who had killed himself. "We'll keep you posted," the reporter told viewers, as though promising a favor. The fifth story of the newscast concerned the arraignment of a Glendale man who had burned down his house, killing his wife and their two children, in retaliation for an affair she was having. Next came another brief report about a conviction in the 1993 shooting of a German tourist, and that was followed by a story about a construction worker who was hurt on the job. Following those seven stories from the police or courts beats, KNBC presented what Tokuda called a "photo-op" story about a set of quintuplets and a brief story about Hillary Clinton's visit to southern California that day. Before the first commercial Tokuda obliquely teased a story about some dogs that had miraculously tracked down their owners.

After the commercial the first story was a superficial account of the release of new maps that showed which neighborhoods might be most susceptible to earthquake damage. The piece featured a reporter sitting at a desk in the newsroom. He was looking at the maps. This was followed by a report about flooding in the Northwest, then the local weather.

The longest story of the newscast occupied the slot after the weather and before the second commercial: a two-minute piece from the courts beat about a group called Second Wives Strike Back, founded by women who challenged alimony and child support payments to first wives. Before the second commercial the station teased the dog story again. After the sports report the dog story finally aired. The second-longest story of the newscast, it concerned three dogs in suburban Los Angeles that had tracked their owner to a hospital three miles away. The piece included detailed interviews with the owners and several segments of video showing the dogs romping. When the reporter threw the story back to the studio, Tokuda was beside herself. She bounced in her chair and said, "That's amazing! Just amazing!"

Next came a tease for the 11 P.M. news. A video clip showed a man and a woman who seemed to be joined by some sort of rope. A voice-over said, "Why is this young woman tethered to an older man, and why won't a judge let her take the tether off? Details at eleven." After a commercial the newscast presented its final story: a British pig trained to herd sheep.

Unfortunately, KNBC's story budget for that broadcast was not unusual. Tens of millions of Americans see the same sort of stories on their local newscasts every day. I recounted summaries of the stories for Paul Klite, a Colorado physician, artist, and activist who founded Rocky Mountain Media Watch, a nonprofit watchdog organization based in Denver. Afterward, he said,

> That newscast sounds like a microcosm of what's wrong with local television. It's titillation, it's terrifying, it's a variety of high-emotional-content subject matter. The violence in the news produces terror and alienation. That increases the anxiety level of viewers. The cutesy stories about animals produce warm, cuddly feelings. Marketing experts call it arousal, and an aroused public

is ripe to accept the advertising around which this "news" is pack-
aged. We're biologically programmed to react to violence and
sex and flashing lights, and TV news broadcasts use those stimuli
over and over to hold an audience. It's great for advertising, but
it's terrible for democracy. While the newscast feeds viewers a
steady diet of emotion, important issues don't get covered because there is no time left.

Like others, Klite ascribes the trend to the tabloid influence. He notes that
scores of stations have adopted the bold graphics, thundering theme music,
and theatrical set designs of the tabloid programs. Many make wide use of
slow motion, grainy images, and black and white, evoking music videos. The
Fox affiliate in Chicago, WFLD, uses those devices as it presents viewers with
a numbing pastiche of celebrity tidbits, sex, and gore. During a sweeps period in 1995 the station featured a series entitled *Chicago Hookers: They'll Fulfill
Your Wildest Fantasies*. WFLD's anchor, Walter Jacobson, who earned a good
deal of respect in nearly three decades at WBBM in Chicago, now appears to
be playing a role. His newscast teases during evening programming are
extravagantly overwrought. He pitches forward in his chair, cranes toward
the camera, squints slightly, and reads his lines with an inappropriate seriousness: "Is Shannon Doherty about to become engaged? Will tonight be the
coldest night of the year? Watch the *News at Prime Time*."

In a famous aside a few years ago Jacobson cut to a commercial by saying,
"More mayhem ahead on Fox." Jacobson later said he was being ironic, but
his use of the word *mayhem* was appropriate. A 1995 survey of one hundred
local television broadcasts by Rocky Mountain Media Watch found that 42
percent of all news time was devoted to mayhem, defined as stories about
crime, disasters, and war.

A mayhem story was the lead item on fifty-seven of the one hundred
broadcasts; "if it bleeds, it leads," the famed broadcast aphorism, is more accurate than ever. KNBC, whose L.A. newscast we considered earlier, devoted 85 percent of its news time to mayhem, second in the country only to the
88 percent at WLKY in Louisville. Other stations that dedicated more than
three-quarters of news time to crime, disasters, and war included KFOR in
Oklahoma City, WGNX in Atlanta, and WCCO in Minneapolis. Interestingly
enough, WCCO in January 1994 became the first station to swear off body-
count journalism in favor of "family-sensitive" stories. (News directors at

WCCO and WLKY say the mayhem ratings lack context because they fail to show the specific stories aired—a police shooting, for example.) Stations with low mayhem ratings tended to be in smaller cities. They included KEZI in Eugene, Oregon; KELO in Sioux Falls, South Dakota; WICD in Champaign, Illinois, and KECI in Missoula, Montana. KTCA, a public television station in Minneapolis, was the only station among the one hundred surveyed that aired no mayhem stories on the evening of the survey.

Eighty-six stations ran stories about O. J. Simpson that night. WSVN, the tabloid-style Miami station owned by Edmund N. Ansin's Sunbeam Television, devoted its first six minutes and twenty seconds to the Simpson case. The stations surveyed aired 224 stories about celebrities, including Simpson. Klite said affiliates of Rupert Murdoch's Fox network featured twice as much celebrity coverage as affiliates of the other major networks. Fluff stories ate up 39 percent of the total news times. The topics included a Miss Bald USA contest, Meat Loaf Week in Florida, women who smoke cigars, and a beauty contest for cows. One station advised its viewers that only ninety-five shopping days were left until Christmas. Five stations carried a story about a kangaroo that fell into a swimming pool in Australia, and twenty-seven stations used video from Mississippi about the birth of a fourteen-pound boy, nicknamed "Sumo Baby."

Klite concluded in the survey summary,

> What we witness in this survey is not a pretty or healthy picture. News content is unbalanced and unhealthy. Tabloid tricks and tactics are seeping into every part of local TV newscasts. Anchors no longer even breathe between items; the next story is panting in the wings. "Jaws"-type music and three-dimensional zoom graphics are being utilized to heighten the hypnotic trance of viewers. As Aldous Huxley noted, every propagandist has his art department. Even re-enactments have become acceptable fare on news shows.

The survey results were not an aberration. The mayhem rating from another 1995 Rocky Mountain Media Watch survey was more than 50 percent. Eighty-six percent of the stations aired stories about the Simpson case, devoting an average of about eighty seconds but ranging up to three minutes and thirty seconds on WJLA in Washington, D.C. The Simpson "news" of the day—a prosecution allegation that he was a chronic spouse abuser—was described in the news reports as "shocking," "startling," and "devastating." On KSL in Salt Lake City, an anchor said, honestly enough, "We'll explore the most sensational elements."

Rational ideas about criminal justice have no chance of being heard over the crime cacophony on TV. As Brad Edmonton wrote in *American Demographics* magazine,

> It's hard to think clearly about crime. When terrorists bomb the World Trade Center, serial killers murder children, and a gunman shoots up a railroad car full of commuters—all in the space of a few months—who can stay rational? Americans couldn't ignore these horrible tragedies last year, especially because television news programs wouldn't let them go.
>
> The three major networks ran 1,700 news stories about crime in 1993, or five a night. That was double the number of stories in 1992, according to the Center for Media and Public Affairs in Washington, D.C. The figure does not include coverage of crime on local news shows, crime-obsessed tabloid tv shows, crime re-enactment shows, and fictional crime dramas. Sitting in their secure living rooms, Americans bathed in this televised crime wave until they were overwhelmed by anger and fear.

As the Simpson case and Klite's surveys showed, the blood lust in television news got worse, if anything, after Edmonton wrote those words in 1994. And as the American media enter their post-OJ phase, what might be next? "How about topless anchors?" Klite asked me, without a smile. "That would draw an audience, don't you think?"

# chapter 2

# Rupert, Amy, and OJ

**A**t this point, it might be difficult for many of us to remember what American journalism was like before O. J. Simpson, Amy Fisher, and Rupert Murdoch. I don't mean to hark back to some Currier and Ives era in our media history during which news coverage was smarter than it is today. Quite the contrary, as we shall see. Modern journalism does a better job of covering most subjects, by and large. The best journalism probably is better than ever. Business and economic reporting are more sophisticated. Coverage of various specialty beats, from education to religion, seems more informed now. Political reporting has been on the media's examination table for at least thirty years; it has been poked, prodded, and diagnosed in scores of books, and the criticism has prompted many changes, if not improvements.

And then there are the foundling beats—crime, sex cases, and celebrities. This journalism is as bad as it has ever been, if not worse. A look back a few years might help demonstrate that these beats have been locked in the orphanage during an era of media enlightenment.

On April 19, 1992, the producers of Fox Television's *A Current Affair* distributed an electronic press release via the PR Newswire Association that hyped a segment scheduled to air on the program the next day. The headline read, 'PRINCE EDWARD IS GAY,' ALLEGES INTERNATIONAL HIGH-SOCIETY COLUMNIST ON NATIONWIDE TELECAST OF 'A CURRENT AFFAIR,' MONDAY, APRIL 20. The text explained that the columnist, Taki Theodoracopoulos, offered the revelation about the British prince "during an in-depth probe by 'A Current Affair' senior correspondent Steve Dunleavy into the scandals rocking the Queen of England and the royal family." The press release offered Dunleavy's office phone number for those seeking further details.

No self-respecting U.S. newspaper would have pursued such a sleazy story on its own. Yet, based upon nothing more than Dunleavy's press release, the *Orlando Sentinel, Boston Globe, Atlanta Journal and Constitution, Newsday,* and many other papers published stories that Monday about Prince Edward's reputed sexuality. The headline in the Orlando paper read simply, PRINCE EDWARD IS GAY, 'A CURRENT AFFAIR' REPORTS. *Newsday* played it cute: PRINCE ALBERT'S IN A CAN; IS EDWARD IN THE CLOSET? Both papers quoted Dunleavy as saying, "We don't 'out' anyone. We're just reporting on allegations."

This was classic peeping-tom journalism, an essential element of the new tabloidization of the mainstream media. Reporters and editors who would not vouch for the veracity of material published in or aired by another legitimate news organization suddenly found themselves willing to peek through the windows of a tabloid TV show and tell readers and viewers all about what they saw. Even though it was widely known that the programs operated free of many of the traditional ethical constraints of journalism, newspapers willingly imperiled their reputations by tacitly vouching for *A Current Affair,* which used scripted questions and answers on some interviews, staged reenactments, and paid for information. The program's version of truth had all the integrity of an infomercial, and every journalist in the country knew that.

Newspapers were willing to risk their most valuable asset—the public's trust and confidence—because the material the tabloid program provided was so titillating that they could not resist. The cross-pollination served both parties. As in the Prince Edward story, *A Current Affair* distributed press releases, videotapes, and photographs to the newspapers, wire services, and TV news programs before a story was to air, and the media touted the upcoming show. The payoff to a paper was a sexy picture or a sexy little story that might increase readership or get a rise out of a bored editor. For the tab TV programs the payoff was increased viewership, ratings, and therefore advertising revenues. Everyone won—except the befuddled news consumer. Jerry Nachman, the broadcast journalist and former editor of the tabloid *New York Post,* said the tabloids began to serve as the crash-test dummies of journalism on sleazy stories. "Slam into the wall, come out undead and have everyone say, 'Oh, good, let's pile on.'"

Dick Morris, a consultant to President Clinton, was the dummy in a prominent tabloid crash in 1996. Morris, reputed to be a family man, had been consorting not so secretively with a Washington hooker. A reporter from the *Star,* a weekly supermarket tabloid, nailed him. Just as *A Current Affair* peddled its Prince Edward story in advance of the air date to try to bump the ratings, the *Star* trolled its story in the legitimate press to increase sales. Most of them bit, including *Newsday,* the Long Island daily that is tabloid in size (small, like a pill or "tab") if not in spirit and content. It has proved to have a particular affinity for stories lifted out of the tabloid trash. F. Gilman Spencer, my former boss at the rival *New York Daily News,* liked to call *Newsday* "a tabloid in a tutu," and it has exposed that schizophrenia by publishing as many tab knockoff stories as any paper in the United States, especially anything related to native Long Islanders Amy Fisher and Joey Buttafuoco. Here is an example from 1993. Again, Steve Dunleavy and *A Current Affair* played a role:

### Amy's Jail Pal Claims Romance
By Phil Mintz, STAFF WRITER

A 26-year-old Long Island woman has told a tabloid television show that she had a "romance" with Amy Fisher in the Nassau County jail and that she now wants to spend the rest of her life with Fisher.

The woman, Yvette Cole, who is to appear on "A Current Affair" (WNYW/Ch. 5) at 7 tonight, said she met Fisher in June and saw her again in the fall. Cole said she held hands with and kissed Fisher, but she "never went all the way."

The show's producers said they have a letter from Fisher to Cole, dated March 17, in which Fisher wrote, "You said you would never hurt me, sweets. I want to believe you because I care so deeply about you . . . You know how very much I love you."

Fisher's attorney, Eric Naiburg, called the allegation "the silliest thing in the world." He said that Fisher knew Cole while in jail, but they were only friends. "It wasn't a sexual relationship. It wasn't even close," he said.

Naiburg declined to comment on the authenticity of the letter, saying he hadn't seen Fisher yet to ask about it.

Fisher is serving a 5- to 15-year sentence in upstate Albion Correctional Facility for shooting Mary Jo Buttafuoco last May, but is currently in the Nassau County jail after testifying before a grand jury last week.

The grand jury is looking into allegations of statutory rape against Buttafuoco's husband, Joseph Buttafuoco, 37, who Fisher says had an affair with her when she was 16. Buttafuoco has repeatedly denied it.

According to "A Current Affair" reporter Steve Dunleavy, Cole said she had been a lesbian since she was 14 and was in jail on an assault charge when she met Fisher. She told Dunleavy that she never asked Fisher about her reported involvement with Buttafuoco, and that was one of the reasons why Fisher befriended her.

"We would hold hands. I would hug her romantically, kiss her . . . she would kiss me back," Cole told Dunleavy. "That's why I felt the love from her, you know, when I'd sit down and talk to her, the way she'd look at me, the way I'd look at her, we would hold each other. It was there."

According to the show, Fisher's letter was in turns sweet and angry. "Don't think you can . . . me over now, and come back later and say you're sorry and you love me, it won't work," she allegedly wrote.

Then, at another point in the letter: "You know, for the first time in my life I fell in love and there was no sex involved. It was so beautiful," she allegedly wrote. "At last you taught me that sex doesn't mean love and love doesn't have to include sex and I'm

not going to write to you anymore if you don't respond to this
letter, OK?"

In the interview, Cole said that she wants to live with Fisher
after she gets out of prison.

"It would be a beautiful life," Cole said.

Someone outside the media pack might wonder why a rational editor at a
good newspaper like *Newsday* would not step forward to question publication of such a story. But by the time that piece was published in 1993, the
legitimate press had run scores of stories copped from tabloid TV. The practice had become so prevalent that it was inconspicuous. And when it came
to Amy Fisher, what was the point of holding back sexy stories? She was a
crime celebrity not because she was a dangerous criminal, after all, but
because she was nubile, a novitiate prostitute still wearing high school plaids.
Sex was precisely the point, just as it has been in most of the sleazy crime
stories that have dominated the news since the mid-1980s.

The peer culture among journalists is as intense as that at any junior high
school. Reporters and editors look to one another—both colleagues and
competitors—to determine what is appropriate. If everyone else is doing it,
that serves as affirmation. Competition can be a warm womb on certain stories. Reporters who would feel silly shouting stupid questions at crime suspects if they were standing alone will lose all inhibitions while in a pack of
peers. Likewise, journalists find comfort in companionship when they are
forced to make decisions about whether to print a particular story—a story
about a prince's sexuality, Amy's alleged gal pal, or Richard Jewell, the Atlanta security guard who briefly became public enemy number one when the
FBI used the media in vetting him as a suspect in the fatal bombing at the
1996 Summer Olympics.

The freewheeling competition is exacerbated in the field of crime news
because that form of journalism is held to a lower standard than others.
Crime still is a *Front Page,* pay-your-dues beat covered largely by untrained
novices. Often, it is the only way for a recent college graduate to get a job
in journalism. Young reporters soon learn that the crime beat regularly gets
their stories on page one or the top of the newscast. In a year or two crime
reporters who have been sufficiently aggressive will make their bones and
move on to more prestigious beats. Perhaps half the news reporters in the
United States have spent some time on the crime beat when they were start-

ing out. "Ah," they will write wistfully in their memoirs, "I remember my first murder."

In the 1980s a new Pied Piper arrived in the follow-the-leader world of journalism. More than any other individual, Rupert Murdoch may be responsible for fomenting the tabloid sensibility that now pervades the U.S. media. Murdoch was born to journalism; his father, Keith, was a protégé of an early British press lord. Returning home to Australia from London after World War I, Keith Murdoch became a successful newspaper executive. In 1952 Rupert, twenty-one and just out of boarding school, inherited a newspaper in Adelaide when his father died prematurely. Murdoch soon began a media acquisitions binge that has not abated.

Today his conglomerate, the News Corporation, has tentacles reaching five continents and includes wide holdings in television, newspapers, magazines, and book publishing. It is difficult to find an example anywhere in the world where Murdoch's influence is regarded as positive. His broadcast enterprises abroad have been criticized for profit mongering and cultural imperialism. Murdoch's broadcast holdings include all or portions of networks in Australia, Europe, South America, Latin America, and Asia. He also owns about two dozen magazines, including *TV Guide* in the United States. His U.S. divisions include interests or outright ownership of Twentieth Century Fox film studio; Fox Video; HarperCollins, the huge book publisher; fX, a cable television network; the Fox Broadcasting Co., a 190-affiliate network; and TV stations in a dozen cities, including New York, Los Angeles, Chicago, and Washington, D.C.

Murdoch publishes more than half of all newspapers sold in his native Australia and about one-third of all newspapers sold in Britain, including the *Sunday News of the World* (parodied as *Screws of the World*), whose circulation of nearly five million makes it the largest-selling newspaper in the English language. He also publishes the *Sun,* circulation 4.2 million, which features a bare-breasted woman on page three each day, as well as the *Times of London,* a newspaper that once was widely respected but now includes a heavy dose of sex, scandal, and royal frivolity. Many blame him for the ruination of the British press, which functions at a full-throated screech. Ill with cancer, Dennis Potter, the British author of *Pennies from Heaven* and *The Singing Detective,* declared a few years ago that he had named his disease Rupert in honor of Murdoch's effect on the international media.

In 1983 Murdoch spent $500,000 for Hitler's "diaries." The *Sunday Times of London,* which Murdoch had purchased two years before, published excerpts. Even after the diaries were revealed to be a hoax, Murdoch bragged that he had lost no money because circulation went up and stayed up. When pressed about issues of decency and public trust, he let fly with a famously dismissive line to which every American should pay heed: "After all," Murdoch quipped to the press, "we are in the entertainment business."

In the United States, ironically enough, Murdoch is esteemed on talk radio as a conservative alternative to the liberal cabal of the mass media. His contributions to American popular culture include the TV shows *Married with Children* and *Melrose Place.* In 1995 he told the author and journalist Ken Auletta that he would not allow his thirteen-year-old child to watch *Melrose Place,* the racy teenybopera on his Fox network. Murdoch in recent years has attempted to shape his legacy by presenting himself as a reformer of politics and a supporter of unbiased news coverage. But legitimacy won't come easily. He has been a powerful force in establishing low common denominators in the mass media of each country he has conquered.

Murdoch became a media player in the United States in the early 1980s, when he began buying television stations and spoiling for a confrontation with the Big Three American networks, which he saw as vulnerable. He surrounded himself with a development team of tabloid acolytes from Australia and Great Britain, and in the mid-1980s they began to assemble programming for his nascent Fox network.

One of the first projects Murdoch approved for development was an edgy newsmagazine show with a title that he borrowed from a prime-time show in Australia: *A Current Affair.* The program's key staff members came from Australia as well. They included executive producer Peter Brennan, a newspaperman from Sydney who had worked in Australian television and as an editor on several Murdoch magazines; Ian Rae, former editor and publisher of the *Star,* a supermarket tabloid owned by Murdoch; and Steve Dunleavy, a former columnist at the *Star* and metropolitan editor of Murdoch's *New York Post,* which had become the most ribald daily newspaper in the United States under Murdoch's guiding hand.

Murdoch and his Australian minions understood that *A Current Affair* needed an American front man, so they summoned to New York a journeyman broadcaster named Maury Povich, who was working as news anchor at a Washington, D.C., television station that, providentially, Murdoch had recently purchased. The program debuted as a local broadcast on July 28,

1986, on Murdoch's WYNY (Channel 5) in New York City. For its first six weeks the thirty-minute program aired at 11:30 P.M., just before Fox's *The Late Show with Joan Rivers* and opposite *The Tonight Show* on NBC and ABC's *Nightline*—an appropriate position, considering its curious mix of news and entertainment. Each edition of *A Current Affair* featured three stories, often presented with quirky incongruity: a piece on the dangers of radon gas might be followed by an interview with Joey Heatherton or a story about the rescue of a dog locked inside a hot car in Manhattan. Cindy Adams, a gossip columnist at the *New York Post,* contributed interviews with usual-suspect celebrities such as Zsa-Zsa Gabor.

Its publicity material described *A Current Affair* as a combination of "tragic, offbeat, and human stories." Murdoch said he wanted a show "that will make news and break news," according to Povich. Staff members called it "reality programming." From planning to inception to daily story selection Murdoch micromanaged *A Current Affair,* an odd role for a billionaire international mogul.

But Murdoch believed that the program's success was crucial in creating a buzz about his new network. He apparently wanted the show to be perceived as a lower-brow alternative to *Nightline*; he was said to be an admirer of that program's host, Ted Koppel. At the same time, Murdoch demanded an activist tone from his reporters, and he favored simple stories that featured clear heroes and villains, in the British tabloid manner. The program was set apart by its content, by Povich's wise-guy delivery, and by quirky reporters who looked nothing like the blow-dried multitude of local TV. The program's set and bold graphics also were fresh, and in a brilliant stroke *A Current Affair* replaced the usual news theme music with a whooshing sound that descended in pitch to a dramatic kicker—ka-chung!—as its distinctive triangular logo banged into the TV screen.

Within days of its debut *A Current Affair* showed up on journalism's radar screen. I had a number of newsroom and barroom conversations with colleagues about the peculiar new program. Was it journalism? We weren't sure. The program was top heavy with freaks, false sentiment, and emotion. But it employed people who walked and talked like journalists, and it certainly looked like they were having fun. Povich too was confused about whether the program was journalism. He said, "I was, in fact, embarrassed by the gaudy nature of some of the stories we were programming for 'A Current Affair.' I didn't think that our rundown should be all focused on tor-

rid sex, ruthless murder, and boundless greed. What about social responsibility?" He summarized that rundown quite nicely as "televangelist spoofs,
tales of quadriplegic killers, reports of Satanic teenage murders, cow-moo-
ing contests, Marilyn Monroe bulletins, Elvis sightings—all presented with
a kind of wide-eyed exuberance by our goofy staff."

As the New York media puzzled over this hybrid, the most unlikely source
granted it affirmation as legitimate journalism. A few weeks after the show's
debut John Corry, a television critic for the *New York Times,* gave an important
endorsement in a review:

> "A Current Affair" is tabloid journalism. Forget now the pejora-
> tive notions that cling to the phrase; "A Current Affair" is tabloid
> journalism at its best. It is zippy and knowledgeable, and when
> it falls on its face, at least it's in there trying. The new weeknight
> series, on Channel 5 at 11:30, is the equivalent of a good after-
> noon newspaper. . . . "A Current Affair" is an interesting, often
> thoughtful, series with a nice sense of humor. It works more
> often than not.

This was a crucial anointing by America's most important newspaper, the
paradigm of good journalism, and an arbiter of what is proper and improper in the media culture. "I could have wept," Povich said.

> All my life I'd been groping for some clear definition of my style
> of journalism and now I had it. I was an afternoon tabloid, full
> of blood and gore and happy mischief. I wanted to sing. Rupert
> was similarly moved. He changed us from eleven-thirty to
> seven-thirty, in the process knocking out one of the station's
> biggest money-makers, "M*A*S*H" reruns. We were on the lip
> of prime time. The business people were shocked and in an
> uproar, but Rupert understood the implications of the rave
> review in the *New York Times.* It changed everything. I thought it
> was nice, having a good review in the *Times,* the good gray lady
> of journalism. It would give me points with my friends and my
> family, it would bestow respect upon the show and extend my
> credibility. But I had no idea of the reach—the long and far
> depths of the impact in the financial community, where respect

and a little sex appeal mean big bucks in advertising. And there was the cultural wallop carried by the *New York Times*. We were no longer that vulgar show you had to hide between the covers of the real news.

The endorsement by the *Times* allowed those who worked at *A Current Affair*—and, ostensibly, like-minded journalists elsewhere—to stand up and say, "I'm tabloid, and that's OK." This was a shift in the media culture that soon would ripple through newsrooms everywhere. New York and the other big cities have had tabloid-style journalism for decades, of course. But *A Current Affair* helped spread the tabloid sensibility to the rest of the country; some staff members called their program "Iowa's *60 Minutes*." The *National Enquirer* sells its share of copies in Iowa, but during its ratings heyday *A Current Affair* had a weekly viewership that approached ninety million, thirty times the national weekly circulation of the *Enquirer.*

Whether journalism would have evolved differently without the influence of *A Current Affair* is impossible to say. But without question the program and its progeny helped enhance tabloidization. Throughout U.S. history the media have reported sexy crime stories. But never before had these stories been in our face in such unbowdlerized form via the hot medium of television. Editors and news directors say that the attention focused upon certain stories by *A Current Affair* made them impossible to ignore. If today's watercooler chit-chat concerns that story on tabloid TV last night, how could the hometown paper and *Eyewitness News* fail to cover it? Thus the media in 1986 began back-alley journalism, stalking along behind the crew from *A Current Affair* as it bounded from one salacious story to the next—the Preppy Murder, Jessica Hahn–Jim Bakker, the Rob Lowe videotape, William Kennedy Smith, the Florida Nympho, Amy Fisher–Joey Buttafuoco, Heidi Fleiss, the Bobbitts, Tonya Harding–Nancy Kerrigan, Michael Jackson, and ultimately O. J. Simpson. Journalists can argue that many of these were legitimate news stories, but it is difficult to defend the extent and manner of the coverage.

Some television historians trace the lineage of *A Current Affair* to the 1950s and programs such as Edward R. Murrow's *Person to Person* and *See It Now*. In the 1960s NBC's *The Big Story* and investigative programs such as *CBS Reports* and *NBC White Papers* were the forebears of *60 Minutes,* the CBS "newsmagazine" that debuted in 1968 and features a mix of serious stories and celebrity fluff.

But the most direct antecedent of *A Current Affair* was not a network program but a syndicated special: *The Mystery of Al Capone's Vaults,* the live TV spectacle hosted by Geraldo Rivera. During the 1980s the number of TV channels available to the average American home increased nearly fivefold, and demand for programming to fill all that newly available air time surged. One ready supplier was Tribune Entertainment, a division of the Chicago-based Tribune Company. The Tribune production company paid $50,000 for the rights to break into two vaults in Chicago that supposedly held booty or bodies left over from Capone's criminal glory days. Tribune Entertainment hired Rivera as host and patched together 181 television stations across the country to air the two-hour live program on April 21, 1986. The show was hyped in the media for weeks before the air date, virtually assuring good ratings. As all the world knows, when the plaster dust settled, Rivera found nothing but a few empty whiskey bottles. After the program a newspaper columnist in Chicago picked over the program's rubble: "There are two things that can be said about 'The Mystery of Al Capone's Vaults.' . . . One, everybody watched it. Two, Al Capone's secrets are still buried. And so is Geraldo Rivera's career in journalism. . . . Equally mysterious is why so many Americans got suckered by this sprawling, spewing, ersatz event."

Little did he know. Credibility and substance were beside the point. The program attracted record viewership for a syndicated program, and a large audience equals money in the form of advertising and syndication fees. Nationwide, nearly thirty million households watched the show. Half the TV sets in the United States that were on at the time were tuned to *Capone's Vaults.* For Murdoch and others those numbers served to confirm that the Big Three were susceptible.

*A Current Affair* focused on Al Capone–style stories—those with potentially high profiles involving sleazy crimes, the courts, sex, and celebrities. The program aggressively pursued stories with an intense buzz factor and often managed to position itself as a participant by paying for information or exclusive interviews, photographs, documents, and videotapes. Despite the ethical taint, thousands of stories on television news broadcasts and in newspapers would cite *A Current Affair* as a source of information. Even the country's high-collar papers began helping themselves to "news" produced by a show that did not operate under the same professional rules.

*A Current Affair* was first cited as a news source (by United Press International) on August 15, 1986, two weeks after the tabloid show's debut, when it aired an interview with Mary Beth Whitehead, the surrogate mother from New Jersey in the "Baby M" custody battle. A few days later UPI cited the show in another story, this time for its interview with Andrea Reynolds, the "other woman" in the high-profile divorce case of Claus and Sunny von Bulow. Late that same month the program aired what apparently was tabloid TV's first reenactment: two actors portrayed Jennifer Levin and Robert Chambers, the victim and perpetrator in the Preppy Murder case, as they met at a Manhattan bar and left together for a fateful walk to Central Park. On the air Maury Povich told viewers that the reenactment was based upon "the facts as we know them."

By the time the Hahn-Bakker scandal emerged in 1987, Murdoch had launched the Fox network, *A Current Affair* had gone national, and the program was being cited on a routine basis as a source of news. Jessica Hahn had come forward to say that she had been forced to have sex with the television evangelist Jim Bakker and another minister in 1980. Once again UPI distributed a number of stories based upon interviews with Hahn by *A Current Affair,* including one aired in September 1987 in which Hahn said, "If the man had come back to my room ten minutes later with one lousy flower and said, 'Jessica, I'm sorry,' I probably could have looked the other way."

Before *A Current Affair* this sort of keyhole peeking was not commonplace in the media. But when Murdoch's minions barged through the boudoir door, the rest of the media followed. Hahn, who bared her soul on TV and her surgically augmented body in *Playboy,* served as a willing case study for gauging just how far journalism would go. The answer, as every American would learn, was all the way. At one point UPI distributed nationally a 750-word story under the headline HAHN: I WAS A VIRGIN. It began, "Bible belle Jessica Hahn insisted Monday she was a virgin when she had sex in 1980 with two TV preachers." The definition of legitimate news had changed. In New York, reporters went so far as to "cover" Hahn's appearances on Howard Stern's radio show.

It is more than coincidence that tabloid television was born during an era in which home video cameras proliferated. For a price the owners of all those newly affordable cameras provided tab TV with America's funniest, sexiest, most pathetic, most violent, and sickest home videos. Viewers had no need to wait for the movie-of-the-week version of a sleazy crime. It came to us daily on tabloid television in the video of the evening.

In 1988 Rafael Abramowitz, a reporter for *A Current Affair* who had worked on documentaries at NBC, obtained a home videotape that showed Robert

Chambers, the accused Preppy Murderer, entertaining a group of young women at a party by acting out strangulation on a doll and on himself. The videotape, for which Murdoch's program paid $10,000, had been made after Chambers had been charged in the Levin murder, and his actions made a grotesque mockery of the allegations against him. The videotape aired on the program over two days in mid-May, and ratings spiked to new highs. A year later the next significant home video contribution to American mass media arrived when *A Current Affair* and *Inside Edition* aired excerpts from a twenty-two-minute homemade sex tape featuring a sixteen-year-old girl that was shot by Rob Lowe in Atlanta during the summer of 1988. The executive producer of *A Current Affair* later said he at first waffled over whether the lurid footage was appropriate for broadcast, even on tab TV. His decision to air the video was sanctioned, he said, when local and network television repeatedly aired the same tape after the tab shows had done it first.

In a matter of months the mainstream press had grown well accustomed to chasing tab TV on these sleazy stories, and the man at the lead of the pack more often than not was Steve Dunleavy, an original member of *Current Affair*'s Australian development team and later its star correspondent. From the Son of Sam to O. J. Simpson, Dunleavy served the United States as both newsman and newsmaker. He became Mr. Tabloid, and he may well have had as much influence on the U.S. media as the parents of modern journalism, people such as Edward R. Murrow, Katherine Graham, James Reston, and Benjamin Bradlee.

Dunleavy is an unlikely model for U.S. journalists. Invariably, he is described as reptilian, partly owing to his pompadour-topped visage, pointy features, and general cragginess. His face evokes a mid-morph fusion of Lyle Lovett and the Wicked Witch of the West. He says that he dropped out of school at fourteen to work in the newspaper business in Sydney. He spent fifteen years as a reporter in Australia, Asia, and London, then came to the United States in the late 1960s to work in the New York bureau of Murdoch's burgeoning News Corporation. Dunleavy and other castaways from Great Britain and its former colonies helped introduce the Fleet Street style here. He first made his mark in the United States by covering the drowning of Mary Jo Kopechne in the Ted Kennedy automobile accident on Chappaquiddick Island in 1969, and he later wrote a quickie book entitled *Those Wild, Wild Kennedy Boys.* Dunleavy has been a scourge of the Kennedys ever since.

In the early 1970s Murdoch assigned Dunleavy to a team that was working to develop a supermarket tabloid to compete with the *National Enquirer,* formerly a crime-and-gore sheet with a meager circulation. The *Enquirer's* readership and profits had begun to climb in 1968 when owner Generoso Pope Jr. shifted its focus to celebrities and scandals. Both Murdoch and Henry Luce took note. In 1974 Luce's Time, Inc., launched *People* magazine, now one of the world's most profitable publications, and Murdoch launched the *National Star,* with Dunleavy as the ace of the staff. James Brady, the gossip columnist who once edited the tabloid, wrote of Dunleavy, "He was wonderful. If you wanted a miracle cancer cure, a flying saucer, a Hollywood scandal, or a rip-off of an upcoming book in the guise of a 'review,' what we called an 'el thievo,' Dunleavy was your man." Dunleavy wrote a column called "This I Believe" that featured the overstatement and mawkishness that would become his trademark TV style. He also proved to have an uncanny ability to cozy up to big stories. When Elvis Presley died, Dunleavy and two other *Star* reporters had just completed interviews with three of Presley's bodyguards for an exposé of the king's dangerous lifestyle. Dunleavy and his collaborators cranked out another quick book, *Elvis: What Happened?* (1977), which became a national paperback bestseller.

When Murdoch bought the *New York Post* in 1976, he brought in Dunleavy, whose personality soon began to define the paper. In 1977, as New York fretted over the Son of Sam serial killings, Dunleavy used one gimmick after another to try to wrest the story from the clutches of the rival *Daily News* and its columnist, Jimmy Breslin, with whom the killer had corresponded. In August 1977 Dunleavy tried to thrust himself into the spotlight by publishing a comically unctuous front-page appeal (TO SON OF SAM) to the killer to give himself up—preferably to the *New York Post.* Dunleavy wrote sappy accounts of interviews with the families of the victims that dripped with false intimacy.

At the traditionally liberal *Post* some staffers laughed, some cried, and some quit, including Robert Lipsyte, later a columnist for the *New York Times.* Lipsyte explained, "Steve is dedicated to wringing out emotion and whipping up frenzy. His prose is not orderly, measured or intelligent, and I can't see what his stories have to do with truth, beauty or even what the public needs to know." To which Dunleavy responded, "If it's accurate, anything goes. If the reader buys it, it's moral."

Dunleavy had a wild ride as metropolitan editor at the *Post.* Reporters who worked for him say he was inspiring, demanding, and unscrupulous. His drinking was legendary, and early-arriving reporters often found Dunleavy snoring at his desk after a late night out with his mates from the large contingent of Fleet Street correspondents in New York. A lottery game, newly enlivened sports pages, and sensational crime headlines, including the famous HEADLESS BODY IN TOPLESS BAR, helped the *Post*'s stagnant circulation top one million. (The famous headline, written by Vincent Musetto, an assistant managing editor, was published on the front page of the early editions of April 15, 1983.) Some years later Dunleavy would say, "How do you tell a sensational story other than sensationally? What should it say: 'Decapitated cerebellum in licensed premises, wherein ladies baring mammaries have been seen, to wit, performing acts counter to social mores?' I don't think so."

Despite its circulation increase, the *New York Post* began to lose more and more money as its reputation flagged and advertisers shied away. At the same time, as Murdoch began to assemble stations for his Fox TV network, Ted Kennedy helped see to it that the Federal Communications Commission invoked long-standing regulations that limited newspaper and broadcast cross-ownership in the same markets. The potential profits of television outweighed the panache of a New York City newspaper pulpit, so in 1988 Murdoch sold the *Post* and turned his full attention to broadcasting.

Riding along in Murdoch's wake, Dunleavy began grooming his act for a broadcast audience. After he worked behind the scenes to launch *A Current Affair,* Dunleavy spent about two years as a correspondent with *The Reporters,* a Fox newsmagazine that failed. He then rejoined *A Current Affair* as an on-air personality, using the same intemperate tone that had served him in print. Any able student of tabloid TV can mimic Dunleavy's trademark introductory word, delivered with an oozing false sincerity and a dramatic bobbing of his pompadoured head: "Tragically . . . "

Dunleavy was the archetype for the Aussie sleaze-TV reporter played by Robert Downey Jr. in Oliver Stone's 1994 film, *Natural Born Killers.* The character, Wayne Gale, pursued the mass murderers Mickey and Mallory Knox for a program called *American Maniacs.* The film acutely portrayed the codependence of sleazy crimes, the tabloid media, and a public that serves as an all-too-willing audience. After a live jailhouse interview Wayne Gale gave Mickey Knox a staged hug and whispered in his ear, "Every fuckin' moron in America just saw that, mate!"

Dunleavy may not go so far as to call his viewers morons. But he is a tabloid traditionalist. Through the ages journalists who have pandered to readers have declared that they are of, by, and for the people. Dunleavy calls himself a populist, and he characterizes any criticism as elitist. He said,

> Simply, I think, traditional television over the years did not real-
> ly in any way, shape or form approach what life is all about. We
> in so-called populist television try to take through a person
> whatever emotions they may go through in twenty-four hours,
> and that may be, of course, disdain for their fellow man, fear of
> a particular situation, whether it be bombings or terrorists or
> violence in the streets, laughter, and sometimes even sadness.
> We're really actually appealing to our viewers. We're actually
> talking to the people who are watching us, and that's the first
> stages, really, of interactive television.

His Australian peer, Peter Brennan, the original executive producer of *A Current Affair,* said, "It ended up with, I think, the major newsrooms deciding for the public what is or isn't news and what is or isn't interesting, and the public never got a vote in that until, you know, these shows came along."

According to Dunleavy, great stories involve such ingredients as sex, happiness, the surmounting of obstacles, bravery, cowardice, elation, pride, humor, fear, distrust, and disgust. Rupert Murdoch's description of a great story is a bit more precise: an entertaining spectacle that fuels envy and resentment about high society and has a visceral Fleet Street attitude of rebellion against social pretense. Expressed another way, the perfect Murdochian story would involve class, tits, and ass—sexy tales about people who live in mansions, presented for the benefit of those who live in trailers.

Thus, when word spread on Saturday, March 30, 1991, that William Kennedy Smith, a scion of America's approximation of a royal family, had been taken into police custody in Florida in connection with a rape allegation, Dunleavy and his crew were on the first jet to West Palm Beach. It was a template tabloid story, by Murdoch's definition, and, gleefully enough, it happened to involve his avowed enemy, Ted Kennedy. The alleged rape had occurred during Easter weekend at the beach home of Smith's grandmother, where Uncle Teddy was also on holiday. Over the next five or six months the Fox program would air more than forty stories about the rape case. The executive producer of *A Current Affair*, said, "We wanted to own that story. That story was very important to 'A Current Affair.'" First, the case allowed

Murdoch to exact some measure of revenge against Kennedy for his role in forcing the sale of the *New York Post*. Second, the program by that time had faced stiff ratings competition from a number of copycat tabloid shows, and the Smith story allowed *A Current Affair* to reassert its dominance. That summer *A Current Affair* posted an average nightly audience of about eighteen million, more than *The CBS Evening News*.

*A Current Affair* ensured that it would own the Smith story, as the producer put it, by paying $40,000 to Anne Mercer, a friend of the woman who had made the rape allegation. An interview with Mercer aired in May, about six weeks after the fateful Easter weekend. Mercer later acknowledged that she exaggerated the details to make her information seem more valuable. (Mercer also said she had been offered $100,000 from the *Globe,* a supermarket tabloid, and $50,000 plus royalties from the *National Enquirer.*) Money was distributed freely to anyone with a connection to the case. *A Current Affair* and a number of other tab TV programs and talk shows paid $1,000 per appearance to interview Michelle Cassone, a bartender who had a bit part. Cassone had been the source of a story that a trouserless and "wobbly" Ted Kennedy had been spotted wandering about the estate on the night of the incident. The *New York Post* called it TEDDY'S SEXY ROMP.

Cassone spent several weeks in the spotlight, but she had entered the tabloid arena at her peril. Malcolm Balfour, a stringer in Florida for the *National Enquirer* and the *New York Post,* bought from Cassone's former boyfriend four photographs—three showing her nude and one showing her engaged in a sex act. Balfour sold the photos to *A Current Affair,* and Dunleavy invited Cassone in for what he called a follow-up interview. He began by asking Cassone whether she intended to pose for *Penthouse* magazine. When she replied that she would never pose nude, Dunleavy ambushed her with the photographs. Cassone responded as one might expect: she was furious, and she tried to grab the photographs. A brief struggle ensued—all on camera—as she kicked and bit Dunleavy while shouting obscenities.

On April 24, 1991, the segment aired on *A Current Affair,* after the usual advance publicity from newspapers and local TV broadcasts that managed to wring some news value out of the stunt. The audience for the episode increased by one third, to twenty-five million viewers. Snippets of the video aired on television news broadcasts across the country, and scores of newspapers ran follow-up stories the next day, April 25. The story was covered by, among many others, *Newsday,* the *San Diego Union-Tribune, Washington*

*Times, Washington Post,* UPI, *USA Today, The Record* of Hackensack, New Jersey, the *Times of London, London Daily Telegraph,* and *Boston Globe.*

The headline over the *Boston Globe*'s story read, FOR A FIGURE IN RAPE INQUIRY, A WEEK OF FIGHTS, RACY PHOTOS. The *Globe* was so titillated that it tracked down Dunleavy for a quote. "'She bit and kicked and strangled me . . . She went berserk,'" Steve Dunleavy, who reports for the show 'A Current Affair,' said in a telephone interview last night." *Newsday*'s version carried the headline AN 'AFFAIR' TO REMEMBER; 'OTHER WOMAN' TRIES TO NIX NUDE PIX IN TV INTERVIEW. Timothy Clifford's story said that Cassone had reacted "with curses, flailing elbows and teeth." The story was accompanied by a photograph that showed Cassone biting Dunleavy.

Once again, newspapers and TV news broadcasts had followed like flies to a stinky story aired by *A Current Affair.* The Cassone incident rates as one of the most freakish moments of the new tabloid era—not so much because Dunleavy did it but because the legitimate press showed such lack of compunction in piling on.

Of course, by then discerning the difference between the leader and the followers was difficult. In a long profile a week before the Cassone ambush the *New York Times* had named the woman who said Smith had raped her. This was an unusual step in a case involving a sexual assault, although newspapers over the years have debated the merit of the policy because it may help to stigmatize rape. More surprising than using the woman's name was the *Times*'s rationale: the paper said it published the name because NBC had already aired it. NBC, in turn, said it was following the lead of the *Globe,* which is among the lowliest of supermarket rags. And the *Globe* pointed an accusatory finger at Britain's raunchy *Sunday Mirror.* Once again, as in the case of the Rob Lowe videotape, the rather ethereal concept of the tabloid influence on the mainstream media reduces to nothing more complicated than the reaction of children caught throwing stones at windows: he did it first.

Florida also was the venue for a 1991 story known as the Florida Nympho case, its tab TV sobriquet. It involved an insignificant prostitution arrest, and it stands as another dizzying example of the new tabloid ethic among mainstream journalists. It began on July 23 when Jeffrey Willets, a deputy sheriff in Broward County, Florida, was arrested for pimping his wife out of their bedroom in Tamarac, a city of forty-five thousand about ten miles northwest of Fort Lauderdale. The authorities alleged that Kathy Willets, thirty-two, had had sex with dozens of paying customers lured by a newspaper classified ad in which she described herself as "fun loving and hot." A client had complained to police after he had heard someone snoring while he and Kathy Willets were in flagrante delicto; the session apparently had lulled to sleep Jeffrey Willets, who had secreted himself and a video camera behind the louvered doors of the closet. It turned out that Jeffrey Willets kept careful written notes and video records of his wife's work.

The kinky couple enlisted Ellis Rubin, the flamboyant Miami attorney who is able to elevate the profile of his cases by divining unique defenses. (Rubin once argued—unsuccessfully—that a teenager who killed his parents was a victim of TV addiction.) Like many defense attorneys, Rubin plays the media with virtuosity, and his firm became a locus of information about the Willets case after the arrest. Coincidentally, Broward County was the scene of a contentious circulation battle among several south Florida newspapers—the *Miami Herald, Fort Lauderdale Sun-Sentinel,* and *Palm Beach Post*—so the case attracted aggressive local competition. WSVN-TV in Miami, one of the most overtly tabloid local news broadcasts in the United States, added to the frenzy by devoting as much as twelve minutes per newscast to the story. Rubin and his lawyer sons, Mark and Guy, were widely available to reporters, and their sexy sound bites drew even more flies to the feast. On July 26 Ellis Rubin revealed that he was planning another kooky defense: Kathy Willets was a nymphomaniac and her promiscuity was therapy to feed an insatiable sexual appetite. Rubin kept the story fresh by dishing new details now and again—that Jeffrey Willets was impotent, so his wife was forced to seek sexual gratification in the arms of others; that Prozac, the antidepressant, may have triggered the nymphomania.

Meanwhile, word leaked to the local press that the business card of Doug Danziger, a Fort Lauderdale city commissioner, had been found in the Willetses' bedroom. Danziger had won election that spring by presenting himself as a Christian family man and morality crusader who opposed spring-break lawlessness, topless bars, and adult bookstores. There were whispers that Jeffrey Willets had made a videotape that captured Danziger in a love clutch with Kathy Willets. On July 29 Danziger resigned.

The story had all the elements, as reporters self-mockingly say. This was tabloid boilerplate. The star, a naughty housewife in corset and garters, was vaguely attractive and utterly shameless. The story featured sexual dysfunction, a lewd twist (voyeurism), a rogue cop, a hypocritical public official, and a showy lawyer. The tab TV producers grabbed their checkbooks and headed for Tamarac. They didn't have far to travel because they had been just up the road in Palm Beach feeding on the William Kennedy Smith case.

On August 14, three weeks after the arrest, *A Current Affair* featured a Steve Dunleavy interview with Kathy Willets in which she spoke about her sexual appetite. ("What would happen if I touched you?" Dunleavy asked. "I would get sexually attracted to you," Willets responded, perhaps proving that she was indeed a victim of sexual dysfunction.) Willets bared her breasts for the program and was paid a reported $30,000.

On the day before Dunleavy's story aired, *A Current Affair* sent an electronic press release to newspapers and TV news programs hyping the Willets striptease. The wire services rewrote the press release into a short news story, and scores of daily newspapers across the country carried that story on the day of the broadcast. In essence, the story promised a sexy good time on that edition of *A Current Affair.* The program's ratings spiked upward by 30 percent, and some of those watching apparently were newspaper assignment editors. Within a couple of weeks many of the country's largest and most prestigious papers had dispatched reporters to Fort Lauderdale. Before the adjective pool was drained, hundreds of stories were published and broadcast about the insignificant hooker case. Even Ellis Rubin, who thrives on publicity, was staggered by the attention. "There would have been some interest years ago because of the sex involved," Rubin said, "but I think the rise of tabloid television shows has taken it to a new depth."

Stories about Kathy and Jeffrey Willets appeared on network news programs and in the most prestigious newspapers in the United States. Most of the biggest newspapers, including the *Washington Post, Los Angeles Times, Chicago Tribune,* and *Atlanta Journal and Constitution,* sent staff reporters to Tamarac. For those that couldn't afford to send staff reporters, the wire services—the Associated Press, United Press International, Reuters, and the Knight-Ridder News Service—distributed stories about the Florida Nympho around the English-speaking world. The south Florida dailies lavished team coverage on the case. In New York the Florida Nympho occupied positions of prominence in the tabloids for days running. In Canada, newspapers such as the *Vancouver Sun* and *Calgary Herald* published about a dozen stories each. In London Willets stories appeared in the *Daily Telegraph,* the *Independent*, and the *Guardian.* (Although U.S. journalists now try to imitate the British press grubbers, the London papers still own the tabloid franchise. A story in the *Independent* carried this headline: SOLID GOLD WAITRESS UNRAV-

ELS SOUTH FLORIDA'S MORAL FIBRE/DAVID ADAMS ON A COURT DRAMA THAT IS TITILLATING AMERICA AND UNDERLINING HYPOCRISY IN THE "SUN AND SIN" STATE.)

In true peeping-tom form most stories in the legitimate press liberally appropriated material from the tabloid TV shows, particularly any quotation about sex. For example, a Reuters dispatch lifted this Kathy Willets quote from *A Current Affair*: "It's (sex) my number one priority. I wake up and my appetite is there and that's how I start my day off."

On August 15, the day after her seminude poolside romp aired on *A Current Affair*, Kathy Willets and her husband were arrested. Had the couple not hired Rubin and gone on TV, the case probably would have led to a quick guilty plea, fine, and the relative oblivion that a prostitution arrest deserves. But prosecutors clearly were not pleased with the attention the Willetses were attracting. They charged the couple with thirty-five counts of wiretapping because they had recorded telephone conversations with some of her customers. The next day, in its story about the Willets arrest, the *Miami Herald* reported the salient details that Kathy Willets's underwire bra and a nipple ring had been confiscated during a strip search. On that same day attorneys for a dozen Willets clients petitioned the court to keep the men's names secret.

Topless TV, a nipple ring, and a secret client list: even the *Washington Post* could no longer resist. It dispatched correspondent Mary Jordan for a first-hand look at the Florida Nympho saga. On August 28 her nine-hundred-word LETTER FROM FLORIDA appeared on page three of the first section of the paper. Jordan reviewed the essential salacious details of the case and quoted Mark Rubin: "All I can say at this point is that she is a nymphomaniac and he's an impotent voyeur."

Over the next four months the *Washington Post* published eight stories about the case, ranging from updates in the national news briefs column to a 950-word piece that ran September 28 on the front page of the Style section. On September 9 the *Atlanta Journal and Constitution* ("Covers Dixie Like the Dew") published on its front page a staff-written, 750-word piece under the headline FLORIDA PROSTITUTION SCANDAL TITILLATES TOWN, TERRIFIES CLIENTS. The case made the front page of the *Philadelphia Inquirer* the next day with a staff-written piece headlined BEDROOM FILES PUT CITY OF "JOHN DOES" IN FEAR. On September 11 the *St. Petersburg Times*, a respected newspaper with a daily circulation of about 300,000, published perhaps the most bizarre story of all. The 440-word story, written by Charlotte Sutton, ran on page 4B:

No Dizziness, No Depression
And No Hint of Nymphomania

TALLAHASSEE—Prozac may have stirred an insatiable libido in a Fort Lauderdale woman charged with prostitution, but another famous user of the anti-depressant drug said he has not had that experience.

"I'd like to find out what brand she's taking, because I haven't had any problems like that," Gov. Lawton Chiles said Tuesday.

Chiles was responding to a reporter's question about Kathy Willets, who claims that although she once had little interest in sex, that changed in 1990 after she started taking Prozac. When her husband, a Broward County sheriff's deputy, could no longer satisfy her increased appetite, she started having sex with other men, she says.

The story went on to recount the governor's history of Prozac use.

In mid-September it appeared that the Florida Nympho story was about to peter out. Kathy and Jeffrey Willets were prepared to plead guilty in exchange for a recommendation of no jail time. But the prosecutor withdrew his plea agreement at the last minute, and tabloid TV played a role. Steve Wilson, a correspondent for *Inside Edition* and Dunleavy's competitor on the story, reported that Guy Rubin had attempted to broker a $100,000 deal between his program and the Willetses. In exchange, Wilson said, *Inside Edition* was to get the alleged sex tape featuring Danziger, the ex-city commissioner, and a nude photo session with Kathy Willets. When Ellis Rubin denied the "diabolical" charges, *Inside Edition* responded by airing secret videotape of the meeting with Guy Rubin. Rubin and Wilson held dueling press conferences.

This development gave new momentum to the coverage. The Willetses turned up on ESPN during national coverage of a University of Miami football game. (They were shown signing autographs.) *Time* magazine checked in on September 16 with a photo-illustrated piece under the headline KATHY'S HOME REMEDY. The story's lead read, "Kathy Willets loved her work." On September 19 the *Los Angeles Times* published a piece that stood out for both its length and lust. The twenty-five-hundred-word story (accompanied by several photographs) began on the front page of the paper's feature section. The piece, written by freelancer Mike Clary and staff writer Geraldine Baum, disingenuously harrumphed about the media circus surrounding the case:

> The media have been slobbering: The Willetses have appeared often in photos on the front pages of the Miami Herald, the Ft. Lauderdale Sun-Sentinel and other Florida newspapers. Inside, there have been reports of developments in the case, as well as accompanying articles detailing Kathy's Roman Catholic schooling, Jeff's disciplinary problems as an officer, and the couple's occasionally violent marital spats and financial troubles—the bank is foreclosing on their house.
>
> In addition to the newspaper coverage, there has been no shortage of TV footage devoted to the case. Last month, when the pair went tripping off to Jamaica's Hedonism II resort, where they could frolic naked and get away from it all, "A Current Affair" captured numerous private moments of the couple, hand in hand, on the island's white sands, as well as Kathy on other beaches, topless, naked or wearing a lacy top.

Clary and Baum, who managed to work in the detail about the confiscated nipple ring, sniped several times about tabloid television's coverage of the case, even as they depended heavily upon tab TV in reporting the piece. They wrote that she "cooed" to *A Current Affair,* "I'm your average American housewife." They used secondhand comments that Steve Wilson of *Inside Edition* had made to WSVN-TV about the content of the Danziger sex videotape ("x-rated," "very explicit"). The piece also quoted extensively from comments that Kathy Willets had made in a call to a radio disc jockey, including the following scintillating exchange:

DJ:  This isn't Kathy from the nympho section?

KW:  This is THE nympho . . .

DJ:  How's the case going?

KW:  It's going great . . .

DJ:   How have you been able to handle the nympho
     problem since you got arrested?

KW:   It's been tough. (She giggles.)

DJ:   You still must have the drive.

KW:   Well, I was down in Jamaica, and I took care of some
     problems down there. (More giggles.)

DJ:   . . . So what do you do now that you're back in the
     States?

KW:   Well, I've been putting Jeff to work a little bit extra.
     (More titters.)

Later in the piece Clary and Baum returned to the phone call while address-
ing the subject of her client list:

DJ:   Any big-time Ft. Lauderdale politicians?

KW:   Maybe.

DJ:   Dade County officials?

KW:   Maybe.

DJ:   Judges and lawyers?

KW:   Maybe.

On September 20 the *Chicago Tribune,* another respected newspaper that had
followed the case by publishing four wire-service reports, ran a one-thou-
sand-word, staff-written story by Mary T. Schmich on page eight. Two days
later the *St. Petersburg Times* revisited the story with a full-treatment, two-
thousand-word, staff-written dispatch on the front page of the local-state
section under the headline SEX, SLEAZE, CASH: THE WILLETS STORY. The *Times,*
quoting the Broward County sheriff's spokesman, had perhaps the most suc-
cinct summary of the case:

> "What you've got," [Ott] Seskin said, "is an attractive woman
> turned prostitute and her husband is a cop and he's booking her
> clients and they get arrested and get attorney Ellis Rubin, who
> can dream up a remarkable defense whether it's viable or not,
> and they have a city commissioner implicated as their customer
> and he was this moralist who went to a high-profile church and
> tried to shut down these nudie bars or at least get them to stop

serving booze, and then the Willets see the pot of gold at the end of rainbow and begin to play this thing for all it's worth on "A Current Affair" and all that, and then . . . "

Seskin pauses to breathe.

"It's a National Enquirer story happening in real life, and it's all true. It's sleazy, and the way attorneys have been posturing makes it more sleazy. And we're all just sitting around and waiting for the other shoe to drop. And wondering whose foot it will come off of.

Indeed, it was all true, except for the misspelling of Ott Cefkin's name.

On September 23 *Newsweek* published a brief item and photograph about "the ever-twisting 'nympho' case." That same week, *People* weighed in with a 750-word, four-photograph piece that, like many others, asserted that tabloid television was largely responsible for the spectacle. Finally, on December 13, 1991, the couple pleaded guilty to thirty-five criminal charges. The story was reported in scores of newspapers across the country. Many used the Knight-Ridder News Service account filed by reporter Scott Higham of the *Miami Herald*. It began:

> After agreeing to testify against their lawyer and turn over a collection of steamy videotapes, Jeff and Kathy Willets ended their sensational sex saga Friday, pleading guilty to 35 pending criminal counts against them.
>
> The couple, who created international headlines with their titillating tale of sex in suburbia, stood stoically as the charges were read aloud in the courtroom.
>
> "All of this took place in your home?" prosecutor Joel Lazarus asked.
>
> "Yes, sir," the Willetses said in unison, closing out a prostitution case that started with a routine police raid and ended in a swirl of passion, fame and frivolity.

"Closing out" proved to be overly optimistic. The Florida Nympho walked out of the courthouse that day into a media sea. There were more stories in February 1992 after sentencing—one year in jail for him and three years' probation for her—and still more when Jeffrey assaulted Kathy after his re-

lease. The *Legal Intelligencer* published several stories about the ethics allegations against Rubin. (He was cleared.) *Playboy* published a seven-thousand-
word story about the case in March 1992, and *Ladies Home Journal,* of all
things, featured the Willets case in a December 1992 piece entitled, THE
STORY BEHIND THE STORY: FOLLOW-UPS TO FIVE SENSATIONAL STORIES FEA-
TURED ON TV. Even *Editor & Publisher,* the sober weekly magazine that caters
to the print media, managed to work the Willets case into its pages—a
January 16, 1993, report on a Florida Supreme Court ruling ordering the
release of the client list. Another flurry of stories arrived in 1993 after the
Florida Supreme Court ordered the release of the Danziger sex videotape
and still more stories when Kathy Willets was sent to jail for a couple of
months because she did not complete a community service requirement of
her original sentence.

On October 18, 1993, the *Miami Herald* published on page c1 a story concerning a book—coauthored by Ellis Rubin—about the case. The headline
read WILLETS EVER END? The answer is no, of course, because the media had
made Kathy Willets famous for being infamous. To this day Kathy Willets gets
occasional media attention. On March 19, 1994, the *Palm Beach Post* published a career update on the front page of its feature section under the headline NYMPHOMANIAC FINDS NEW LIFE ON STRIP CIRCUIT; HER PRISON LIFE
OVER, WILLETS FLASHES SEQUINS, RED LIGHTS. The *Post's* man on the scene
reported that, in her act, Willets wore a gold chain suspended between nipple rings and that she used whipped cream to simulate the shaving of her
pubic region. She has continued to work as a stripper, and she has had some
success as a B-movie and porno-flick actress. The south Florida media have
reviewed her films, and her name pops up every month or so in one newspaper or another, often in stories about Prozac or in a piece about her latest
film or strip-tease show. Most stories manage to declare some degree of
moral indignation about her turpitude.

Scott Higham, one of a half-dozen reporters who covered the story for the
*Miami Herald,* had a down-front seat during the Kathy Willets frenzy. I asked
him what it was like. "I know that there's no way I'll ever work on a story that
bizarre for the rest of my life," he says. "It was one of those classic Florida
cases where just when you think it can't get any stranger, it does. After a
while, I began to feel like it was all being done for the benefit of the media."

Higham, who moved to the *Baltimore Sun* in 1995, keeps at his desk a photograph shot by a *Herald* photographer that shows Kathy Willets standing in

the center of an immense media crush outside the courthouse on the day that she pleaded guilty. He says he still puzzles over the attention the case received from the out-of-town media.

> I guess it had all the right elements a reporter looks for in a story: corruption, duplicity, sex, a videotape. . . . It was just so lurid, and it became so competitive because all these reporters came in from out of town, from the tabloid TV shows, from Fleet Street. The British guys were unbelievable. There were just no constraints put on these guys. They were doing everything— trying to pay off people for information, posing as priests and detectives. It was just amazing for me to see how high the stakes could get on a story like that. It was the strangest thing I ever worked on in my life. Yes, it was kind of fun at first, but then it just got out of control and took on a life of its own. . . . I know it's not the reason that I got into journalism.

It seems clear in retrospect that the two Florida stories from 1991— William Kennedy Smith and Kathy Willets—served as a watershed for media mores. An anything-goes ethos had elbowed aside self-restraint. The use of tabloid television and even supermarket tabloids as sources of information and as news agenda setters became institutionalized.

At the same time, curious attempts at self-affirmation began appearing in the mainstream press about the new legitimacy of the tabloid media. During an appearance on CNN a news executive at WPIX-TV in New York City praised *A Current Affair* for its handling of the Smith case, the Cassone ambush apparently notwithstanding. "They gave good dimension to the Kennedy Smith rape trial in Florida," he said. "I thought they did a totally responsible job on that." The *Columbia Journalism Review* featured a cover story that concluded that paying for information was not always bad because sources who need money can benefit. A couple of issues later, *CJR* published a piece about the *National Enquirer's* new credibility. Andrea Sachs wrote that the paper was "edging toward respectability" and, for their handling of the Simpson story, compared two editors at the tab to Woodward and Bernstein.

The question was who was edging toward whom. The tabloid grunges, accustomed to toiling in the cellars of journalism, suddenly were being invited to press parties in the penthouse, and they were clear-minded about what had happened. "We haven't changed," said Valerie Virgo, a photo editor at the *National Enquirer.* "The rest of the press has changed. They're becoming more tabloid." "Five years ago," Brian Wells, a former executive editor of the *National Enquirer,* told *Maclean's* in 1994, "the mainstream press and television would hardly have touched these stories. Now, there are all these tabloid TV shows reporting everything—and the mainstream press follows TV. By the time the tabs come out, the stories have been done to death." Howard Rosenberg, a *Los Angeles Times* writer and a perceptive critic of the tabloidization, observed that was a case of "the forest coming to Dunsinane."

Those that didn't actively pursue sleazy stories darted about the edges of the media wolf pack. Dan Goodgame, a White House correspondent for *Time,* explained: "You let the tabloids go out and pay people for stories and do the dirty things establishment journalists hold themselves above. Then you pick up and cover the controversy, either directly or as a press story. You write: 'Oh, how horrible the press is.' Then you go into the details." The media frequently used that tactic to peek through media windows at the British royal family. An example from the *New York Times*:

EXTRA!

PRINCESS IN PHONE SHOCK!

By William E. Schmidt

Special to *The New York Times*

LONDON, AUG. 27—When readers picked up their Sunday morning edition of the News of the World two weeks ago, the weekly—one of Britain's more sensational tabloids—offered a juicy exclusive.

A girlfriend of a man who was once a confidante of the Princess of Wales had been receiving a series of harassing telephone calls, the newspaper reported, and detectives at Scotland Yard had traced the calls to private telephones inside Princess Diana's residence.

Then, a week later, the newspaper published a second, and even more detailed exclusive, albeit one that appeared to contradict their original story. This time, the paper said, it was a man—a married London art dealer who is a close friend of both the Princess of Wales and her estranged husband, Prince

Charles—who had been receiving the crank calls, all of which were also traced by the police to telephones inside and near the Princess' residence.

Whatever the precise truth of the tale, The News of the World's highly detailed allegations—the newspaper's account included a minute by minute log of some of the calls to Mr. Hoare's home—made the front page of every British newspaper last week, spawning wild speculation about the state of Princess Diana's mind, as well as outraged indignation among British politicians demanding to know who might have leaked police files.

The story went on to recount a number of "exclusives" about the royal family that appeared in the *News of the World,* the *Sun,* and *Daily Mirror,* the raunchiest tabloids in Britain.

*Since September 1997, journalists and their critics have been pointing quivering fingers while psychoanalyzing the celebrity obsession that, directly or indirectly, led to Princess Diana's death. The sad truth is that we all are culpable because the paparazzi work for each of us—the photo service that buys the image, the magazine or newspaper that publishes the photograph, the reader who ogles it. We've all become window-peepers.*

Perhaps the most infamous of the peeping-tom stories broke just a couple of months after William Kennedy Smith's acquittal, when the *Star,* the supermarket tabloid that Murdoch had founded and later sold, featured a front-page story about a woman named Gennifer Flowers who was paid a reported $150,000 to reveal the details of MY 12-YEAR AFFAIR WITH BILL CLINTON. Its publication coincided nicely with the beginning of the primary election season. When the *Star's* editor convened a press conference in Manhattan on January 27, 1992, to help publicize the story, about three hundred journalists showed up.

Clinton was in New England campaigning at the time, and many newspapers cloaked their coverage of the press conference as "reaction" stories from Clinton about the *Star's* big scoop. Of course, each piece managed to work in the sexiest of Flowers's allegations. The *Washington Post* ran one thousand words on the front page of the Style section under the headline THE BRIGHT & SLIMY STAR: CHECKING OUT THE TABLOID THAT RAN WITH THE CLINTON STORY. Gannett News Service offered its subscribers an 850-word piece under the headline CLINTON DENIES ANEW ALLEGATIONS OF MARITAL INFIDELITY. The piece began, "For the second time in a week, a supermarket tabloid is alleging marital infidelity by Democratic presidential candidate Bill Clinton, this time with reports of tapes. Clinton again called the reports false."

Many journalists were disgusted by the media's performance on the story, including Paul Reynolds, managing editor of the *Daily News* of Bangor, Maine. At the time, he told the *Los Angeles Times*, "We didn't give the Clinton-Flowers story as prominent a play as many papers. But still we kept asking ourselves: 'Why are we doing this? What the hell has happened to journalism?'"

I ran across Reynolds's comments while reviewing the Flowers coverage. I telephoned and read the quote back to him, nearly five years after he said it. Reynolds paused for a few seconds, then said, "That's an accurate reflection of how I felt at the time, and journalism has gone downhill from there. We've fallen into the abyss at this point." After a twenty-three-year career at the *Bangor Daily News,* the last ten as managing editor, Reynolds left daily journalism not long after the Flowers case. He taught journalism at the University of Maine for a couple of years and now works as a spokesman for a division of the Maine state government. He says, "I think the popular press continues to outdo itself in appealing to the lowest common denominator. I never stopped being shocked by it, and I still get angry. I keep watching and reading, maybe because I want to see how low they will go."

He says the obsession by the media with trivial titillating stories presents the country with a skewed sense of what is important. "There is an overwhelming willingness to fabricate news out of nothing, as happened in the Flowers case," Reynolds says. "The relative weight assigned to any given story on any given day is likely to place it well beyond the boundaries of what a reasonable person would say it is worth. It's discouraging, because it's going to distort the average voter-citizen's perception of reality."

A friend of mine, a reporter, compares the media's obsession with sleaze to an addiction. One jag leads to another, she said, but the dosage must be increased with each binge to reach the same effect. The media were ripe for another bender following the presidential primary, and along came Amy Fisher, a troubled Long Island teenager who shot her lover's wife on May 19, 1992. Several thousand felonious assaults occur each year on Long Island, but the Fisher case stood out for its classic tabloid combination of sex, nubility, and videotapes. Cash-for-trash flowed from the tabloid spigots. An investment group paid $60,000 to bail out Fisher. A one-time client of the neophyte prostitute sold a videotape showing her at work. *A Current Affair* paid a reported $500,000 to the victim, Mary Jo Buttafuoco, and her philandering husband, and another $200,000 advance was paid to the couple in a movie deal. (Ultimately, three films would be produced about the case.) *Hard Copy* paid $10,000 for a "surveillance tape" that showed Fisher talking suggestively with one of her lovers. In several dozen instances legitimate news organizations cited information bought by tab tv—everything from Fisher's alleged lesbian dalliance to how she performed in bed to the fidelity of Mary Jo Buttafuoco.

It was hard to imagine that journalism could sink much lower, but along came the summer of 1993 and an astonishing procession of sleazy crime stories. First, Heidi Fleiss was arrested on pimping charges in Los Angeles, which prompted a particularly puzzling frenzy. The first story about the arrest appeared in the *Los Angeles Times* on June 12, three days after it occurred, and rated play only on page three of the local news section. Yet the story was destined to go national, apparently because her client list included marquee names (the actor Charlie Sheen, for example). Ultimately, the U.S. media would publish or broadcast tens of thousands of stories about the hooker case.

On June 23, eleven days after Fleiss's arrest, Lorena Bobbitt sliced off the penis of her unfaithful husband, John, and the tabloid pack toted its klieg lights to Prince William County, Virginia, bestowing extravagant attention upon yet another sex-related story of dubious importance. The *Washington Post*, whose local circulation area includes Prince William County, would publish several hundred stories that mentioned the Bobbitt case, according to the Lexis/Nexis electronic clipping service. The *New York Times* also dedicated an astonishing number of column inches to the story, including a front-pager about the miracle of penile reattachment. CNN provided live coverage of Lorena Bobbitt's assault trial, and John Bobbitt's life has been tracked unremittingly by reporters ever since, a media icon until his obituary is written.

The final stink-bomb story of the summer of 1993 broke in August, when police raided Michael Jackson's estate in California while investigating allegations that he had sexually abused a boy. Because the authorities would not say much about the case and Jackson was reclusive, the media turned within to cover the story. The burgeoning practice of journalists interviewing other journalists bloomed during the coverage of William Kennedy Smith. In a fifteen-hundred-word piece after the Smith trial writer David Margolick of the *New York Times* described Steve Dunleavy as "the ringmaster" of the case and compared his role to that of H. L. Mencken at the Scopes monkey trial. Margolick used a telling scene setter in his piece: "One reporter watches another reporter interview a third reporter as a woman from 'Entertainment Tonight' asks Mr. Dunleavy whether it's a thrill that the long-awaited trial is finally getting under way."

In the Jackson case a source from the California Department of Children's Services apparently leaked documents about the investigation to *Hard Copy,* Paramount's entry in the tabloid TV world. The program also paid about $125,000 for interviews with Jackson's bodyguards and a former maid. Diane Dimond of *Hard Copy* assumed Steve Dunleavy's newsmaker role. She was interviewed by dozens of newspapers and television broadcasts, from *USA Today* to *CBS This Morning,* and she freely dished theories, rumors, and innuendos that were presented as news. In *Tabloid Truth,* a revealing documentary film about the media coverage of the Jackson story, the journalist and author Richard Ben Cramer concluded, "The carnival sideshows are now the main event."

The next circus act was the bizarre knee-capping of the ice skater Nancy Kerrigan on January 6, 1994. Once again tab TV came carrying heavy wallets. *Inside Edition* paid between $300,000 and $600,000 to Tonya Harding, the rival skater who was widely suspected in the assault, according to the *Portland Oregonian. Hard Copy* paid $20,000 for the first interviews with two of the alleged assailants, Derrick Smith and Shane Stant. (The two later appeared on *Geraldo* to tout their $4.99-per-minute 900 number, promising "explicit new details.") As a journalist was conducting a live interview at a Portland radio station with a minor player in the story, a reporter from *Hard Copy* rapped on the studio glass and shouted, "Don't say another word until you talk to me! I've got money!" ABC interrupted its daytime program for live coverage of a press conference by Jeff Gillooly, Harding's ex-husband. The mania reached low tide when *A Current Affair* got its mitts on what might be the all-time cringe-inducing videotape, purchased from Gillooly for a reported $1 million. It showed his bride undressing on their wedding night.

The videotape was nearly as beguiling as the arguments devised by the various tabloid TV operations as they pointed fingers at one another to rationalize the cash-for-trash wackiness. First, they pointed out that network TV and *60 Minutes* have occasionally paid for interviews and information. (Which is true, although it probably can be declared with some certainty that CBS has never paid for photographs of a woman performing oral sex on her boyfriend or for a videotape of a wedding-night striptease.) Next, they blamed market considerations. Bill O'Reilly, a former host of *Inside Edition,* said, "The competition for ratings and stories is now so intense that 'Inside Edition' must pay for some big scoops to survive. If we didn't pay, we'd be off the air. Simple as that." The overhead, not the ethics, seemed to bother Rupert Murdoch most. "You can't just let Paramount come along and run over you with 'Hard Copy,'" Murdoch said. "We'd rather not pay at all or certainly pay a lot less, but it's not something the networks haven't done." That seems a bit like Genghis Khan saying that he was a victim of the overzealousness of his enemies.

Because tabloid TV owned most sources involved in the Harding story, the TV networks and newspapers took the easy route by copying paid-for material and otherwise working the fringes. (The exception was the *Oregonian,* which used quaintly old-fashioned reporting—asking questions, getting answers—to stay ahead on the story.) Connie Chung of CBS attached herself to Harding like an ankle bracelet. To get Harding to agree to talk, Chung first had to promise not to ask questions about the case. In her first interview with Harding, Chung asked such questions as, "How are you handling all of this?" Apparently embarrassed by the first, in a second interview Chung got tough, prompting Harding to storm off, which probably was the intent all along. The huff-inducing interview was recounted in the press and rebroadcast many times on network and local television. Steve Dunleavy surely smiled and recalled his Michelle Cassone ambush as he watched Chung's performance.

At that point it probably was too late for Chung to rescue her reputation. All of America knew that she had had one too many breakfast table conversations with her husband, Maury Povich, the original host of *A Current Affair* who had gone on to further fame as an insincere and obsequious talk-show host. As Newt Gingrich's mother would put it after Chung's famous "just-between-you-and-me" interview in January 1995, "It catches up with you."

The tabloid jag clearly was leading somewhere, and that destination turned out to be Brentwood, California, and the home of O. J. Simpson, accused in the June 12, 1994, murders of his ex-wife, Nicole, and Ronald Goldman. The story was the logical culmination of all the sleazy crime coverage of the previous eight years, through Hahn, Smith, Fisher, Fleiss, and Harding. By the time OJ came along, the tabloid techniques had been buffed to a high sheen by the earlier frenzies. First, the media mucked up the inves-

tigation by paying off a number of witnesses—standard operating proce-
dure. The mainstream media then borrowed generously from material
bought by both TV and supermarket tabloids. In one bewildering example,
the *New York Times* twice cited the *National Enquirer* for its report, based upon
an unnamed jail guard, that Simpson had exclaimed, "I did it!" during a jailhouse conversation with Roosevelt Grier, the minister and former professional football player. The *Times* reporter and his editors argued that the
*Enquirer* had proved to be a responsible and accurate source of information
on the Simpson story. By contrast, Linda Deutsch, the level-headed journalist who would impress her peers with her work as lead reporter for the
Associated Press at Simpson's criminal trial, threatened to pull her byline
after her editors tried to insert the same quote from the *Enquirer* in her story.
Her bosses backed down. "It was an unattributed story from an unreliable
source," Deutsch said. "All it did was sensationalize it, which it certainly
doesn't need at this point. . . . To me, it was astounding that The New York
Times did that."

The Simpson coverage featured the usual myopic focus on minuscule
events that were presented as huge developments, each the biggest since yesterday. There was the silly obsession with trivia (Marcia Clark's hairdo).
There was shoot-from-the-hip theorizing by all manner of prognosticators in
the press, on the Big Three networks, and on CNN, Court TV, and E!, which
gave themselves over to OJ. There was hypocrisy by papers that tut-tutted
people like Faye Resnick and Kato Kaelin on the editorial page, then quoted
them as sources of information on page one. When the reporters weren't
interviewing demisources, they were interviewing one another. ("For Steve
Dunleavy, it just doesn't get any better than this," began one Simpson story
in the *San Francisco Examiner*.) It was the same old tabloid stuff but more of
it. The media gratuitously attempted to self-rationalize the coverage by
blaming the public's obsession or by arguing that the case was some sort of
societal parable or, failing that, a fine civics lesson. As one writer put it, "The
closely watched Simpson trial provided an education to the entire nation
about some of the finer points of forensic investigation."

God help the legal system if the Simpson debacle was an example of the
finer points of anything. The coverage of O. J. Simpson taught us more about
the media than it did about the U.S. court system or the attraction-repulsion
dynamic of our culture. We learned, once again, as we had in the Lindbergh
kidnapping case in the 1930s and many times since that the media can be a

corrupting influence in a high-profile criminal case. We learned that the notion of self-restraint, an unspoken underpinning of the First Amendment, can be subjugated by competitive considerations whenever two journalists cover the same story. We learned that the public perceives the media not only as interlopers but as manipulators.

"The O. J. Simpson (criminal) trial was the absolute low point of low points," Paul Reynolds, the former managing editor in Bangor, Maine, says.

> I can't imagine any working journalist not agreeing with that. I've asked myself again and again why we allowed it to happen, why newspapers stooped so low. I think there are two answers. First, quite frankly, with declining circulations and the increasing threat of the electronic era, newspapers are running scared and probably do things today that violate their own ethical standards. Another factor is that the culture is changing, driven to a large extent by our reflection as we see it on television. When we see something on television, either wittingly or unwittingly, it has an effect on the decisions made in newspaper newsrooms about what stories go on which page. It is difficult to do battle against these influences, even if you believe them to be negative influences.

One day soon members of the U.S. media may well awake from the tabloid stupor and find themselves in roughly the same position as one of those people who land in the supermarket tabloids after claiming that they were ABDUCTED BY ALIENS!!! Having been released from Rupert Murdoch's flying saucer, the men and women of the media will be standing in the middle of a vast North Dakota field that bears a perfect rendering of *A Current Affair*'s logo carved out of the waist-high wheat. How did we get here? they will ask one another. And how do we get back to 1985? They'll have to find their way back without the help of Steve Dunleavy and *A Current Affair*. Tragically, as he might say, Dunleavy was taken off the air in 1995 as the program tried to spruce up its image. In 1996, as its ratings continued to sag and advertisers grew disenchanted with its audience demographics (down market and predominantly female, like the supermarket tabloids), stations began to cancel the show or move it out of prime viewing slots. Finally, Murdoch pulled the plug on *A Current Affair,* which earned $50 million a year during its peak.

It leaves many survivors, including scores of staff members who learned the Fleet Street craft there and now practice it at other newsmagazine shows. At various times U.S. television has offered nearly two dozen versions of the newsmagazine/current-events/true-crime program. The format is popular with network executives because such shows cost half of what a sitcom costs to produce. Many programs use the same types of reenactments and dramatizations as *A Current Affair*. Most famously, *Dateline NBC* in 1993 rigged a GM truck to create an explosion in a crash. But *Dateline* is not alone. ABC's *20/20* used a dramatic reenactment of Lorena Bobbitt's flight from her home after the assault on her husband. During a prison interview with Charles Manson *Turning Point* (also ABC) used a point-of-view camera to re-enact the approach to the house where Manson and his followers murdered the actress Sharon Tate and her friends.

Producers move freely among the programs, and they all compete for the same mass-murderer interviews and sleazy crime story of the week. Don Hewitt, the executive producer of *60 Minutes,* said, "It's like a carnival show. Barbara (Walters) is saying, 'Step right up to the most horrible murders anybody's ever seen. John Donvan (the correspondent) will take you through it, and when it's over I'll meet you on the outside.'"

At this point, *A Current Affair* would be redundant to the entertainment programming on television, anyway. The Australian accent may be gone, but the Aussie sensibility lives on, with Murdoch's Fox network still the sleaze-trend leader. Reenactments are now passé. TV viewers today can watch programs that show *real* people being injured or killed in planes crashes, car crashes, animal gorings, fires, and natural disasters. We can sit in our living rooms and witness tragic moments in the lives of others while munching popcorn or eating TV dinners; Oliver Stone's *American Maniacs* seems less like fiction now. The snuff genre—"When Disasters Strike," "When Animals Attack"—was the perfectly logical next step in bad taste.

Meanwhile, in 1993 Murdoch managed to buy back the *New York Post,* rescuing it from closure, after members of Congress—Ted Kennedy not among them—pressured the FCC to waive the regulations barring cross-ownership. A brief item that appeared in the *Post* in early 1997 is a nifty little example of the symbiosis within Murdoch's empire. The gushy brief appeared on the TV page of the *Post:* "Overwhelming viewer demand has led Fox to schedule a repeat telecast of 'The World's Scariest Car Chases,' a thrilling hour of dramatic video footage of police pursuits which scored huge ratings in its first broadcast this past Sunday." Up at the front of paper Steve Dunleavy is back at the *Post* as a columnist, postulating with the same heavy hand about junk justice and liberals and the moral deterioration of the America he so dearly, dearly loves. In the photograph that accompanies his column in the *Post,* Dunleavy appears to me to be winking.

# chapter 3

# Seven Little Sins, So Many Stories

**O**ver the past several years I have listened patiently to a number of arguments by journalists about the news value and relative merit of the stories that helped define the new tabloid era. Beyond the fact that two people were dead, they will say, the O. J. Simpson case was important because it addressed the country's confusing racial dynamics and the secretive subject of spousal abuse. They say the Dick Morris prostitute scandal was news because it unveiled political hypocrisy—a presidential consultant who espoused family values and sucked a hooker's toes when he wasn't playing bridge with the wife.

The Gennifer Flowers allegations against President Clinton called into question the character of a man who wanted to be president, and it bespoke the possibility of abuse of power by a politician. Harding-Kerrigan was a morality tale about power, money, and rivalry in U.S. sports. The Jim Bakker–Jessica Hahn case was about sexual power and financial deceit in the religion racket. Heidi Fleiss was about power, somehow, in Hollywood. Rob Lowe was about the abuse of a star's power. Ditto Michael Jackson—all about power. William Kennedy Smith was a case of alleged sexual abuse by a man born into a family with political power. The Bobbitts? The empowerment of a woman against an abusive spouse. Amy Fisher? Uh, how about the empowerment of a nubile paramour against her lover's spouse?

Is it mere coincidence that most of these stories involved sex? Not likely. For centuries the scribes of the world have been well served by lust and the other six sins: pride, envy, sloth, intemperance, avarice, and ire. These basic ingredients have formed the stock of the news stew since well before parchment replaced cave walls as the medium of choice. During the Middle Ages traveling news balladeers and storytellers earned their daily bread by dishing details of executions, wars, natural disasters, adultery, and lawlessness. When Johann Gutenberg perfected movable type in the German city of Mainz in the fifteenth century, the method was used to print an edition of the Book of Psalms. But it surely was not long before enterprising writers expanded upon the religious motif: perhaps a true-life tell-all account of a love triangle involving the local minister and his mistress from the chant choir in Antwerp.

Crime, death, and immorality have been part of the standard repertoire of what we now think of as journalism since its birth. That is not surprising because those same themes form the spine of both classic literature and folk legends—the more respectable cousins of journalism—in most cultures. In particular, humankind has proved to possess an enduring and robust appetite for tales about coitus and death—how life begins and how it ends. Why do stories about sex and murder make our pulse race? Is the interest purely prurient and morbid? Is it triggered by a primordial survival instinct of some sort, like animals that obsessively sniff at the carcass of a fallen member of their family unit, as though looking for clues to how to avoid the same fate? Or, as a reporter in Cleveland suggested to me, are sexy crime stories so popular "because people like to read them"?

Whether the appeal is shallow or deep, the popularity of this type of news has created a convenient codependency between seller and buyer—convenient in that each can blame the other for its propagation. Today, as always, an irreconcilable combination of lust and disgust greets blood-stained and sexy news. Readers and TV viewers consistently say that they wish to be spared most of the gore and gossip, but news directors and editors point out, correctly, that circulation figures and ratings beg to differ. Clearly, someone is stealing peeks at the stuff.

The fretting over the low and corrupting content of certain news stories is not a modern phenomenon. Hand-wringing always has attended publication of crime news. In fact, the history of crime reporting is strikingly linear, from topic to content to form. Journalists can take comfort that their crime-reporting ancestors were no more thoughtful than they are. For centuries lustful stories of dubious worth have been disguised as important educational stories that serve as societal parables, just as we see today. Allowing for changes in language usage, there is a continuum in crime reporting from the penny press era of the 1830s to the yellow journalism of 1900 to the jazz journalism of the 1920s to the tabloid TV–tinged journalism of the 1990s. In all likelihood, Amy Fisher would have been no less a celebrity criminal had the pubescent hooker attempted to slay her lover's wife 150 years ago. So although it can be said that coverage of crime has never been any better than it is now, it has never been any worse, either. But to fully understand the present of crime reporting, it is necessary to look at the past.

The crime news in newspapers and on television descends from pamphleteers who peddled their melodramatic accounts of death and misdeeds to blushing bluenoses three hundred years ago. As early as the mid-1600s a number of periodicals that catered to the educated class in England carried red-hot accounts of crimes. The tsk-tsking followed closely. In 1648 the periodical *Mercurius Anti-Mercurius* chastised these "Newsmongers . . . ready to gather up the Excrements of the Kingdom." In 1719 the *London Daily Post* censured its raw competitors, apparently the forebears of today's tabloids:

> 'Tis the Misfortune of the Town to have much News but little Intelligence, Truth ill-told, Lies ill-covered, Parties ill-served, and, in a Word, the Readers vilely imposed upon on all Sides. . . . Almost every transaction is set in a false Light. Misrepresentation is, as it were, the Business of every Writer, and whether they speak of private Persons or of publick, the character of no Man seems safe, but Scandal and Slander make havoc of Men's Reputation without Mercy.

The tabloid pedigree of U.S. journalism traces to the founding fathers, or at least a founding uncle. James Franklin, the older brother of Benjamin, was a printer in Boston who is said to have acquired a brash entrepreneur-ial spirit while working as an apprentice in England in the same journalistic era described by the *London Daily Post.* In 1721 he established the *New-England Courant,* which set itself apart from the other Boston periodicals by combining stories of sex and crime with strident political polemics. A writer for the competing *Boston News-Letter* called the *Courant* "full freight-ed with Nonsense, Unmannerliness, Raillery, Prophaneness, Immorality, Arrogancy, Calumnies, Lyes, Contradictions, and what not, all tending to Quarrels and Divisions, and to Debauch and Corrupt the Minds and Man-ners of New England."

James Franklin had a famous contentious streak. He was opposed to inoc-ulations for smallpox, which he equated to quackery. He fought bitterly with the local postmaster, whom the *Courant* called a "Butter-headed Churl" after he had canceled one of Franklin's printing contracts. He railed against Puri-tans and clergymen, including Cotton Mather. In one story not long after the paper was founded, a writer charged that the Reverend Thomas Walter, a nephew of Mather, was a boozy womanizer who had spent an intimate eve-ning in the bedchamber of "two sisters, of not the best Reputation in the World." Benjamin Franklin, a sixteen-year-old apprentice printer, learned journalism at his brother's knee. Young Benjamin wrote his famous satirical essays for the *Courant* under the nom de plume Silence Dogood about such topics as overimbibing and women's underwear. He possessed more than a modicum of his brother's insolence. "I speak this by Way of Warning to all such whose Offences shall come under my Cognizance," the teenager wrote, "for I never intend to wrap my Talent in a Napkin." In June 1722 the *Courant* published a brief note about the Massachusetts government's slow-footed response to the most pressing crime problem of the day: pirates. A bucca-neer ship had been working the waters outside Boston harbor, and James Franklin wrote sardonically that the authorities planned to send a pursuit ship "sometime this Month, if Wind and Weather permit." Franklin was hauled before the legislature for this sarcastic faultfinding on crime policy and was imprisoned for a month.

In 1821, ninety-five years after Franklin's *Courant* folded, crime reporting was institutionalized in the Western press when the *London Morning Herald* appointed John Wight to look in on the night sessions at Bow Street Court, where cops presented a procession of drunks, thieves, and petty criminals, most of them poor East Enders and Irish immigrants. Wight wrote brief accounts of the court proceedings, often quoting the suspects in dialect and spicing his stories with humorous asides that belittled the uneducated court denizens. Wight explained police reporting:

> The reader is placed without personal sacrifice amidst the various and somewhat repulsive groups of a police office and made acquainted with the states and conditions of human nature, with which, from the sympathy due to the more unfortunate part of the species, he should not be entirely ignorant; it is by such means alone that the prosperous and orderly portion of society can know what passes among the destitute and disorderly portion of it.

This type of news proved shocking—and extremely popular. Newspapers of the early nineteenth century were a combination of political sheet and commercial catalogue, often featuring long lists of cargo from each ship arriving and departing. They were expensive and were read primarily by educated merchants and the gentry. The ignominious goings-on at a city court were not considered appropriate material for a dignified newspaper. Wight's work scandalized London, although many who professed to blush at his stories must have been closet readers because the *Herald*'s circulation promptly tripled. Soon, nearly every newspaper in London had its own crime and courts reporter, and American journalists took keen note of the development. Wight's court reports grew so popular that they were compiled as a book, *Mornings at Bow Street* (1826), which was sold throughout the English-speaking world, including the United States.

In the 1820s the installation of steam-driven presses at big-city newspapers increased the demand for timely fresh copy to fill all those faster-moving pages. In 1828 the *New York Morning Courier* began reprinting Wight's work, and some papers made sporadic but timid attempts at original crime reporting. The city's press had a jolly time debating whether such material was appropriate. In a June 1828 edition the *New York Statesman* had its say:

> We deem it of little benefit to the cause of morals thus to familiarize the community, and especially the younger parts of it, to the details of misdemeanors and crime. It is a contemplation that, without any possible good, at once exposes the heart to

taint and the mind to perversion. Besides, it suggests to the
novice in vice all the means of becoming expert in its devices.
The dexterity of one knave, arrested and sent to State Prison, is
adopted from newspaper instruction by others yet at large. . . .
And then we ask whether it is congenial to pure feeling and sentiment, either to register these matters on the one hand, or to
delight in their perusal on the other? We think not.

The *New York Evening Post,* edited by the young poet William Cullen Bryant,
was so inspired by the *Statesman*'s finger waggling that it reprinted the rival
newspaper's editorial about "those indecent police reports." This is the ances-
tor of the same *New York Post* that today trafficks with such relish in those
indecent police reports.

Just as modern American tabloid journalism teems with Britons trained
on Fleet Street, the first full-time police court reporter in the United States
was British. His name was George W. Wisner, and he had reported from Bow
Street Court for London newspapers. Wisner was hired by the *New York Sun,*
a four-page tabloid daily that was the first U.S. newspaper to make local
crime a staple ingredient. Founded by Benjamin Day, a twenty-three-year-
old printer from Massachusetts, the *Sun* also was the first paper targeted at
a mass readership. At the time broadsheet newspapers sold for six cents a
copy in an era when skilled artisans earned roughly $2 a day and unskilled
laborers $1. The *Sun* cost just a penny, a price that placed it within the eco-
nomic grasp of nearly anyone who could read.

Wisner was assigned to report from New York Police Court, then located
in City Hall Park in lower Manhattan. Many of those who passed through
court came from Five Points, a Manhattan slum on the Lower East Side popu-
lated by Irish immigrants, blacks, and destitute Native Americans. Like Wight
in London, Wisner used accents and dialect in his reports. The *Sun*'s first
issue, published on September 3, 1833, carried this report: "John McMan,
brought up for whipping Juda McMan, his darling wife—excuse was, that his
head was rather thick, in consequence of taking a wee drap of whiskey. Not
being able to find bail, he was accommodated with a room in Bridewell [the
city jail]."

Using the names of suspects in police stories proved highly controversial. (In some countries it still is deemed inappropriate; accused criminals
are identified only by a first name and last initial.) The Chichesters, a Five

Points gang, occasionally retaliated against police reporters who named them in stories. In one instance, William H. Attree, an abrasive police court reporter, was stabbed while on a Sunday stroll in Hoboken, New Jersey. His attacker was the brother of a man Attree had named in a story about an assault. In July 1834 the *New York Transcript* defended its policy of naming crime suspects:

> Fellows who are not ashamed to behave so scandalously as to be brought before the police are nevertheless apt to be very scandalized at seeing their names in print, and away they post to the newspaper offices to swear and storm at the liberties thus taken. A word with you, gentlemen, if you please. We assure you it grieves us to the soul to be obliged to speak in disparaging terms of such "honorable men"; but one thing we advise you, and that is, if you wish to keep clear of Police reports, to steer clear also of the Police Office.

James Gordon Bennett, whose *New York Herald* earned a reputation as the most sensational paper in the United States, reveled in naming suspects and airing the dirty details of crime stories. Bennett knew that crime reports and police court news had a certain licentious appeal to his readers, and his *Herald* lived up to its reputation with its watershed coverage of a New York prostitute's murder. In April 1836 Ellen Jewett was found hacked to death with a hatchet and set ablaze in her bed at Rosanna Townsend's brothel on Thomas Street in Five Points. Police arrested Richard Robinson, an eighteen-year-old Wall Street mercantile clerk who had been a customer of Jewett on the night she was killed. Neither murder nor harlotry was any less common then than it is today, but the *Herald, Sun,* and others among the ribald penny press Buttafuocoed the story. The *New York Transcript* printed a special Sunday edition about the crime during an era when publication on the sabbath was considered sacrilege. Out-of-town papers rushed to the frenzy as well. The *Boston Times,* for example, filled twelve of its sixteen columns in one edition with Jewett stories—all below a disingenuous editor's note that castigated the New York papers for covering such lewdness, in a choice early example of peeping-tom journalism.

Bennett visited the crime scene himself and for days running filled the *Herald* with florid accounts of Jewett's life and death—her beauty, her refinement, her seductive manner. Although the body was bloody and charred, he somehow managed to conjure a titillating image of the condition of the young prostitute's corpse: "the perfect figure, the exquisite limbs, the fine face, the full arms, the beautiful bust, all surpassed in every respect the Venus de Medici. . . . For a few moments, I was lost in admiration of this extraordinary sight." Although most papers fingered Robinson as the killer, Bennett served up unabashed speculation about the guilt of the madam of the brothel.

Some scorned Bennett for his newspaper's sensationalism, and he responded with a self-serving editorial note that brings to mind the attempts by some journalists today to rationalize the excesses of the O. J. Simpson coverage. Bennett wrote, "Instead of relating the recent awful tragedy of Ellen Jewett as a dull police report, we made of it the starting point to open up a full view upon the morals of society . . . the opening scene of a great domestic drama that will, if properly conducted . . . bring about a total revolution in the present diseased state of society and morals." Poor Bennett's revolution ultimately failed—Robinson was acquitted, and the murder was never solved. Justice may not have been served, but penny press circulations tripled.

The American public—at least that part of it that was not buying the papers—was nettled by intemperate coverage of such crimes during the 1830s. Perhaps not coincidentally, citizens also became increasingly alarmed in that decade by a perceived increase in lawlessness and immorality. It is not entirely clear whether the crime run-up was real or a press concoction based upon the spread of police and courts reporting; it probably was a combination of both. The criminal justice system was undergoing a period of important change. The United States had become a world leader in the use of imprisonment to reform rather than simply punish lawbreakers. Many convicted criminals were able to gain clemency by collecting signatures of supporters who swore that the inmates had been repaired while in prison. Efforts were afoot to abolish capital punishment, and the juries of the day often were lenient, mystifying the authorities.

Philip Hone, a patrician politician and businessman from Manhattan, kept a diary in which he inveighed against the influence of newspapers that catered to the immoral masses. He believed debauchery was inborn among immigrants and that the penny press and its crime reports appealed to their worst instincts. Hone wrote:

Mankind, even such as despise petty crimes, are prone to look with some degree of admiration upon those of a more daring and attrocious [sic] character, and their admiration leads them insensibly to sympathize with perpetrators. I cannot help believing that such publications, by familiarizing the mind of ignorant persons with the commission of crimes of a high grade, and showing the indifference with which their consequences are met, do greater harm to society than the wretches who committed them. In catering for the depraved taste of the multitude, our papers from all quarters are filled with revolting accounts of murders, from cold blooded parricides to the more ordinary slaughters of the Bagnios, Rapes, seductions, arsons, Robberies from those of the valiant Knights of the Road to those committed by the unpitied wretch, who steals to escape starvation, and forgeries of "high and low degree." Until crime becomes familiar to every sort of comprehension, and men cease to shudder at what appears to be the ordinary occurrences of life.

Bennett's *Herald* responded to this type of criticism in an editorial: "A good police reporter in such a city as New York is a useful person to society. Half the misery of the world is occasioned by secret impulses, unrestrained by public opinion. An exact and correct record of crime—ingenious crime, not vulgar drunken brawls—is useful as a warning and a beacon for others to avoid."

Journalists today ponder these same motifs at conferences and in professional journals. What *is* the purpose of crime reporting? Does it suffice for journalists to simply chronicle each crime as a freestanding anecdote, in all its numbing detail? And can these anecdotes collectively serve as beacons, or does the reading and viewing public gain nothing but a false understanding based upon marquee crimes presented without context? The answers seem apparent. Yet, with a few exceptions, crime reporters do not see themselves as policy specialists who are supposed to help the public better understand crime and its ramifications. Ask crime reporters what they do, and they are likely to respond, "My job is to cover murder and crime stories."

A prototype crime reporter was a man named George Goodrich Foster, who wrote for Horace Greeley's *New York Tribune*. He produced thousands of Bennett's "useful beacons" (or Hone's "revolting accounts," depending upon your point of view) during a long police-reporting career. He was enormously popular, and his stories were collected into a half-dozen books, including the best-selling *New York in Slices* and *New York by Gaslight*, both published in 1850.

The books are filled with florid accounts of Foster's travels on the seamy side of New York City. He led readers on tours of police court, the city jail, brothels, gambling dens, and other unsavory places where polite citizens did not go. In one of his books Foster described his idea of a journalist:

> What the triod of the Pythoness, the omens and oracles of the seers and soothsayers, the inspirations of the prophets, and the direct revelations from heaven were to the earlier ages—what the two tablets of stone, given to Moses on Mount Horeb, were to the patriarchal epoch of the race—the press ought to be to the present generation; what chivalry and knighthood were to the dark ages, the knights of the press to be to this: The defender of the assailed, the protector of the weak, the vindicator of the innocent—the terror of the oppressor, the scourge of the false, and the standard of all courtesy and honorable dealing. No institution or power on earth, sacred or secular, ever held so high a trust, or ministered from so lofty an altar, as the free press of the nineteenth century.

It might seem an impressive homily about these saints armed with ink and paper, standing as bulwarks against crooks and corrupt officials on behalf of the common person. But Foster failed to mention one widely practiced means by which lawbreakers could manage to keep their names out of the police reports during that era: they could pay off the police court reporters.

Appropriately, Charles Dickens, who toured the country and then offered his impressions in the book *American Notes and Pictures from Italy*, published in 1842, was less moved than Foster by the sanctimony of the New York newspapers. He wrote:

> What are the fifty newspapers, which those precocious urchins are bawling down the street, and which are kept filed within, what are they but amusements? Not vapid waterish amusements, but good strong stuff; dealing in round abuse and blackguard

names; pulled off the roofs of private houses, as the Halting Devil did in Spain; pimping and pandering for all degrees of vicious taste, and gorging with coined lies the most voracious maw; imputing to every man in public life the coarsest and the vilest motives; scaring away from the stabbed and prostrate body-politic every Samaritan of clear conscience and good deeds; and setting on, with yell and whistle and the clapping of foul hands, the vilest vermin and worst birds of prey.

Three decades after Dickens's visit Joseph Pulitzer borrowed freely from the penny press story budget of murder, sin, and sex as he developed a style of reporting and marketing that became known, rather misleadingly, as "new journalism." The Pulitzer style of journalism stands alongside the penny press as important exhibits in the history of U.S. crime reporting.

Pulitzer, a native Hungarian, had emigrated to the United States to serve as a mercenary in the Union army. After the war he settled in St. Louis, where he had connections in the large German-American community, and landed a job as a reporter with the *Westliche Post,* a German-language daily there. In 1878 Pulitzer bought the *St. Louis Dispatch* for $2,500 at a sheriff's bankruptcy sale, then merged his new property a few days later with another local daily, the *Post.* The *P-D*'s coverage was dosed heavily with scorn for the wealthy and elite. Pulitzer filled the pages with stories of tippling clergymen, defiled virgins, love triangles, prostitution, and sundry adulteries. Within three years the *Post-Dispatch* was the city's leading evening newspaper, and soon a grander stage beckoned.

New York, America's largest city, awaited Pulitzer's sensational sensibilities. Journalists of the day were well aware that great wealth was within reach of any publisher who was willing to pander to the rabble. In 1879 Whitelaw Reid, who had succeeded Horace Greeley as editor of the *New York Tribune,* wrote, "There is not a newspaper editor in New York who does not know the fortune that awaits the man there who is willing to make a daily paper as disreputable and vile as a hundred and fifty thousand readers would be willing to buy. It is the newspaper opportunity of the time." Pulitzer was the man, and the *New York World,* a money loser that he bought for $346,000 from financier Jay Gould, was the paper. As it would turn out, Pulitzer produced a newspaper that was so disreputable and vile that ten times the number Reid predicted were willing to buy.

In a signed editorial in his first issue, published on May 11, 1883, Pulitzer dusted off the same mission statement he used in St. Louis:

> The entire World newspaper property has been purchased by the undersigned, and will from this day on be under different management—different in men, measures and methods, different in purpose, policy and principle—different in objects and interests—different in sympathies and convictions—different in heart and head.
>
> Performance is better than promise. Exuberant assurances are cheap. I make none. I simply refer the public to the new World itself, which hence forth shall be the daily evidence of its own growing improvement, with forty-eight daily witnesses in its forty-eight columns.
>
> There is room in this great and growing city for a journal that is not only cheap but bright, not only bright but large, not only large but truly Democratic—dedicated to the cause of the people rather than that of the purse-potentates—devoted more to the news of the New than the Old World—that will expose all fraud and sham, fight all public evils and abuses—that will serve and battle for the people with earnest sincerity.
>
> In that cause and for that end solely that new World is hereby enlisted and committed to the attention of the intelligent public.

As the news pages of the *World* carried the predictable mix of sex and blood, the editorial page thumped a drum against greedy corporations and government complicity. Pulitzer was an inveterate writer of staff memoranda, and he freely shared his news philosophies in terse maxims punctuated by exclamation points. In one, he urged the staff to focus "on what is original, distinctive, dramatic, romantic, thrilling, unique, curious, quaint, humorous, odd, apt to be talked about." Other memos drilled home the Pulitzer dictums that would become part of the training for generations of journalists to come: "Accuracy! Accuracy!! Accuracy!!!" "Never drop a big thing until you have gone to the bottom of it. Continuity! Continuity! Continuity until the subject is really finished." "Terseness! Intelligent, not stupid, condensation."

After the Civil War, literacy had increased with the institution of mandatory education, and Pulitzer tapped that growing pool of readers by positioning his papers as advocates for the working class. The *World* endorsed increased taxes for the wealthy, social reforms for the poor, and reconstruction of the corrupt civil service system. It embarked upon a number of public crusades, including fund-raising for the Statue of Liberty. Most important, it "reveled in lachrymose titillation," as one journalism historian put it, especially as related to the seven deadly sins. Once again, the *New York Evening Post,* forebear of what would become the country's most sensational daily paper, waggled a finger at this latest form of sensationalism, just as it had during the penny press era: "A yellow journal office is probably the nearest approach, in atmosphere, to hell, existing in any Christian state. A better place in which to prepare a young man for eternal damnation than a yellow journal office does not exist."

The single-minded Pulitzer probably paid little heed to criticism. The *World*'s new journalism—a combination of crime, public advocacy, and patronage of the working class—resonated with New Yorkers like no other newspaper had. In its first year the *World*'s circulation quadrupled, to sixty thousand, then it quadrupled again, to a quarter million, by 1887.

A half-century after the penny press practiced sensationalism, technological advances and a broadened readership base had raised the stakes of irresponsible journalism. Faster presses made newspapers such as the *World* more readily available when lurid news was breaking. Color printing, cartoons, photographs, and writers who were more skilled than ever in the tabloid arts of mawkishness and feigned indignation could create a public furor in a single edition. The large circulation, increased immediacy, and skilled use of hype gave the *World* unprecedented influence, and editors across the country began to take note.

During the 1880s and 1890s new daily newspapers opened at a rate of more than one per week in the United States; English-language dailies increased from 850 in 1880 to nearly 2,000 in 1900. As these papers jockeyed for a place in the crowded news market, many chose to try to emulate the success of Pulitzer in St. Louis and New York by adapting his excessively self-promoting methods. Papers such as the *Chicago Tribune, Philadelphia Record,* and *Boston Globe* featured the same overwrought emotion that defined the *World.* The *Denver Post,* published by a former saloon keeper and a real estate speculator, used huge headlines in red ink over stories stuffed with

*World*-like purple prose. The paper, which billed itself as "Your Big Brother," operated out of offices with walls painted barn red. Thus its nickname: the Bucket of Blood.

In 1887 George Hearst, publisher of the *San Francisco Examiner,* was appointed to the U.S. Senate to fill an unexpired term, and he left his newspaper in the care of his son, William Randolph. The twenty-four-year-old upstart declared that he would transform the *Examiner* into the *New York World* of the West. "What we're after is the 'gee-whiz' emotion," said one Hearst minion. "We run our paper so that when the reader opens it he says, 'Gee-Whiz!'" Hearst quickly transformed the *Examiner* from a rather obscure sheet into a profitable, powerful newspaper. And like Pulitzer, Hearst was not satisfied to toil in the provinces. In 1895 he paid $180,000 to buy the *New York Journal,* and one of the most intense newspaper rivalries in history commenced.

Hearst offered his New York paper at a penny, so Pulitzer cut the *World*'s price to match his foe's. The two papers often battled most intensely on crime stories; readers were treated for weeks running to story upon story about the duly designated crime of the moment. The antagonism between the two men was personal, and each relished swiping prized staff members from the other. One such raid helped create the nickname Yellow Journalism, given to the Pulitzer-Hearst era. It was derived from "The Yellow Kid," a popular color cartoon by Richard F. Outcault published in the *World.* The cartoon, which depicted life in a Lower East Side tenement, featured a recurring character, a bald, big-eared, overgrown infant who wore a nightshirt that always was colored yellow. When Hearst enticed Outcault to leave Pulitzer for the *Journal,* the *World* created its own version of "The Yellow Kid." Promotional posters for both papers featured the rival Yellow Kids, and the color stuck in a shorthand description of the competition between the *World* and the *Journal.*

The rivalry created "a shrieking, gaudy, sensation-loving, devil-may-care kind of journalism which lured the reader by any possible means," according to journalism historian Edwin Emery. He called it "journalism without a soul." Another historian wrote, "The louder the yellow press screamed, the greater waxed its popularity and the stronger its grip grew upon American journalism. Publishers can ignore truth, decency and ethics, but they cannot disregard the methods which prove themselves by selling more papers."

The papers certainly did sell. Their circulations climbed to unimagined levels—500,000, 750,000, 1 million—as Hearst and Pulitzer tried to one-up each other with everything from shamelessly trivial stories about sex and crime to blatant fabrications about Martians and miracle cures. Hearst specialized in the confessions of criminals and the alleged true-life stories of debauched virgins. The *World* and the *Journal* presented stories with doctored photographs, five-color illustrations, apocalyptic headlines, and breathless text. In that day, circulation was based almost entirely upon street sales, so page one was particularly raw. An editor from the *World* explained the packaging secrets:

> Suppose it's Halley's comet. Well, first you have a half-page of decoration showing the comet, with historical pictures of previous appearances thrown in. If you can work a pretty girl into the decoration, so much the better. If not, get some good nightmare idea like the inhabitants of Mars watching it pass. Then you want a quarter of a page of big-type heads—snappy. Then four inches of story, written right off the bat. Then a picture of Professor Halley down here and another of Professor Lowell up there, and a two-column boxed freak containing a scientific opinion, which nobody will understand, just to give it class.

At the end of the nineteenth century, as Hearst and Pulitzer were mastering the craft of public hype, a number of influential Americans, including Theodore Roosevelt, Henry Cabot Lodge, John Hay, and Josiah Strong, were preaching that the country could succeed on the world stage only by turning toward imperialism. They enlisted the *World* and *Journal* to help whip up a jingoistic frenzy of support as they shopped quite publicly for colonial properties. Behind the American imperialists was a newly modernized navy that was ready for a fight.

In March 1895, a few months before Hearst bought the *Journal,* an insurrection began against Spanish colonial rule in Cuba. The U.S. government supported the revolutionaries with money and advice, and public sentiment weighed heavily toward the Cubans. As the fighting intensified in early 1896, many large American newspapers, including the *Journal* and *World,* sent correspondents to Cuba with instructions to find atrocities and report them in microscopic detail. The *World* was positively frenzied in its coverage. James Creelman, Pulitzer's man in Cuba, provided his readers with this phlebotomitic sentence: "Blood on the roadsides, blood in the fields, blood on the doorsteps, blood, blood, blood!"

But the *Journal* managed to outscream even the *World*. Hearst's melodramatic accounts presented the noble native Cubans as battling valiantly but in vain against Spaniards who were characterized as butchering conquistadors. The paper reached a hyperkinetic state after 266 American sailors died in the sinking of the battleship *Maine* in Havana harbor. On the day after the explosion, before it had any evidence, the *Journal* blamed the Spanish and published a crude illustration that showed the *Maine* anchored above a floating device that was labeled SPANISH MINE. Hearst offered a $50,000 reward for information leading to the conviction of those responsible, although the paper said it would proffer the cash only if the snitch talked exclusively to the *Journal*. Two days later the paper's front-page banner headline read THE WHOLE COUNTRY THRILLS WITH WAR FEVER. Hearst got his war, of course. Some years later Theodore Roosevelt, an assistant secretary of the navy during the Cuba crisis, would say, "It wasn't much of a war, but it was the best war we had."

Emery, the journalism historian, estimated that one third of all metropolitan U.S. newspapers were "yellow" by the turn of the century. For more than twenty years Pulitzer and his peers had a rollicking good time with scandal, international intrigue, murder, and sex. There were the unsolved case of Jack the Ripper, who killed five prostitutes in London in 1888, the murders of Andrew and Abigail Borden in Massachusetts in 1892, and the first "crime of the century," the 1906 love-triangle slaying at Madison Square Garden in New York of the renowned architect Stanford White by Harry Thaw, heir to a railroad fortune. The object of their mutual affection was a Broadway show girl named Evelyn Nesbit, who also happened to be Thaw's wife. A journalist who covered the Thaw trial called it

> the most spectacular criminal case . . . that ever sucked dry the descriptive reservoirs of the American press. You see, it had in it wealth, degeneracy, rich old wasters; delectable young chorus girls and adolescent artists' models; the behind-the-scenes of Theaterdom and the Underworld, and the Great White Way . . . the abnormal pastimes and weird orgies of overly aesthetic artists and jaded debauchees. In the cast of the motley show were Bowery toughs, Harlem gangsters, Tenderloin panders,

Broadway leading men, Fifth Avenue clubmen, Wall Street manipulators, uptown voluptuaries and downtown thugs.

A modest public backlash against the sensationalism followed the White-Thaw trial. George W. Alger, a social critic of the times, criticized yellow journalism for "its vulgarizing influence on its readers; by its bad taste, by its daily offenses against the actual, though as yet ideal, right of privacy, by its arrogant boastfulness, mawkish sentimentality, and a persistent and systematic distortion of values in events." Joseph Pulitzer himself, who earned a fortune by purveying bad taste, had a famous change of heart at about the same time. Blind and afflicted by a severe nervous disorder, Pulitzer attempted to chisel a revisionist version of his personal legacy after so many years of stooping low to sell papers. He mounted one final crusade: to establish a professional school where the study of journalism could become one of the world's major intellectual pursuits, like the law, philosophy, and religion.

When he died in 1911, Pulitzer left a $2 million endowment to the school, which opened the following year. Today the Columbia University Graduate School of Journalism and the Pulitzer prizes, the most prestigious awards in the field of journalism, stand as rather ironic monuments, for it is not difficult to argue that Joseph Pulitzer brought a measure of dishonor to the profession. His most profound accomplishment may have been that he helped make the reading of a newspaper a daily habit for twentieth-century Americans. How he did so—sensationalism—is quite another issue. Of course, Pulitzer has had great postmortem public relations. Biographies about him have had such subtitles as *An Adventure with a Genius* and *Liberator of Journalism*. In a 1965 biography, W. J. Granberg went so far as to say that Pulitzer was caught unaware by sensationalism. According to Granberg's account, Pulitzer was ill and under doctors' care in Europe during the mid-1890s when Arthur Brisbane, the *World*'s managing editor, introduced the yellow style of crime coverage to keep up with Hearst. Granberg wrote that Pulitzer sent a plaintive cable from Europe: "WHO DEGRADED THE PAPER?" The author concluded, "Shaken by the knowledge that his newspapers were hated and scorned, Pulitzer worked as best he could to reform them. But he was too distant from the scene to exert much real pressure in the news room." To which there is only one appropriate response: Yeah, right.

During the height of his power Pulitzer had found an admirer in an aspiring British publisher named Alfred C. Harmsworth, who, after gaining title, became known as Lord Northcliffe. During the 1890s Northcliffe had visited New York to observe the methods of the *World* and the *Journal*. He took what he learned back to London and created a series of newspapers, including the *London Evening News, Daily Mail,* and in 1903 the *Daily Mirror,* a halfpenny illustrated paper that was printed in the tabloid format. A tabloid, measuring roughly eleven by sixteen inches, typically is the size of a broadsheet turned on its side. It became popular in big cities because commuters on trolleys and subway trains are able to handle the papers more adeptly in places with little elbow room. *Tabloid* can refer to the abbreviated content and tone of the paper as well, and at one point Northcliffe ordered editors of the *Daily Mail,* whose slogan was "The busy man's paper," that no story should run longer than 250 words.

The *Daily Mirror* was a circulation success, and it spawned a number of tabloid imitators in London. Northcliffe became convinced that an illustrated tabloid could be highly profitable in any of the world's biggest cities, including New York. During World War I, Northcliffe   by then an influential press baron—became a mentor for a number of determined young journalists from throughout the English-speaking world who passed through London while covering the war. One was an Australian named Keith Murdoch, Rupert's father, who impressed Northcliffe with a moving account of the war from Gallipoli. The two developed a father-son relationship, and Northcliffe offered Murdoch guidance and support when he returned home and went to work at the *Melbourne Herald.*

Another Northcliffe protégé was a young U.S. Army officer, Captain Joseph Medill Patterson. At war's end New York City still had no tabloid, and Northcliffe summoned Patterson to a business meeting to discuss that void. For five years Captain Patterson and his cousin, Colonel Robert R. McCormick, had inhabited rather awkward positions as copublishers of the *Chicago Tribune,* which had grown to prominence under the editorship of their grandfather, Joseph Medill. Following Northcliffe's advice, the cousins agreed to use *Tribune* profits to establish the New York tabloid that the British press lord knew would thrive. McCormick would continue to publish the *Tribune,* and Patterson would carry the title of publisher of the new paper. The captain and colonel returned to the United States to assemble a staff, and on June 26,

1919, the undersized *Illustrated Daily News* bowed in New York City. It would help define crime reporting for several generations of U.S. journalists. A mission statement was printed in the first edition:

WHO WE ARE

THE ILLUSTRATED DAILY NEWS is going to be your newspaper. Its interests will be your interests. . . . It is not an experiment, for the appeal of news pictures and brief, well-told stories will be as apparent to you as it has been to millions of readers in European cities.

We shall give you every day the best and newest pictures of the interesting things that are happening in the world. . . . The story that is told by a picture can be grasped instantly. Ten thousand words of description cannot convey to you the impression you received when you look at Millet's painting, "The Angelus." . . .

No story will be continued to another page—that is to save you trouble. . . . You can read it without eye strain.

The policy of the Illustrated Daily News will be your policy. It will be aggressively for America and for the people of New York. . . . It will have no entangling alliance with any class whatever. . . .

Because the doings of the very fortunate are always of interest we shall print them as interestingly as possible in our society column. Because fiction will always be appealing we shall print the best and newest that is to be had. We shall print the best features that are to be found.

In the same day's edition of the *New York Times*, Captain Patterson bought an ad that summarized more succinctly a primary appeal of the *Daily News:* SEE NEW YORK'S MOST BEAUTIFUL GIRLS EVERY MORNING IN THE ILLUSTRATED DAILY NEWS. The paper was a lively compendium of brief crime news, sexy stories, fiction, and column upon column of gossip. About one fifth of the daily editorial space was dedicated to photographs. To understand how jarring this was to the public, consider that on most days the rival *Times* and other broadsheets generally carried not a single photo. In terms of design it was like turning *USA Today*'s layout staff loose in a journalism world occupied only by *Wall Street Journals*.

By the spring of 1921 the *News* was selling 400,000 copies a day, more than any other New York paper except Hearst's *Evening Journal*. A year later, with the *News*'s circulation climbing ever higher, an aging Hearst responded with a "Lady Luck" lottery, borrowed from a newspaper war in Chicago between his *Herald-Examiner* and Colonel McCormick's *Tribune*. When Hearst announced a grand prize of $1,000 in New York, Captain Patterson offered his paper's lottery with a $2,500 top prize. When Hearst went to $5,000, Patterson offered $10,000. Simon Michael Bessie, a newspaper historian, wrote, "Lady Luck so absorbed the staffs of both papers that news accounts were reduced to the minimum and the offices were in a state of excitement bordering on demoralization." Circulations of the two New York papers increased by a total of a half million during the lottery frenzy. Ultimately, Hearst blinked when Patterson increased the payoff to $25,000. The master of publicity had met his match.

As the dominant paper in the most important U.S. city, the *Daily News* developed a national reputation for its over-the-top coverage of murder and mayhem. Predictably, it proved no less controversial than the earlier versions of sex-and-crime sheets that had scandalized the bluenose crowd. Bessie wrote that Pulitzer and Hearst had prepared the way "for the cheap illustrated daily which sank its tentacles still deeper into the strata of the faintly literate." He quoted one social critic of the 1920s as saying that tabloids "reduce the highest ideals of the newspaper to the process of fastening a camera lens to every boudoir keyhole." The *Independent* called the *Daily News* "baudy, inane, contemptible," and the *Saturday Review of Literature* worried over where the tabloid sensibility was heading. "What will the grandchildren of the tabloid readers be like?" the editors asked. "In emotion, ideals, intelligence, either wrought into fantastic shapes or burnt out altogether. Soiled minds, rotten before they are ripe."

Despite—or perhaps because of—its rotten influence, the *Daily News* was an instant institution, as New York as stickball and Coney Island. The content, tone, and presentation met with a readership that apparently had been waiting for just such a paper, as Lord Northcliffe had long predicted.

Inevitably, the success of the *Daily News* spawned imitators, including the *Daily Graphic* and the *Daily Mirror,* Hearst's tabloid answer to the *News* in

New York, and others in the country's largest cities. The brash little papers developed a style that came to be known as *jazz journalism* as they helped America forget the world war. They covered celebrity gossip with relish, and they helped sear into our national history certain names and lifestyles: speakeasies, flappers, molls, Al Capone, Legs Diamond, Dutch Schultz. The newspapers made celebrities out of sports figures like Jack Dempsey, Knute Rockne, Babe Ruth, Bobby Jones, and Bill Tilden.

But crime and criminal trials attracted the brightest tabloid spotlights. The second "crime of the century," after the murder of Stanford White, came in 1921, when Fatty Arbuckle, a silent film star, was acquitted of a manslaughter charge after he beat a starlet who later was seized by convulsions and died. In 1924 the tabloids helped transform the murder of a young boy by two teenagers, Nathan Leopold and Richard Loeb, into yet another national obsession. The case featured a defense, prepared by Clarence Darrow, that the accused killers were victims of their own upbringing and genetic composition. The following year, when Darrow took his oratorical talents to Tennessee to defend John Scopes against heresy charges for teaching evolution, the New York press tagged along, with the *Daily News* at the lead.

During the summer of 1926 the circulation of the *Daily News* passed one million as it featured an extraordinary stream of sleazy stories about triple murders, secret love nests, and child brides, including the marriage and divorce of "Daddy" Browning and his fifteen-year-old wife, Peaches. Trying in vain to compete with the *Daily News* circulation juggernaut, Hearst's *Mirror* on July 28 dredged up the Hall-Mills case, a four-year-old double suicide of a minister and his choir-member mistress in New Brunswick, New Jersey. The *Mirror* claimed that it had new evidence implicating the minister's wife, Frances Stevens Hall. The *Daily News* featured the story as its front-page "wood"—the type for the largest headline of the day was carved from wood because metal type of that size was unavailable—for nearly a month running, dedicating as many as five pages per day to the stories, photographs, and maps. The *News* helped make an obscure story a national sensation, just as today's papers have in the Buttafuoco, Fleiss, and Florida Nympho cases.

The story was knocked from the front page only a handful of times during that frantic season. On August 7 Gertrude Ederle earned the wood when she swam the English Channel. On August 20 Irving Berlin's marriage managed to bump Hall-Mills for the day. On August 24, when Rudolph Valentino died, the *Daily News* devoted six full pages to the story. Its wood headline that day read, VALENTINO POISONED. A tiny parenthetical after-thought was tucked beside the main headline: BROADWAY HEARS DOCTORS DENY. On September 3 a wave of murder made the wood: SEVEN KILLINGS IN 15 HOURS.

The year ended with the very public trial and acquittal of Francis Stevens Hall. Acquittals in highly sensationalized criminal trials have formed something of a pattern in this century, from Fatty Arbuckle to O. J. Simpson. One exception came in 1927, the year after the Hall acquittal, in yet another love-triangle murder made famous by the tabloids. Judd Gray, a corset sales-man, and Ruth Snyder, his married lover, were accused of killing Snyder's husband. From the filing of charges in March through the trial in May the newspapers assigned a squadron of reporters to the story, with speculative pieces about Gray's other lovers and the relative culpability of the killers. Snyder and Gray were convicted, and the press eagerly awaited their execu-tions. On January 12, 1928, Ruth Snyder faced execution at Sing Sing prison in upstate New York. On the day before the execution the *Daily Graphic* enticed readers with a full-page tease: "Don't fail to read tomorrow's Graph-ic. An installment that thrills and stuns! A story that fairly pierces the heart and reveals Ruth Snyder's last thoughts on earth; that pulses the blood as it discloses her final letters. Think of it! A woman's final thoughts just before she is clutched in the deadly snare that sears and burns and FRIES AND KILLS! Her very last words! Exclusively in tomorrow's Graphic."

But the *Daily News* managed to do the *Graphic* one better. As the hour of Snyder's electrocution approached, a *Daily News* man, Tom Howard, took a front-row seat in the section reserved for observers and journalists. At 11:06 P.M., as the electrical current was activated, Howard discreetly raised the cuff of his baggy trousers and snapped a single shot from a forbidden camera strapped to his ankle. The *News* published the photograph in an extra edition on January 13, then printed it again on the front page on January 14. The rather blurry photo showed a blindfolded Snyder sitting in the electric chair with straps around her torso, arms, and legs. The caption below began, WHEN RUTH PAID HER DEBT TO THE STATE! On the second day that the photo ran, the caption described Tom Howard's snapshot as "the most talked-of feat in the history of journalism." The competition shrieked, the moralists fret-ted, and the public bought. The *Daily News* sold an extra half-million copies that day.

The photograph was a ghastly crowning achievement of crime-news coverage. Ever since James Gordon Bennett had rhapsodized over the scorched corpse of Ellen Jewett, U.S. crime reporters had tried to carry readers ever closer to the crime scene through description, details, anecdotes, illustrations, and, later, photographs. Tom Howard had taken *Daily News* readers so close to Ruth Snyder's execution that they could almost smell her singed hair.

With such coverage the *Daily News* had considerable influence in the culture of crime reporting during this century. It maintained and sanctioned the penny press archetype that had been preserved by Pulitzer and the other new journalists. The paper specialized in aggressive coverage of anecdotal cases but gave little attention to crime policy. It lavished disproportionate attention on sex and violence. It was friendly to the point of complicity with the police authorities and thus fomented the idea that police officers ("New York's Finest," the *Daily News* calls them) are adept at solving crimes and catching criminals. As the country's largest newspaper, the *News* helped certify what was acceptable and expected in coverage of police news.

A 1987 study of crime stories that ran in the *New York Times* during the first half of this century concluded that crime was covered by anecdote, with little attention to stories about solutions and policy decisions. The researcher analyzed nearly fifteen hundred crime stories published in 156 sample editions of the *Times* from 1900 to 1950. She concluded:

> Most were brief, superficial, descriptive accounts of offenses, lacking in interpretations and background analyses. . . . The most significant finding is the similarity of crime coverage over the five decades analyzed. Despite massive changes in most other realms, and substantial professional and technological innovation within the press, crime news reporting remained relatively constant. . . . Indeed, it is the police blotter that serves as the main source for crime news coverage from 1900 to 1950 and beyond. . . . The results point to a picture of crime rendered superficial through the routinization of a method that answers questions such as: who, what and when and only rarely why.

Today most newspapers still cover crime as a reactive beat, by chasing the mayhem that reveals itself via the police department, either in a crackling radio transmission or as a "major case" that is summarized on the blotter. This model of news is so ingrained that most journalists might think it absurd to cover crime in some other fashion. Journalists can't necessarily influence what the public thinks, but they do influence what the public thinks *about*. The arrested development of crime coverage has prompted the public to think about seven things: lust, pride, envy, sloth, intemperance, avarice, and ire.

# chapter

# Anything Particularly Cruel

## THE WORLD OF CRIME REPORTING

It probably is folly to expect much more than stories about the seven deadly sins from the crime beat. After all, at most newspapers the reporters who cover crime are the catfish of the newsroom. They occupy the bottom of the reporting hierarchy, down near the obituary writers. If other reporters look upon them with a degree of respect, it is only because they must cover a beat that most would rather not.

Crime reporters tend to be more blue collar than blue blood, and they can be lumped into two subgroups: cubs and lifers. Cub reporters, almost always green and fresh from college, are not yet qualified for the more prestigious beats, such as city hall, education, the courts, or the statehouse. A newspaper can hire them for $400 a week and send them off to the police beat, which will teach them the basic skills needed to crank out two or three stories a day under pressure of deadline. They will learn to "work the phones" and develop resourcefulness. They learn how to summon the nerve to interview cops. (For some reason, even reporters who can spar at press conferences with mayors, governors, and presidents tend to clench up at the thought of asking a question of the police.) Most important, young police reporters will hone the most vital skill that a journalist can possess: the delicate art of wheedling information, anecdotes, and photographs out of living crime victims, relatives of dead crime victims, and the authorities.

Only rarely are young police reporters treated to formal training. Typically, a cub reporter simply is pointed toward the police state by an editor who probably has never been there. "Go for it," the editor might say. These young reporters wouldn't know a patrol strategy if they tripped over it, and they don't know a UCR (uniform crime report) from a VCR. The experience of Ilene Prusher, who was hired in the early 1990s to cover crime in a collection of suburban towns for the *Philadelphia Inquirer,* is typical. "I had no training whatsoever," she says. "They just told me that I was the police reporter. The former police reporter was gone, so no one could introduce me to the key sources or give advice. My boss gave me a list of phone numbers for the police departments and told me to call them." Most cub reporters hope to cover a few murders, bank a handful of front-page bylines, then advance to a more attractive beat after eighteen months. Their news hormones rage as they chase around the city after car accidents, fires, robberies, and homicides. Experienced reporters recall their time at the cop shop—the days of innocence and energy—with dewy eyes.

On the other hand, reporters who find themselves covering police news for more than a few years are viewed in the newsroom as lifers on the police beat. These reporters often are the most valuable in a newsroom during the frequent scavenger hunts for a crucial detail—a name or an address, for example—that another reporter has been unable to come up with. Yet lifers on the police beat can be seen as somehow defective, unable to adapt to a better beat. A police reporter at the *Baltimore Sun* who had covered the cops for two years told me that he was advised by a snot-nosed newcomer to the paper that he ought to get off the police beat. "You're too good to cover the cops," the callow fellow counseled.

Although cubs go into police reporting because it's a foot in the door of journalism, some lifers cover cops because they were too short, fat, or crazy to get into the police academy. Lifers identify with cops and often hang out with them. They keep police scanners at their desks, in their homes, and in their cars. They wear beepers to bed. They might enjoy the aroma of a warehouse fire. They have dreams about crime scene chalk lines and taxicab yellow POLICE: DO NOT CROSS tape. Long-term exposure to crime can breed an insidious and unhealthy cynicism in these reporters, just as it does in cops. Some lifer police reporters develop a reputation as loners. They become isolated in the newsroom, taking desks behind pillars, around corners. Now and then a longtime police reporter breaks down. He might get into a fistfight with an editor or a police sergeant, or he might disrobe and go screaming naked at a dead run up the center stripe of Main Street. Generally, police reporters do not have the patience or disposition to make good Cub Scout leaders and T-ball coaches.

By trade, police reporters traffick in human misery and deviance. In a chapter about police reporting in one respected journalism textbook, the author quotes a police reporter from the *Sacramento Bee* as she reviewed the blotter of reports of the previous twenty-four hours, searching for crimes that she could spin into stories. "I'm looking for anything strange, anything particularly cruel," she said.

That is police reporting in two phrases: anything strange, anything particularly cruel. In its typical antediluvian form, crime news is cheap and easy, and almost anyone can produce it. Send a warm body to the police station and tell her to scan the blotter to find an anecdote that is strange or cruel. Talk to the police, talk to relatives, write a story. That's how crime news happens. This has been so for 150 years or more, at least since the days when James Gordon Bennett declared that the function of a newspaper is to startle. Today most reporting about crime begins and ends with the famed five ws asked by scribes and mystery writers for centuries: Who killed her? What killed her? When was she killed? Where was she killed? Why was she killed?

Of course, modern journalists would never say aloud that their professional mission is to startle. Instead, they use codified phrases that hark to the gee-whiz journalism of William Randolph Hearst. An axiom popular among editors is that the best stories are those that get a rise around the breakfast table. They are called "Holy Shit!" or "Hey, Maude!" stories now—stories that make Mr. and Mrs. America drop their false teeth in the corn flakes and shout, "Hey, Maude! Listen to what I've just read about Joey Buttafuoco in the *Tribune*." More often than not, "Hey, Maude!" stories come from the police beat.

Each day, news about crime and the courts system fills about one-third of the space of the typical U.S. newspaper and nearly half the news minutes on local television broadcasts. The media select that news from a vast menu of possibilities. Roughly five thousand violent felonies and thirty-five thousand nonviolent crimes are reported to police each day in this country. Tens of thousands of other cases are wending through the courts system at any moment. Police reporters provide great comfort to assignment editors, who arrive at work each morning to find blank pages that must be filled by deadline. These reporters go to the police station and collect accounts of local misery by reviewing arrest reports, crime reports, and accident reports.

The daily pressure to produce fresh tales about late-breaking mayhem is, without question, the most difficult part of the crime beat. That pressure also can be a pretty good excuse for superficiality and the occupational attention deficit disorder from which journalism suffers.

In the late spring of 1990, overwhelmed by crime news and increasingly troubled about my role in its presentation to the public, I resigned my position as chief of the police headquarters bureau for the *New York Daily News.* When I cleaned out my desk in the pressroom at One Police Plaza in lower Manhattan, I took with me several dozen files that contained story clips, notes, and background information on some high-profile cases that I had helped cover—the killings of cops, the ascension of mobster John Gotti, and so forth. I also took six folders labeled MURDER, each overflowing with story clips organized by date. They form a crime reporter's diary: MOM HELD IN FATAL SCALDING: 3-YEAR-OLD HAD ANGERED HER BY SOILING HIS DIAPER, COPS SAY (March 22, 1988); MOTHER ADMITS "I DROWNED MY BABY"; KIDNAP TALE FALSE; SHE TELLS POLICE: "I COULDN'T TAKE HIS CRYING ANY MORE" (April 22, 1988); BOY, 3, IS SHOT WHILE BEING USED AS SHIELD (February 2, 1989); HEADLESS BODY IS I.D.'D AS TENANT ORGANIZER (June 20, 1989); GORY DETAILS POUR OUT: "BUTCHER" CALLED CLASSIC PSYCHO FULL OF BOASTING (September 21, 1989); FOR "NICE GIRL," A DATE WITH DEATH (February 22, 1990); B'KLYN BOY SET ABLAZE; COPS NAB SUSPECT, 13 (March 8, 1990).

The sad fact is that, less than a decade later, I don't remember any of the stories, any of the victims. They consumed a day of my life, then I was off on the next chase. That is crime reporting—a blank page each day, fresh human suffering with which to fill it. The pack goes on to poke and prod at new human detritus. No one can afford the time to remember yesterday because the competition, the crank that turns the wheel of crime news, is preparing for tomorrow. Journalists are condemned to live "wholly in the present," as Horace Greeley noted more than 150 years ago.

This is what Stanley Walker, the Texas gentlemen who was city editor of the *New York Herald Tribune* from 1927 until 1946, meant when he said, "Most of the music in journalism is played by ear." There is no time to study the sheet music. Ray Ring, a former Arizona newspaperman, described the anxiety-inducing tension of daily journalism in his novel *Arizona Kiss*:

> I can tell you what it's like to work for a newspaper. Imagine a combine, one of those huge threshing machines that eats up a row of wheat like nothing, bearing right down on you. You're running in front of it, all day long, day in, day out, just inches in front of the maw, where steel blades are whirring and clacking and waiting for you to get tired or make one slip. The only way to keep the combine off you is to throw it something else to rip apart and digest. What you feed it is stories. Words and photos. Ten inches on this, fifteen inches on that, a vertical shot here and a horizontal there, scraps of news and film that go into the maw where they are processed and dumped out on some page to fill the spaces around the ads. Each story buys you a little time, barely enough to slap together the next story, and the next, and the next. You never get far ahead, you never take a breather, all you do is live on the hustle. Always in a rush, always on deadline, you keep scrambling to feed the combine. That's what it's like.

The business is difficult, often frenzied, and the results probably can be no better than imprecise. As Walker, the *Herald Tribune* editor, put it, "News is the inexact measure of the ebb and flow of the tides of human aspiration, the ignominy of mankind, the glory of the human race. It is the best record we have of the incredible meanness and the magnificent courage of man."

The media expend a great deal of time, space, energy in documenting that meanness and magnificence. Newspapers in all but the largest cities dedicate a column or more a day to a small-type accounting of neighbors' transgressions and misfortunes—arrests for driving drunk or passing bad checks, reports to police of break-ins and thefts, convictions for larcenies and welfare fraud. These minor nonviolent crimes are vastly more prevalent and probably more important to most residents than the violence on the front page, but they get scant attention. In big cities, where there is so much crime that the local paper can't afford the newsprint to thoroughly report even all the murders, crimes such as burglary and car theft are ignored as minutiae unless the victim happens to be a politician or a newspaper editor. A 1988 study found that newspapers in the mid-1980s covered violent crimes (murder, robbery, rape, assault) four times more frequently than property crimes (burglary, larceny, theft), even though property crimes are nine times more prevalent.

In addition to local crime news, a broad selection of mayhem from afar is available via the wire services. To an outsider, it might seem like a mystery of journalism that editors at hundreds of newspapers across the country on a given day should decide a certain story is worthy of space in your home-town paper, whether you happen to live in Little Rock, Arkansas, or Big Stone, Minnesota. But there it is, day after day: the duly designated crime of the moment. The news services help sustain the sameness. All but a handful of the 1,550 daily newspapers in the United States are member-subscribers of the Associated Press, for example. The AP also serves six thousand TV and radio stations across the country and another eighty-five hundred media outlets elsewhere in the world. It draws material not only from its own staff members but from reporters who work for its subscribers. From a pool of thousands of possibilities AP editors fish out perhaps two dozen stories for each wire—local, regional, national, and international—and transmit those stories electronically to print and broadcast members.

Certain sex-related stories—the Florida Nympho or Amy Fisher—are selected based purely upon their prurient content. Others are chosen based upon mindless habit of editors who recognize a name from previous installations; the criminal travails of the Menendez brothers, finally convicted in 1996 of murdering their parents after two trials and tens of thousands of news stories, is one example. But why is it that most of America manages to read or hear about a particular death of the day—often a grotesque murder—that happened in a faraway city? It might be a love-triangle murder in Maine. A teenager stuffs a pipe bomb into the mouth of a girl in South Carolina; it explodes. Six municipal workers are slaughtered by a suicidal former colleague in Florida. There's been a triple murder in California, a quadruple in Texas. An innocent bystander has been killed in Brooklyn. A knife fight in a pizza parlor in Chicago, a drive-by shooting in the Cleveland suburbs, a riot at a high school basketball game in Texas, a disco bomb in Madrid, a fatal arson in Kentucky.

After the last page is turned, after the credits roll, news consumers sit in easy chairs across the nation, eyes dry and mouths agape, no better informed than they were thirty minutes earlier. The stories make no attempt to answer the question that should arise in virtually every story about crime: so what?

Linda Heath, a research psychologist, analyzed the crime content of thirty-six newspapers, then assessed attitudes about crime in interviews with their readers. Her conclusion might help explain the conventions of crime-news selection. She wrote:

> The more newspapers print articles about criminals in other places running amok, picking victims at random, and trampling social norms, the more secure readers feel in their own environments. In essence, readers like the grass to be browner on the other side of the fence, and the browner the better. Far from frightening, reports of grisly, bizarre crimes in other cities are reassuring. Readers are still exposed to some reports of crime that occur locally, but the severity and outrageousness of such crimes appear to be judged in comparison with crimes from other places. When crimes are occurring on the local turf, however, the tables are turned. . . . Readers do not appreciate criminals choosing their victims at random (or, at least, media accounts that make it appear so). Reports of crime that lack rhyme or reason are frightening. If the victim apparently did nothing to precipitate the crime, then the reader can do nothing to avoid the crime. If, on the other hand, the victim took some action that made him or her more vulnerable to the victimization, then the reader can avoid that action and presumably remain safe. . . . The unexpected, the quirky, the heinous crimes that are reported in newspapers increase fear of crime among readers in that crime locality, even if the reporting style itself is nonsensational.

At the center of Heath's study is a concept known to sociologists as *perceived control*. It is crucial to our national sanity that we perceive that the authorities have the upper hand on lawlessness. Police reporters provide the public with stories that serve as daily updates about the degree to which police are maintaining control. A crime has been committed in your hometown, the story will say, but an arrest has been made; besides, the victim courted danger by a reckless lifestyle.

During more than a decade of police reporting at three daily newspapers I never pondered my role in this issue of perceived control, of course. Like most reporters, I flatly rejected attempts by outsiders to explain or criticize my craft. But as I read Heath's study, her conclusions resonated. That same week, in April 1995, I was on a meandering car trip in the Southwest, and I was struck by the similarity of the wire-service crime news from one city's newspaper to the next, even beyond the O. J. Simpson case. In many papers the national news page functions as a coast-to-coast crime blotter. I found that local TV news broadcasts managed to squeeze in a faraway crime atrocity or two, particularly if bloody video was available. One day while driving through the haunting canyon country of southern Utah, I listened to a top-of-the-hour installment of *ABC Radio Network News* that included three stories: a Simpson update, a Newt Gingrich press conference, and a twenty-five-second, two-sentence account of a Florida case in which a man killed his wife, his two children, and himself.

Heath's point about the societal need to rationalize crime by blaming the victim brought to mind the Preppy Murder slaying, the 1986 case in which a teenager named Jennifer Levin was killed in New York's Central Park by Robert Chambers. In the days just after the killing, my newspaper, the *Daily News,* ran front-page headlines that read, GIRL'S SLAYING SUSPECT: SEX PLAY "GOT ROUGH" and HOW JENNIFER COURTED DEATH. A few days later, a follow-up story under the headline CAUGHT 'EM IN THE ACT reported that a jogger saw Chambers and Levin "making love." The story said Chambers had confessed "he strangled Levin accidentally while resisting sexual pain she inflicted during an amorous encounter." The stories implicating Levin's lifestyle in her death came from police sources based upon statements made by Chambers and witnesses; Levin wasn't around to give her version. I don't suppose that Ellen Levin, Jennifer's mother, had read Linda Heath's theories about perceived control, but she was wise enough to recognize the concept. Some years after the slaying Ellen Levin wrote, "Suggesting reasons why a particular person was singled out, that the victim was somehow culpable, makes the public feel fairly safe that this fate could not befall them. This is what most violent crime news is about."

It would have been no less tragic had Jennifer Levin's life ended without notice. But the New York media decided that Levin counted—that her death was important news. In New York, which averaged five or six murders a day while I was working as a reporter there, not every homicide victim counts. Many slayings in big cities don't rate a simple five-W story in the newspaper or a single sentence on any news broadcast. Even in less populous places, where every murder is news, there are degrees of coverage.

No secret crime-reporting manual exists, and no editor ever took me aside to explain the nuances of which crimes are newsworthy and which are not, which victims count, and which don't. But the rules do exist, and every crime reporter in the United States learns them.

The first canon is that any crime, no matter how petty, that is witnessed by a journalist—especially an editor—will tend to be big news. Any crime committed by or against a politician or sports figure also will get special attention. Journalists view crimes involving wealthy or prominent people as more important than crimes involving poor or obscure people. Journalists are more race sensitive today than they were a generation ago, and no one would be willing to say that the murder of a white person is more important than the murder of a black, Asian, or Hispanic person. But crime victims with certain occupations, which connote socioeconomic status, are sure to rate the front page: bankers, stock brokers, lawyers, doctors. Crimes against the secretaries, clerks, and cooks who work for them may not.

Location also is a crucial factor. Any heinous act committed "in broad daylight" on the town square is big news. Every city has a handful of venues that attract heightened media attention when they are visited by crime—a sports facility, city hall, theaters, the courthouse, town green or central park, tourist attractions, subways or elevated trains, Main Street, certain highways. Most cities have silk-stocking Zip codes or neighborhoods whose names send tingles to an editor's fingertips: Main Line, Gold Coast, Country Club. Likewise, there are "location" phrases that abrogate news value: "inner city," "housing project," "known drug location," "prostitution venue." The slaying of a hooker at a high-class downtown hotel might be big news. The murder of a transvestite hooker in a back alley off the renovated waterfront is smaller news. The murder of a crackhead hooker at a motel on the seedy edge of town is not news.

Other criminal subsets, including organized crime, have their own degrees of newsworthiness. In New York and most other large cities in the

Northeast and Midwest, the murder of an Italian mobster, who probably is involved in the drug trade, is big news, no matter how low his position on the crime-family totem pole. A Mafia killing is not just a murder; it's a rub-out. Editors have visions of gangster movies and Al Capone, so the story goes on page one. The murder of an Asian mobster also can be big news. Editors see the Asian gangs as mysterious and menacing, like the bad guys in a Bruce Lee movie. The story goes on page three. The murder of a South American narcotics mobster may or may not be news, and the murder of a black drug-gang member probably is not news. All were involved in the same dangerous business—purveying narcotics—but the murders are rated differently based upon media conventions about what is interesting.

In New York in the late 1980s crack-related killings became so prevalent that the bodies of one or two unidentified young black men would turn up each morning in vacant lots in Brooklyn, the Bronx, Queens, or upper Manhattan. The crime summary form in the police press office would include the bare details—time and location that the body was found, mode of death, and so forth. Under the section reserved for further details, a police officer would scrawl in longhand, "No ID. No Motive. No Suspect. No Weapon. No Nothing. Possibly Drug Related." The information was insufficient for even a who-what-when-where-why story. My editor, Bill Boyle, and I began refer-ring to these anonymous murder victims as *unblees,* from unidentified black males. Unblees rarely rated a story unless three or four turned up at the same location. We paid little attention to these routine murders because the police paid little attention. They were roadkill in the crack scourge.

Some journalists argue that the media give their customers what they de-mand—that the decisions on the relative worth of a particular crime are based upon the will of readers or viewers who play puppeteer to the media marionette. It seems to me much more likely that the conventions of crime coverage are self-promulgated by the media, with the aid and comfort of law enforcement agencies. The authorities tend to highlight crimes that they are likely to solve, and they convene press conferences to trumpet their achieve-ments, whether an arrest in a murder or a mass indictment in a drug case. When law enforcement officials identify a crime pattern that they haven't been able to solve—a rapist working a particular neighborhood or a burglary gang in a certain subdivision—they are reluctant to call the media together to warn the public to lock the doors and draw the blinds. That might give the impression that the police are not in control.

I have found it fascinating to watch police officials and politicians stumble over one another to claim credit for the crime decline in the United States during the 1990s. William Bratton, who was police commissioner in New York City just long enough to pose for his official portrait, magnanimously accepted responsibility for the precipitous crime decline there, even though it had begun before he arrived and continued unabated after he was gone. Bratton was dispatched from the position by Mayor Rudolph Giuliani, who decided that he deserved full credit.

Bratton was an early acolyte of the theories of George Kelling and James Q. Wilson, criminologists who since the early 1980s have held that crime migrates to neighborhoods in disrepair (hence their recommendations are known as the *broken windows strategy*). The New York City Police Department has followed a spinoff anticrime program, known as the Quality-of-Life Initiative. Bratton and Giuliani explained that the drop in crime was prompted by increased enforcement of petty crimes such noise violations, drinking in public, and turnstile jumping to avoid paying subway fare. Reporters parroted their explanation that these new police strategies were responsible. Conveniently enough, crime has declined since the NYPD put the Kelling-Wilson broken windows theory to practice. Privately, many law enforcement authorities say that an improving economy and a slowdown in the use of crack, the drug that caused the crime run-up in the 1980s, deserve most of the credit for the drop in crime.

During the crack epidemic, when the monthly release of crime statistics was a bad-news story, the New York City Police Department often would slip the new stats down to the press room late on Friday afternoon, thereby assuring that the story would be a brief item in the thin Saturday papers, the poorest-selling edition of the week. No official ever volunteered to take credit for the increase in crime, least of all Police Commissioner Ben Ward and Mayor Ed Koch, who attempted to absolve themselves of responsibility for the proliferation of crack usage in the city. Instead, they offered reporters a sacrificial lamb, typically a young captain from the crime analysis unit who would say, "Well, yes, homicide *did* increase by nineteen percent and robbery by seventeen percent, but felony assaults went up only eleven percent."

Bratton may or may not be an innovator in enforcement strategies, but I know firsthand that he is a brilliant strategic thinker. In 1990 and 1991, after I left daily reporting, I worked as a consultant with the Metropolitan Transit

Authority in New York. Primarily, I wrote scripts that Bratton, the transit police chief from 1990 to 1992, used in a series of videotapes for his officers and later for the public. The MTA had a financial motivation in hiring Bratton: subway ridership had declined steeply, and the city's confidence in subway safety had ebbed. Soon after he arrived from Boston, Bratton decided to produce the videotapes, each featuring simple messages about image and public confidence. Crime *will* decline, he vowed. Arrests *will* increase. The subways *will* be safer. Then he added a unique twist. He said that he should be held personally accountable for crime and arrest statistics. Next, Bratton flooded the trains and platforms with uniformed cops and encouraged them to make arrests and issues summonses. This ensured an increase in arrests and a decline in crime—the quantification Bratton needed. Finally, he set his public relations man to work to make sure that the press and public learned the good news about crime in the subways. These stories became incessant, like a woodpecker's tapping, in the print and broadcast media. The MTA trumpeted certain arrests. It invited reporters to observe and photograph the periodic mass-arrests for turnstile jumping. To ensure maximum media exposure the agency churned out a press release announcing each new crime statistic that signaled a downturn.

This cooperation was typical of the relationship between journalists and the police. As Mark Fishman, a Brooklyn College sociologist, wrote, "Crime news is mutually determined by journalists, whose image of crime is shaped by police concerns, and by police, whose concerns with crime are influenced by media practices. . . . News organizations may choose what crimes to report, but the pool of occurrences from which they draw is preselected and preformed within police departments."

Big-city police departments are able to screen the hundreds of crimes reported each day and present the media with detailed information on only a handful of "major cases." As a young police reporter in Omaha, Nebraska, I would scan the blotter at the beginning and end of my shift, but I also had direct access to each investigative unit and detective. I could go from office to office and desk to desk if I needed details on a case. Tom Hallman Jr., a senior reporter with the *Oregonian* in Portland, said he had a similar experience during eleven years of covering the crime beat. Today, he said, the pervasive use of public information officers in police departments means that reporters get second- and thirdhand information. "I think that many police reporters today never ever get a chance to talk with a real cop," Hallman says.

In New York, where citizens might dial 911 ten thousand times in a single day, the police-staffed press office winnows that mass of mayhem into perhaps a dozen major cases per day for the media's eyes. They know from past experience that journalists will show interest in certain crimes involving celebrities, sex, racial bias, and murder.

Periodically, other crimes—assaults on joggers, drive-by shootings, carjackings, youth violence—will draw special attention, almost always sparked by a particularly egregious anecdotal example. Because of the interest by journalists, the police pluck these cases from the vast pile and feed them to the media, which present the stories in the form of a crime wave. Often, the same types of crimes had been occurring in happy obscurity all along.

Lincoln Steffens, the famed muckraker who worked as a police reporter for the *New York Evening Post* one hundred years ago, understood this perfectly well. He wrote,

> Every now and then there occurs the phenomenon called a crime wave. New York has such waves periodically; other cities have them; and they sweep over the public and nearly drown the lawyers, judges, preachers, and other leading citizens who feel that they must explain and cure these extraordinary outbreaks of lawlessness. Their diagnoses and their remedies are always the same: the disease is lawlessness; the cure is more law, more arrests, swifter trials, and harsher penalties. The sociologists and other scientists go deeper into the wave; the trouble with them is they do not come up.

There are abundant examples of public hysteria driven by flawed or false news reports of outbreaks of lawlessness. In one, the crazed press in Cleveland reported with some glee that a tsunami-sized crime wave had descended upon the city in the latter half of 1919. News coverage of crime increased sevenfold, with each newspaper trying to outdo the next in whipping up anxiety among its readers, according to one study. In the end, it turned out that crime had in fact increased. But the numbers proved to be underwhelming: 345 felonies were reported during the first six months of 1919 and 363 from July through December, an increase of 5 percent.

In 1976 New York got worked up about its own crime wave as the media publicized a purported startling increase in violence against senior citizens, including an act that became known as a "push-in" robbery. Young toughs would accost the elderly while they were unlocking their apartment doors and push into the homes. The crime-wave reporting began in November after several elderly people were slain. In the next seven weeks the *New York Daily News, New York Post,* and one local TV station managed to run fifty-six stories about crimes against senior citizens.

The reaction followed the pattern predicted by Steffens. The mayor condemned the juvenile justice system. The police expanded its Senior Citizens Robbery Unit. The state legislature passed laws to make juvenile records available to judges, to mandate prison sentences for those convicted of violent crimes against the elderly, and to deny juvenile status to youths accused of such crimes. Network television and newspapers across the country picked up the story, and the following spring a Harris poll showed a significant uptick in the national fear of crime.

One hitch: The trend was a myth. Fishman, the Brooklyn sociologist, conducted a study that revealed the facts behind the frenzy: "It is doubtful that there really was a crime wave or any unusual surge of violence against elderly people. No one really knows, least of all the journalists who reported the crime wave. The police statistics from the N.Y.P.D. do not show a crime wave. In fact, for one type of crime, homicide, the police showed a nineteen percent drop over the previous year's rate of elderly people murdered."

As often is the case, there was a story behind the crime-wave stories. Beginning in 1974 the issue of crime against senior citizens had been high on the research agenda in national law enforcement circles. It was a popular subject for grant applications by police departments to the federal Law Enforcement Assistance Administration. A national police organization held a conference on the topic in 1975, the year that the NYPD's Senior Citizens Robbery Unit (SCRU) was created, and in February 1976 *Police Chief* magazine devoted a special issue to the subject. When the slayings that touched off the reported crime wave happened later that year, journalists were directed to SCRU, where the commanding officer was pleased to feed them quotes and anecdotes that helped raise the unit's profile, justify its existence, and prompt an expansion of its staffing.

And a coda: Although both houses of the state legislature had quickly and quite publicly passed the three initiatives to stop the crime wave that didn't happen, the bills lingered on the desk of the governor, whose signature was required to make them law. On August 19, 1977, ten months after the hype had begun and eight months after it had subsided, New York governor Hugh Carey quietly vetoed all three bills.

Reporting during 1993 and 1994 on the carjacking–Florida highway murders–Polly Klaas crime wave followed the pattern described by Steffens and Fishman. In fact, crime was declining as coverage on network television and national newsmagazines focused on "a scary orgy of violent crime," as *U.S. News* called it in its January 17, 1994, edition. Predictably, these horrible but isolated anecdotes were met with reactionary crime legislation. In sociology *bias* refers to errors in systematic measurement. This bias in crime measurement is precisely what happens each day as the media focus on one atypical crime at a time. The crime of the day is presented as the biggest thing since yesterday's biggest crime of the day, without benefit of context. In his 1991 study of crime and the press, Roy Edward Lotz concluded that this "know-nothing approach" was deeply entrenched in crime reporting. As a result, he wrote, crime stories

> are lean on information and practically barren of implication. Rules of objectivity force reporters to isolate crimes and treat each as a sample of one; they virtually forbid generalizing to the wider picture. Reading about a person mugged in a subway, we don't not know whether subways are generally experiencing a rising or declining crime rate. . . . News people find gratification in small details and rudimentary facts, such as ages, names, dates, times, and addresses, but pay scant attention to relationships between victim and offender or the cultural setting of the crime. Cautioned against any signs of critical thinking, crime reporters hug the shoreline, relying heavily on perfunctory findings by police and treating each crime in splendid isolation. . . . In its cautious approach of raising small questions and sticking to the case at hand, the press appears as a paper tiger. Articles often dwell on the narrowest of particulars, leaving crime in general alone. The omission of broader discussions rarely startles readers, who have been conditioned not to expect them. After years of such narrowness, it has become sanctified by journalistic custom.

These customs and conventions, not a cunning conspiracy, are responsible for the uniformity of crime coverage from one year to the next and from one media organization to the next. No mysterious media commission gives thumbs up to Buttafuoco but thumbs down to deep contextual reporting. Journalism fosters nearsightedness, mostly because paying heed to the big picture is difficult when you are busy pouring either gasoline or water on the brush-fire story of the moment.

Although I tried to be conscientious as a police reporter, I really did not begin pondering the essential questions of crime journalism until, ironically, I left the *New York Daily News.* In September 1991, about a year after I had left the paper, I learned of a report compiled by a group of New York prison inmates that said 85 percent of the state's prison population was black or Latino and 75 percent came from one of seven predominantly minority neighborhoods in New York City. At about the same time I contacted an advocacy organization called the Correctional Association of New York concerning a magazine story about crime policy that I was beginning to research. Its executive director, Robert Gangi, gave me statistics showing that, as a result of mandatory sentences in nonviolent narcotics cases, the percentage of inmates who landed in jail as a result of drug cases had increased from 11 percent in 1980 to 46 percent in 1990. Meanwhile, the percentage of nonviolent felons in prison had increased from 33 percent to 60 percent.

My colleagues and I had written extensively in 1988 and 1989 about drug sweeps—known as "buy-and-bust" operations—by a special New York police unit with a headline-grabbing name, the Tactical Narcotics Team, or TNT. TNT used these sweeps predominantly in the seven minority neighborhoods cited in the prison study. Mass-arrest strategies were not unique to New York. Police departments in dozens of U.S. cities used a variation of the same technique against gangs and drug dealers during the late 1980s and early 1990s. But in New York the media had helped prompt mass drug arrests as they pressured the police to do something palpable about the crack problem that had afflicted the city since 1985. We applied heat, in particular, after a young cop named Edward Byrne was shot in the head and killed by "drug scum," as his father put it, on February 26, 1988, as he sat in his patrol car in South Jamaica, a black neighborhood in Queens where the crack problem had been particularly acute. Five days later the *Daily News* developed its own anticrack strategy with five full pages of stories following a front-page headline that read, NEW WAR ON DRUGS. Here are the opening paragraphs of a story that explained the plan:

Vowing to drive crack dealers out of South Jamaica like "rats from an open trench," Mayor Koch yesterday endorsed a model plan to join police, public officials and community leaders in a battle to clean up the drug-riddled neighborhood where a police officer was gunned down last week.

The idea to set up a pilot program for a so-called "drug-free zone" in a targeted area of Queens was proposed by the Daily News yesterday at a special leadership forum on the city's crack plague.

The forum—attended by top law enforcement officials, community leaders and drug experts—was convened to search for answers to the question posed by Matthew Byrne, father of Edward Byrne, the 22-year-old rookie cop assassinated last Friday: "What are the decent people of the world going to do?"

Speaker after speaker called for leadership and decried the lack of coordination among police, city agencies, drug programs, education efforts, community patrols and religious leaders.

Under the pilot program, a community would be selected for intensive attack under a single leader. As much as possible the aim would be to create a drug-free zone, and, if successful, duplicate it in other neighborhoods.

After the forum, Koch, who did not attend, said, "I think it's a grand idea."

"Arrests are not enough," said Koch, who added he had been discussing the need to take dramatic and immediate action in South Jamaica in the hours preceding Byrne's funeral Monday.

"We are going to make it so hot and heavy for the drug push-ers in the area . . . we will drive them out like rats from an open trench."

Thus my newspaper hatched an initiative that the police were all but required to act upon, and TNT was born. The police department's press office kept a running total of the unit's drug arrests, which numbered one hundred or more on some days, and the New York media gave daily updates to read-ers and viewers during the first few weeks.

Reporters were invited along to take pictures and observe the buy-and-bust operation, so one afternoon I found myself huddled inside an unmarked police van in Queens, watching through tinted windows and scribbling notes as cops collared one druggie after another. Crack had made cocaine financially accessible to everyone, and its convenient form made it the narcotic equivalent of fast food. It was sold in two vial sizes—$2 for small, $5 for jumbo. It could be smoked, so there were no messy needles and no need to worry about gusts of wind. Powder cocaine tended to be sold in quantities that cost $100 or more and lasted a few days. But crack customers were likely to buy a vial or two several times a day, so dealers were forced to offer twenty-four-hour sales service. This created employment opportunities for thousands of kids in America's poorest neighborhoods.

As I sat in the van in Queens, it became apparent that everyone arrested that day was a skinny whiskerless black teenager. Clearly, police were nabbing only the small fry of the crack gangs—kids who were given a few dozen vials and told to stand on a street corner. A few years later, when I read the prison statistics from Gangi's Correctional Association, I understood that my former newspaper and I had played a role in the arrests of all those young black men sitting in prisons in New York State. In 1987, before the TNT sweeps began, 32 percent of those entering state prisons had been sentenced for drug offenses. By 1989, the year after TNT started, the figure had increased to 45 percent. In whole numbers the difference was 4,657 people. Many had been caught in the TNT dragnet that I helped hype.

I know that the narcotics problem is a deep dilemma, and I don't mean to minimize the culpability of those who choose to sell drugs. As it turned out, several young black men not unlike those I observed from inside the van that day were arrested, charged, tried, and convicted in the murder of Byrne, the young cop. His slaying was among the most sobering affronts against civilized society that I covered as a newspaper reporter. According to the authorities, it was a premeditated $8,000 contract hit on a cop chosen at random to avenge the arrest of a vile Queens drug kingpin named Howard "Pappy" Mason.

But while my colleagues and I were pumping air into TNT as the last hope for New York, we failed to sufficiently raise the big-picture questions—questions concerning official responsibility for the crime rate, deconstruction of the public's fear of crime, the racial inequities of crime policy, the burgeoning prison population as a result of mandatory sentences, the issue of alternatives to imprisonment for nonviolent drug sellers.

Instead, our message to readers was clear: lock 'em up and everything

will be OK. It was simple but simplistic. While we were sitting in vans count-
ing arrests, we missed the most important story on the crime beat: the collapse of the U.S. criminal justice system as an effective means of fighting
crime, maintaining order, ensuring public safety, and meting out equitable
justice. Between 1980 and 1990 the national prison population more than
doubled, yet crime had not decreased, and the public was more fearful than
ever. I came to conclude that the media had been scooped by myopia, sleazy
story distractions, and an unhealthy devotion to the official police agenda.

With thousands of bright reporters across the country covering crime,
how did that happen? My fairly typical career as a daily newspaper crime
reporter might serve as a case study. When I started out, I didn't know
enough to ask the right questions. At the end, flagged and disheartened by
crime shell shock and troubled by the swelling tabloid sensibility, I didn't
have the spirit to pick the fights that I should have picked.

I suppose that my first journalism hero, Jimmy Cagney, would have. I was
drawn to the profession while watching television one night in the early
1970s in my hometown of Omaha. It was after midnight, and the late late
show featured a cheesy melodrama from 1933 called *Picture Snatcher*. Cagney
starred as Danny Kean, an ex-convict in New York who is turned away from
one job after another because of his bad-guy background. He finally stum-
bles into a place so low in the social pit that his criminal history doesn't matter: a newspaper office. The Cagney character is hired on the spot by the city
editor (Ralph Bellamy) as a picture snatcher. His job is to get inside the home
of a murder victim or dead hero–firefighter by any means necessary, even if
that meant posing as a life insurance agent or minister. While the grieving
widow is distracted making coffee or fetching a document, the picture
snatcher grabs photographs of the dearly departed off the walls, tables, and
bureaus so they can be reproduced and plastered in the next day's paper.
Watching this on TV at two o'clock one hazy morning in my sixteenth year,
I thought that I might become a newspaperman.

By college my father had steered me toward the more pragmatic study of
business, but serendipity interceded. During the third semester a buddy and
I decided to take a class together. We scanned the course catalogue and found
only one offering that seemed suitably easy and would fit into both schedules:
Introduction to Mass Communication. The professor was Warren Francke, a
ruddy-faced redhead with a bushy blond mustache that he stroked and yanked
as a prop to his lively lectures about the delicious history of media titillation.

He told us about the important work of the muckrakers—Lincoln Steffens, Jacob Riis, Ida Tarbell, Upton Sinclair—and their exposés of the Standard Oil Company and the Chicago meat-packing houses. It was the Watergate era, and I daydreamed that perhaps I too could "find fault with things as they are," as Steffens described his work.

That same semester my economics professor was a tiresome fellow who spoke in monotone and sucked on an unlit pipe. He wore purple three-piece suits and matching shoes—a cross between Adam Smith and Barry White, the portly disco love machine. I dropped the business class and became a journalist.

On a chilly morning in the fall of 1977, my first day as a professional reporter for the *Council Bluffs* (Iowa) *Daily Nonpareil,* a newspaper with a savagely ironic name, another reporter led me across Pearl Street and a couple of blocks south to police headquarters. He showed me the blotter, a clipboard to which the police had attached copies of several dozen form reports about car accidents, drunken driving arrests, lawn mower thefts, and break-ins that had occurred during the previous forty-eight hours. He took me upstairs to meet the chubby little chief, who grunted a gruff hello. We backed out of the office, feeling cowed. My tour guide, three months out of college himself, wished me luck and fled to his beat at the courthouse. My formal introduction to police reporting had lasted fifteen minutes.

I covered the police beat part time at the *Nonpareil,* which was owned by Thomson Newspapers, a chain that publishes scores of newspapers in the United States and Canada and owns a reputation for squeezing dimes out of its local franchises. The paper had a circulation of about twenty-five thousand and a news staff of ten. As any journalist would in a first job, I learned a great deal there—how to write quickly, conduct interviews, take notes. I also learned a few things that I wish I hadn't. For example, one editor offered the useful advice that newspapers must be written for readers with a sixth-grade education. I also began to understand at the *Nonpareil* that journalism was not necessarily the pure-of-heart occupation that my iconoclast college friends and I believed it to be. Council Bluffs had about six large supermarkets. Five advertised with the paper, and one did not. The publisher deemed that the offending store be blackballed from the news columns. When someone included the store in a roundup story about the availability of some commodity in short supply at the moment—rock salt or bottled water—the publisher handed down to the newsroom a ban on using that supermarket's name unless he cleared it first. As luck would have it, fire broke out in a storeroom at that supermarket a few weeks later. It was not news in the *Nonpareil*.

One Saturday morning I went to the police station to collect the day's crime tidbits for a wrap-up column called "Seen and Heard." The blotter that day included a report about the suicide of a young man who had shot himself in the head at his home. Following *Nonpareil* convention, I wrote a two-sentence item, citing the cause of death as a self-inflicted gunshot wound to the head, according to police. That afternoon, as usual, the funeral home located across the town square delivered to the newsroom its daily death notices for the obituary page. The second line of the death notice for the young man said that he had died at home "after a brief illness." This struck me as dishonest, and I impetuously called the funeral director to tell him so. He told me that he was no medical expert and that he based the cause of death on what the survivors had told him. I asked him whether he had done the embalming, and he responded that he had. By chance, I asked, did you happen to notice the hole in his head? Ten minutes later the irate publisher called and demanded to know why I was harassing his advertisers. After eighteen months in Council Bluffs it was time to pack my pencils.

I was rescued by Carl Keith, the night managing editor of the *World-Herald,* just across the Missouri River in Omaha. He hired me as a copy editor on the night shift at the *World-Herald,* a decent employee-owned paper with a circulation of about 250,000, split between its morning and afternoon editions. Keith had assembled a youngish night staff of smart pragmatists peppered with intellectuals and eccentrics. I found my colleagues to be informed, open minded, well read, and interesting, just as I believed journalists should be. We had a dandy time putting out the five editions of the morning paper.

The *World-Herald* was not a great writers' paper. Stories were edited with a heavy hand, so reporters tended to write cautious formulaic pieces. The best writing produced in the newsroom often could be found in memos posted on the copy desk clipboard—a witty style note by the copy desk chief, a brief heads-up by Keith, who delighted in using double entendre and dry humor to skewer the extravagant criticisms and anal prescripts passed down from his boss. (The editor once decreed that it was insufficient to write "the Omaha area." The correct usage, he said, was "the greater Omaha–Council Bluffs metropolitan area.") On deadline late one night a respected veteran editor named

Charles Poell hurriedly wrote a headline over a breaking story about federal intervention in a dispute involving Native Americans at Wounded Knee, South Dakota. The full name of the town would not fit in the one-column, three-line headline, so Poell wrote, approximately, FBI AGENTS/SWARM INTO/WOUND KNEE, dropping the *ed* in *Wounded*. It wasn't a great idea, and predictably enough an editor responded with a scathing note that banned any future use of the shortened version of Wounded Knee. Keith posted the note without comment on the copy desk clipboard. When he arrived at work late that afternoon, Poell read the nasty criticism, walked to his desk, and banged at a typewriter for a few seconds. He went back to the clipboard and affixed his response atop the editor's note: "I Fuck Up. C. Poell."

One night, after I'd spent three or four months on the copy desk, the police reporter called in sick, and Carl Keith asked me to fill in on the beat. I found the police station, located the blotter, talked to some cops, and felt my way around. I managed three bylined stories in the next morning's paper, and Keith never returned me to the copy desk. I spent most of the next five years as a police and courts reporter at the *World-Herald,* which turned out to be a fine place to learn the craft. My hometown of 330,000 people averaged just under a homicide a week. Killings got plenty of attention, of course, but the paper covered all types of crime, serving as an old-fashioned newspaper of record. Each violent crime was reported, and in agate type the paper gave a daily accounting of nonviolent crimes of any financial consequence reported to police.

Jim Fogarty, a courts reporter, kept an elaborate file system that tracked every arrest reported in the paper to its final disposition, whether that was a dismissal, plea bargain, or trial, conviction, and sentence. Each day Fogarty would write five or six short stories that updated the cases as they wound through the legal system. At the end of his shift each evening he spent thirty minutes or more making notations on the cards in his crime files—"Prelim. hearing 11/12/79; bound over for trial" or "Dismissed 12/1/79; story done." Fogarty's commonsense idea was that readers deserve to know the outcome of every arrest that the paper reported.

Another conscientious courts reporter was David Thompson, a proud Notre Dame graduate who carried himself with professional dignity and railed against excesses in news coverage. He recognized that restraint and context in stories are essential if the media are to hold the public's respect. "Too many journalists follow a creed that anything worth doing is worth overdoing," Thompson told me one day. "In the long run the readers won't buy hype." I picked up other tips from Bob Dorr, who reported with persnickety exactness, and Jim Flanery, whose extensive Rolodex and intricate note-keeping system awed his peers. Fred Thomas, a pioneering environmental reporter, showed by example that a degree of advocacy and sensitivity toward sources were not necessarily journalistic defects.

Of course, functioning as a callow rookie among all this precision and aptitude was intimidating. During my first couple of months as night police reporter I often would lie awake until dawn, going over my stories word for word in my head, imagining errors under my byline in copies of the newspaper that were being distributed at that very moment throughout the greater Omaha–Council Bluffs metropolitan area. I would bolt upright: Oh my God! Did I write that the 7-Eleven robbery happened on Fontenelle Avenue, not Fontenelle *Boulevard?*

I also began to dream about crime—dreams that continue to this day. In some dreams I am called upon to cover catastrophes that I cannot locate. I know that the competition is there, collecting quotes and colorful details, and I am lost as the clock ticks toward deadline. I am too shamed to call the office for directions for fear of being unmasked as an incompetent fraud. In another recurring dream I am a falsely accused perpetrator, and I always end up in prison, unable to convince the authorities that they have the wrong man. (Many police reporters have the same dreams, I later learned.)

In my early years on the police beat I found it increasingly difficult to watch action films or television programs. During each car chase or wild shoot-out all I could think about was how I would write the story:

- A mute survivalist known only as Rambo shot, stabbed, and bludgeoned to death with his bare fists an estimated 22 bad guys as a complex government conspiracy came to bloody conclusion today in wooded rural Pennsylvania.
- A brawl broke out today among plainclothes detectives in the Hill Street police precinct station house as a cop known as "Dirtbag" cast verbal aspersions upon the virtue of the wife of a uniformed sergeant. Two shots were inadvertently fired. A locker was damaged, but no one was injured.

When I told my editor, Joanne Stewart, about this problem, she laughed heartily. But her laugh tumbled quickly to a full stop. She looked at me slightly askance and suggested with a tight smile that perhaps I should try to get a bit more rest.

I came to enjoy the police beat, including its unique rhythms—frantic one day, languid the next—and the relationships that developed over time. It was a less restrictive era. Cops and reporters were not so suspicious of one another then, and I had open access to the detective bureau at police head-quarters in downtown Omaha. I learned that I had a certain kinship with cops. Like many of them, I came from an ethnic background. Some com-manders who served as my sources patronized the shot-and-a-beer taverns in South Omaha that my relatives owned, and my sensibilities were not unlike those of many of the younger college-educated officers.

I spent time with police officers both on the job and off. I wiled away slow evenings in a police radio car with James Skinner, an aggressive young detec-tive sergeant who later would become police chief in Omaha. After hours I would hang out with vice cops conducting prostitution sweeps in downtown Omaha, sometimes riding along in the decoy cars or chatting with the wo-men as they waited in a police wagon for the trip to jail. I occasionally fished and hunted with cops on my days off, and after a time they began to invite me to their parties, which included periodic *Onion Field*–style gatherings at which they cut loose. They would rent a suite of adjoining rooms at a local hotel and invite plenty of women but no wives. The cops had a favorite party gag. First, they would dismantle the light in the bathroom. Then they would stretch cellophane tightly over the toilet bowl. As the unwitting foil stood in the dark and peed, the urine would splash on his trouser legs and eventual-ly leak onto the floor. Within a couple of hours the bathroom would be an inch deep in urine.

During one of my first nights at the police station a young lieutenant named Anthony Circo recited for me a tongue-twisting sentence that he used as a humorous response to naive questions by reporters about why a crime suspect had done one thing or another. "Always remember," Circo said, "that intelligence is not a prerequisite characteristic to the perpetration of a criminal act." Nor, I learned from that party gag, is intelligence a pre-requisite for the possession of a police badge.

I think I came to understand cops pretty well during my years on the beat in Omaha. Some have a deep persecution complex about their profession. Many see themselves as underpaid crusaders battling a morally corrupt society that, more often than not, sides with the criminal. Some develop the *Robocop* mentality, described aptly many years ago by a childhood friend who took a job as a small-town cop near Omaha: "When I put on that uniform, I feel like I can kick anybody's ass." Of course, most cops—like most of the reporters who cover them, I suppose—are decent, earnest people. But the ranks of each profession will reflect society, from the best to the worst, whether in Council Bluffs or New York.

It was a fluke related to competition that I ended up working as a crime reporter in New York City. After about eight years at newspapers in the Midwest, I took a year off to get a graduate degree at Columbia University in New York. I had good clips and a decent résumé, so I was in a position to interview with a number of large newspapers during the school year while planning my next job. Early in the spring semester I talked with the *Atlanta Journal and Constitution* about a job as an assistant city editor. I flew down for an interview, and afterward I was certain that I would go to work there. I enjoyed New York, but it seemed a debilitating place to live. I'm not sure why, but a few days after the Atlanta visit I sent a résumé to *Newsday,* which was making an aggressive circulation move into New York City in the early 1980s.

During the school year Dick Blood, a former *Daily News* editor who was one of my professors at Columbia, told me that I might fit in well at his old paper, and he sent a letter of introduction on my behalf to Gil Spencer, the editor of the *News.* I sent a résumé a few days later but got no response; jobs in Nebraska and Iowa didn't carry much weight at the *News.* Coincidentally, Spencer was visiting Columbia that month as a member of a Pulitzer jury, and I managed to bump into him in the hallway. He sized me up and said, "You look like a reporter." I introduced myself and mentioned Dick Blood's letter, and he told me to call him. A few weeks later I went for an interview at his office at the Daily News Building on East 42d Street, a striking art deco build- ing made famous in exterior shots of the *Daily Planet* in *Superman.* Spencer began by telling me that he absolutely, positively had no job to offer me. After five minutes of chit-chat he asked whether I was interviewing with other pa- pers. I told him that I had spoken with the *Philadelphia Inquirer, Fort Lauderdale Sun-Sentinel,* and the Atlanta papers. Almost as an afterthought I said that I had an appointment the following week at *Newsday.* Before both syllables of the name of his rival paper were out of my mouth, Spencer grimaced and said, "Oh, don't tell me that!" I knew at that moment that I was going to work for the *New York Daily News.*

With its gigantic headlines, oversized photographs, and short stories, the *Daily News* seemed like an anachronism, journalism from another era. I knew of the *News* primarily through its star columnist, Jimmy Breslin, whose work was syndicated nationally. Breslin's reputation reflected that of the paper— brash, brawling, maybe a little boozy. I had never imagined that I would go to work there.

For decades the *News* had spoken the language of the common people of New York—the ethnics, the Irish and Italian immigrants, union members, cops, and fire fighters. "Tell it to Sweeney," the longtime publisher, Captain Joseph Patterson, would admonish his writers as they banged out punchy stories. It was said that immigrants learned English by reading the *News,* and detractors like to wisecrack that this explains why New Yorkers speak as they do. Like Joseph Pulitzer's populist papers, the *News* looked out for its read- ers. It celebrated the city's heroes, it struck out against its goats and foes. Its famous front-page headline in 1974 after President Gerald Ford decided against a federal bailout as New York teetered on the brink of bankruptcy is the enduring example: FORD TO CITY: DROP DEAD.

For decades crime news had been the paper's bread and butter, and read- ers apparently couldn't get enough. During the 1940s and 1950s, the *Daily News*'s circulation had climbed to peaks of 4.5 million on Sunday and 2.5 million on weekdays, making it by far the largest paper in the United States. It was part of the fabric of the city, and if you loved New York, you had to love the *Daily News*. While Mom and Dad were reading the *News* in the liv- ing room of the apartment, the kids were out in the street chanting a rope- skipping rhyme:

> Toots and Caspar went to town
> Tootsie bought an evening gown,
> Caspar bought a pair of shoes
> Buttercup bought the *Daily News.*
> How many pages did he read?
> Five, ten, fifteen, twenty . . .

But as the Sweeneys of New York moved to the suburbs and turned on their new television sets, the *Daily News* failed to make the same connection with the city's ever-changing ethnic population. Circulation began to fall. By the time I arrived at the paper, it was selling about two million copies on

Sunday and 1.5 million on weekdays, and its relevance to hundreds of thousands of residents of the city appeared tenuous.

The *Daily News* was an old-fashioned newspaper in that the vast majority of the staff had risen through the ranks, from copyboy to reporter trainee to reporter and, in some cases, to editor. The institutional history of the paper hung heavy in the newsroom. There were certain customs and a vocabulary to which I was not privy. The editors who were told that I was coming aboard knew that I had no experience as a reporter in New York and that I was arriving from a college. As a result of these bits of my biography, along with the fact that I had not served time as a copyboy on the *Daily News* "bench" (the status was insufficient to rate a chair), I was hazed.

I presented myself at the city desk one day in June 1985 at promptly 9 A.M., as instructed by the city editor, Bob Herbert.

"Who're you?" the editor on duty demanded.

I repeated that I was a new reporter who had been instructed by Herbert to report at 9 A.M. that day.

"Well, Bob Herbert is on vacation for two weeks, and he didn't tell anyone about you," the editor said.

"So you're telling me I should come back in two weeks?"

"Nah, hang on."

After a quick confab with a colleague he returned to give me my first assignment, even before I had taken a seat in the newsroom: I was to go to a private club in Manhattan to cover a midmorning speech by Mayor Koch. He told me that he did not care much about what Koch might say during the speech, but he wanted me to ask him about a story that was in the *New York Post* that morning.

"Ask him what his reaction is to—-," he said, explaining the story at some length. "And if he says this, then you ask him that. And if he says that, then you say this. And if he says . . ."

This went on for several minutes, with the editor suggesting at one point that I might want to write down what he was telling me. A dutiful scrivener, I went off and asked the questions as directed. I had a list of a half-dozen primary queries from the boss, plus double that many provisional questions, depending upon Koch's responses. I recorded the mayor's answers, walked back to the newsroom, and approached the city desk. Ten paces before I reached the desk, the editor looked up and glared at me.

"What are you doing back here?"

"Well, the speech was over, and I asked the questions and"

He cut me off.

"Never come back from a job before calling the city desk first. What if we wanted to send you somewhere else? What if there was an event right next door that needed coverage. What if . . . ?"

During the upbraiding a couple of his editing colleagues sat at the desk with heads bowed, trying to stifle smiles. He sent me off with a wave of his hand and told me to "dump your notes" to Frank Lombardi, a political writer. Lombardi wasn't in yet, so I sat down at a desk and began transcribing Koch's comments from my tape recorder.

Soon, a shadow was cast upon the desk.

"What are you doing?" the editor asked.

I told him that I was transcribing my notes.

He crossed his arms with staged drama and said, "We don't really use tape recorders at the *Daily News*."

I was vexed.

"You mean, there is an official newspaper policy against the use of tape recorders?"

"Not officially," he said, "but *Daily News* reporters generally do not use tape recorders."

I could see this wasn't going to be easy. I stared until he went away.

About an hour later a plump little man who was too old and misshapen to wear leather trousers—but who was doing so nonetheless—arrived with a flourish and sat at the desk beside my temporary quarters. He greeted me warmly. "Oh, you're the Nebraska guy. Yeah, we heard (which I heard as *hoid*) about you," he said. After a few moments he unlocked a bottom drawer in his desk and withdrew a large envelope. "You like Oriental girls?" he asked. I'm not sure whether I shrugged or nodded, but the reaction was sufficient to prompt him to wheel his chair over beside mine and guide me through his collection of photographs, all showing naked Asian hookers. He told me their names (Suzies, mostly), their country of origin, and their professional specialties. He told me that he could recommend Asian massage parlors in any of the city's five boroughs, and he confessed that he possessed a powerful case of "yellow fever."

This was the *Daily News* in an anecdote: I've got a fetish; let me tell you about it. I certainly had not encountered anything quite like it out on the prairie. For some *Daily News*ers I was fresh meat. A federal courts reporter teasingly asked how many skyscraper fires I had covered in Nebraska. How many grain elevator explosions have you covered? I responded. A crime reporter gave me an ID quiz: Who's Phil Rizzuto? I believe that I answered correctly: the TV spokesman for The Money Store, a regional mortgage company.

During a month of honing pithy retorts to insults, I managed to settle into a routine of arriving early so that I could read the papers. Several times I was joined in the nearly empty newsroom by Pete Dexter, a columnist from the *Philadelphia Daily News* who had been brought in by Spencer to add a fresh point of view to a stable of native commentators. Dexter, who was destined for distinction as a fiction writer (*Paris Trout, The Paperboy, Deadwood*), had agreed to write a few columns to see whether he would fit in. His first efforts were nothing like Jimmy Breslin's. One was an obtuse account about an odd injury—a lacerated nipple—that Dexter had sustained while doing some brush hogging at his rural home. It seemed funny to me, but I was from Nebraska. New Yorkers don't know from tractors.

Dexter had no office, so he wrote his columns early in the morning on a backup-system computer across from my desk in the middle of the newsroom. The news staff didn't know what to make of Dexter, and Dexter surely didn't know what to make of the *Daily News.* He and I developed a fleeting relationship, not unlike two American strangers meeting unexpectedly in a Nepalese mountain village. "Let me ask you something about this place," Dexter would say, screwing his face into a whorl. "Have you noticed that—?"

Early one morning, as Dexter typed his column, a preppy young man strode up boldly, thrust forward his hand, and introduced himself. The young man, whose name was Chris and who happened to be the son of a well-known writer at the *New York Times,* introduced himself by name but not by job title. After quick hellos Chris leaned down close to Dexter and stage whispered, "I got to tell ya, man, the column is not going over. I mean, that lacerated nipple thing, nobody understood what the fuck you were talking about."

Dexter nodded solemnly, and there was an awkward moment as he seemed to try to take measure of both critic and criticism. I knew that Dexter had a reputation in Philadelphia as something of a pugilist, and it occurred to me that he might just lunge from his seat and wallop our young Chris. Instead, he leaned back in his chair and said reflectively, "They didn't understand it?"

"Nah, not at all," Chris said, talking fast. "I mean, people in New York don't get lacerated nipples from farming accidents. You've got to get out and do more columns like Breslin."

"Like Breslin," Dexter repeated quietly.

Chris, perhaps sensing that he had deflated Dexter, clapped him on the back and told him not to give up. "You'll catch on," he said. "Try going out and doing real reporting. Go to a crime scene or something. That's what people want to read."

Dexter managed a wan smile as Chris strode off, whistling confidently. I pretended that I hadn't heard the conversation, and Dexter pretended to go back to work. But after a few moments he turned to me and said, "Isn't that guy kind of young to be an editor?" I told him that Chris was no editor. He was a copyboy. Dexter's laugh began slowly and ascended in a crescendo as he fell off his chair onto the carpeted floor, holding his gut. I believe that the column he finished that morning was his last for the *Daily News*.

Although the *Daily News* newsroom provided some great listen-to-this-one material for my friends back in Omaha, I found little mirth in the work. As a general assignment reporter in Manhattan and later in Queens I spent most of my time at crime scenes, explosions, fires, construction accidents, and building collapses.

Five days before Christmas 1986, Michael Griffith, a black man from Brooklyn, was beaten and chased into the path of a car by a group of whites in Howard Beach, Queens. Early that morning an editor called me at home in Brooklyn and told me to go interview the dead man's mother, Jean, at her apartment on Pacific Street in Bedford-Stuyvesant. I took a car service to her building, stepped through the locked door on the ground floor (the glass was missing), climbed two flights of stairs, and knocked. I was a stranger, and her son had been killed just hours earlier. She could have spit in my face, and I would not have blamed her. But she invited me inside, served me coffee, and talked in a musical lilt about Michael and her life in America since emigrating from Trinidad in 1973. She pointed out the packages under the Christmas tree from and for her dead son.

It was a great interview. I was the first reporter to visit Jean Griffith that morning (a TV crew knocked at the door as I was leaving), and her noble grace under the circumstances was striking. She was not bitter or hyperbolic. She was sad and understated in a way that wrenched my heart. As a human being I should have wept with her. But as a journalist I could barely contain my exhilaration because I was getting, in the occupational parlance, "great stuff."

The conventional wisdom is that reporters develop a membrane over their feelings. I'm not sure that that is possible, ultimately. It is a bizarre business, chasing after quotes from the bereaved, snatching (figuratively) their most personal photographs, seducing them with little lies: we merely wish to put a human face on the tragedy surrounding your loved one, to show viewers and readers how he was special, that he will be remembered. Reporters rationalize this by telling one another that speaking with a stranger can have a cathartic effect on someone who has undergone trauma. We all have anecdotal examples of those cases. But sometimes I wanted to tell people like Jean Griffith, "Don't talk to me. Slam the door in my face. It is not in your best interest. You will be used and forgotten."

I managed to stifle that absurd notion, and based in part upon the reporting and writing that I did on the Griffith story, I was named chief of the *Daily News*'s five-reporter bureau at police headquarters about eighteen months after I arrived at the paper. Our job was to report the major cases of the day, monitor crime trends, and cover the police department as an institution. We worked out of One Police Plaza, at the foot of the Brooklyn Bridge in lower Manhattan. The pressroom there was a warren of a half-dozen small offices on the second floor occupied by reporters from the four daily newspapers, the *Daily News, Post, Newsday,* and the *Times,* as well as the Associated Press, United Press International, two Spanish-language dailies, and a Chinese daily. The beat was very competitive—perhaps the most competitive beat in the most competitive news town in the country. Rival reporters regarded one another warily for the most part. Many of us were in our late twenties and early thirties. After a time there, our common characteristics were pallid complexions, festering cynicism, and a tendency to glance over our shoulders every few minutes.

An exception was Joseph Cotter, the veteran early-morning man for the *New York Post,* who by tenure was the dean of the "police shack," as the old-timers called the pressroom. Cotter was gracious and dignified, and as he collected the details of the previous evening's death and destruction for America's raunchiest daily newspaper, he listened to classical music on the radio.

Like Cotter, most of the reporters assigned to headquarters were native New Yorkers. I was an anomaly, as was Todd Purdum of the *Times,* another midwesterner with an Ivy League degree. We developed the same sort of isn't-this-weird relationship that I had briefly with Pete Dexter. Not long after I was assigned to One Police Plaza, a senior police official wondered aloud whether Purdum and I were not out of place there. I'm not sure whether she thought we were overeducated to be police reporters or out of our natural habitat among New York cops. Whatever she meant, it is true that we had similar frustrations related to police reticence and the superficial nature of crime coverage. But while I seethed internally, Purdum acted out by hurling telephones against the wall every few days. Purdum, who would go on to *Times* assignments as White House correspondent and Los Angeles bureau chief, proved to be a brilliant writer with an analytical knack that probably was wasted on routine crime news. We had conversations that often were incongruous to the content of our stories. He once complimented me, for example, after I wrote a story about a murder at a restaurant for correctly rendering the English translation of the French prix fixe meal as a "fixed-price meal" rather than the incorrect but more commonly used "price-fixed meal." And he once chastised me after I wrote a story that referred to agents of the federal Bureau of Alcohol, Tobacco and Firearms as *G-men*, a designation that he said was reserved for FBI agents. "I believe that, technically, ATF agents must be called *T-men* since they work for the Treasury Department," Purdum said.

Any accounting of the denizens of the press shack must feature prominently Patrick Doyle, who spent thirty-seven years as a reporter for the *Daily News,* many of them on the night shift at police headquarters. Doyle had managed to get himself listed in the 1985 edition of the *Guinness Book of World Records* for covering twenty thousand murders between 1945, when he joined the *News,* and 1982, when he retired. The quintessential police-beat lifer, the lean and natty Doyle was known as The Inspector because he would occasionally identify himself as "Doyle from headquarters" or "Doyle from downtown" while seeking information by telephone from a far-afield police precinct, and he certainly couldn't be blamed if the cop on the line inferred that he was a ranking police officer. Doyle also was known for chronicling the dying words of murder victims—"Ya got me," or "See ya in hell, boys," or "Tell Laura I love her"—even if the words were spoken in Canarsie, Brooklyn, while he was sitting at his desk in Manhattan. It seems that anyone who has spent time as a crime reporter in New York during the past fifty years knows a few Pat Doyle stories. A vestigial connection to the old school, Doyle was at once beloved and puzzled over. During his later years at the shack Doyle's behavior had grown increasingly peculiar. He would lock himself inside the *Daily News* office at headquarters for the duration of his shift. He cooked his nightly meal on a hot plate, and it was said that he didn't leave the office even to use the bathroom. Some people believed that he simply didn't want to miss a phone call. Others believed that years of crime reporting had left him paranoid.

When I got to police headquarters, Doyle was working there as a stringer for WNBC television, earning a weekly stipend. On most mornings he arrived at 11 A.M. dressed in well-worn clothing straight out of *The Front Page*—a fedora (or straw in summer), topcoat, wingtips, jacket, and a tie whose width had come into style and gone out again several times since it was new. Each morning he would remove a half-full bottle of Chivas Regal from a desk drawer and prop it beside his manual Underwood typewriter. Then he would light a cigar and begin banging away on the keys. He told me many times that he was writing his memoirs. After a couple of hours Doyle would stash the scotch bottle, don his hat, and head up to P. J. Clarke's, the Third Avenue saloon where he had a table on permanent reserve and a special press-parking zone out front. Before leaving he often would poke his head in the *News* office. Although I was a whippersnapper, he seemed compelled to pay homage because of my position as bureau chief for his old paper. Doyle had an extensive collection of magazines in which his name had appeared in stories about famous crime reporters. Every week or so he would pitch one of them onto my desk. "Pretty good rag," he'd say. "Have a look." A paper clip would be inserted at the top edge of the page on which he was mentioned.

One day he gave me a sample from his memoirs, a two-thousand-word account of the slaying of a New York mob figure, Paul Castellano, told vaguely in the style of Raymond Chandler. Here is the first paragraph:

> I walked on Paul Castellano's blood. It was just after the ventilated bodies of New York's multi-millionaire Don and weight-lifting bodyguard were punctured with quarter-ounce slugs pumped into them by swearing hit men December 16th on a street busy with Christmas shoppers in a classic mob set-up. Ninety minutes later and not too tenderly, morgue attendants hoisted the sheet-draped stiffs onto stretchers and laid them on the floor of a dark-colored van. Destination: Bellevue morgue.

On November 5, 1987, a few weeks after he gave me the Castellano excerpt, Doyle was driving southbound on the FDR Drive near 120th Street on Manhattan's East Side when, at precisely 10:48 A.M., his vehicle inexplicably veered sharply to the right, jumped a concrete divider, and slammed into an empty parked car. He was dead on arrival at Bellevue Hospital. It was to have been his last day as a stringer for WNBC, which had cut Doyle and two hundred others from the payroll to save money. Doyle was sixty-two, and Joe McNamara, the great *Daily News* rewrite man, wrote in the obituary that he was "like a frozen piece of Broadway."

When news of Doyle's death got around that morning, Vinnie Lee, a *Daily News* old-timer, called me to suggest that I should go through Doyle's desk and locker before his family arrived, just in case there was something there that they shouldn't see. There wasn't much to find; it almost seemed as though Doyle was prepared for the end. Typing paper was neatly stacked on top of the metal desk. The center drawer held office supplies. The drawers to the left contained telephone books, a police roster, and other reference materials, and the drawer to the right was filled with cigar butts and ashes. We borrowed bolt cutters from the police to open his locker. Inside we found a few articles of clothing. On an upper shelf we found something that gave credence to the stories of Doyle's reclusiveness during his later *Daily News* years: four jars filled with tawny-colored urine.

The *Daily News* staff at police headquarters for most of my time there included Larry Celona and Patrice O'Shaughnessy, both well-sourced reporters with New York savvy; John Marzulli, a cop turned reporter, and Peter McLaughlin, a *News* veteran whose time was devoted largely to his position as president of our union, the Newspaper Guild. Our office clerk was an older gentleman named Tony Cristiani, and the night shift reporter, successor to Pat Doyle, was James Duddy, a *Daily News* thirty-year man. Young reporters came in for brief training periods.

As with the crime beat anywhere, our work could be thumb twiddling one day and full frenzy the next, often depending as much upon the space available in the paper as on the events of the day. The killing of a cop always got us on page one, as did most Mafia murders and any crime that involved allegations of racial bias. Crime-wave stories about pit bull attacks or violence at schools would ebb and flow. Often, events away from the crime beat dictated whether a particular story would be a big headline, a small headline, or no headline. One day the murder of a Brooklyn grandmother might have been front-page news. The next day our dead granny could end up on the spike, the city desk's story graveyard.

Wasting a day of reporting on a story that failed to make the paper was not unusual. The competition for space was particularly frustrating for

Duddy, who arrived for work at 5 P.M., just as the first edition of the paper was being readied for the presses. Duddy, like Doyle, worked the phones from police headquarters. A tall ruddy Irishman, Duddy rarely went out of the building on assignments, and he never wrote his own stories, instead dumping his notes to a rewrite uptown at the main office.

At the end of his shift at 1 A.M., before he left for the subway ride home to Queens, Duddy would type a memo to me that recounted the events (or lack of events) of the evening. The memos, which I filed and saved, illustrate the pressures and rhythms of the daily crime beat as a reporter must appease his editors ("the city desk" in the memos) while squeezing information from the police ("upstairs"), keeping an eye on the competition (primarily the *New York Post*), and dealing with the problem of trying to crowbar good stories into a crowded newspaper. Here is a sample:

> Dave: The night was about as dull as the ballgame. Cops caught a fourth suspect in the old homicide they had a press conference on. I added his name to the scroll of sinners. . . . A priest and a male nurse got a couple of stitches at St. Luke's Hospital after they tried to calm down a batty teenage resident of the Holland Hotel waving a razor blade in each hand and menacing people out in front. City desk said it would be incorporated into an upcoming feature someone is doing on the hotel and the violence in it. Duddy.

> Dave: I gave in the story of the teen-stud who, it turns out, was shot in the groin during a dispute over a girl (ironic, no?) in front of Julia Richmond High School. Cops are still looking for the suspect, who can only be described as a sharp-shooting little ball-breaker. . . . Also, no suspects in the retired cop who was working as a limo-driver. He was shot once in the back and is in stable condition. And the tattooed woman still remains unidentified, or, more correctly, they think they know who she is but can't locate next of kin for a positive ID. Duddy.

> Dave: The city was as quiet as a comatose monk. Duddy.

> Dave: Hispanic guy took a bullet in the head while sitting in a parked car in the Sunset Park section. DOA. Appears to be drug

location. No known mob overtones at this time. . . . ME's office declared death of a two-month-old boy a homicide due to fractured skull. His mother brought him into Harlem Hospital, or rather to the 32d Precinct and then to hospital, two days ago, claiming she didn't know why he was in a coma; police questioning her, no arrest yet. . . . Upstairs gave out a pix and flyer on a six-year-old taken into a car from in front of a midtown welfare hotel and driven off about four days ago. City desk pissed on all of the above. Duddy.

Dave: Did another case of child abuse, this time neglect and malnutrition of a five-month-old girl in the Bronx. Mother and father arrested. Kid in serious condition. . . . Picked up a little more info about the bank robber, plus a great quote. They made the jerk available for a photo-walk here in the building as he was coming out of the Major Case Squad. Someone in the media asked him, "Do you know you are being compared to Willie Sutton?" To which he responded, "Who is Willie Sutton?" Duddy.

Dave: The paper went to bed early due to Happy New Year and such. I am just so happy that they called down here to wake me up. Duddy.

Dave: Story on the Irish girl who was raped was tough because the Sex Crimes sergeant in charge was not giving out anything much at all. I got a little more from upstairs, but there still were several holes in the yarn. Cops say they know who his female accomplice is. I am not sure, but it might be his wife. . . . Urselina Santiago, 19, of 304 Mosholu Parkway, found DOA in tall weeds near a ballpark at E. 202nd St. and Mosholu Parkway about 6:30 P.M. Homicide, fully clothed, possibly strangled, exact cause of death up to ME autopsy. No room in paper. . . . Earlier in the day in Brooklyn, about 2:30 P.M., a 12-year-old girl (you guessed it—cops would not give her name) was brought into Methodist Hospital. She had a bullet in the chest (not serious) and said her uncle had shot her and left her off at the hospital, then left. A real sweetheart of a guy. She said she was visiting him and other relatives but could not remember their names. She is from Las Vegas. No room in paper. Duddy.

Dave: Wacko tries to commit suicide. Shoots himself in the head 12 times with a pellet pistol. Taken to Queens General Hospital. Must be some kind of record. Duddy.

Dave: You might get a return call from a woman who called here last night wanting to know why we were not going to cover an ax murder in Harlem yesterday. She said the victim was a sweet little old man who lived in an SRO building [a low-rent hotel] 39 W. 126th St. and was loved by all, except one of the tenants, who gave him a free shave and a haircut. Turns out the old man started the fight with his ax, which was taken from him and then applied to him by the other chap, who is with him in a local hospital, both in critical condition and both facing assault charges, upon recovery and plastic surgery. . . . Duddy.

Dave: So you're gonna write a book some day, eh? It was a slow night, slow and damn lonely here at 1 Police Plaza. There was a fairly well-known rap singer who was shot in the Bronx. He is in Lincoln Hospital, his soul hanging somewhere between heaven and hell. The medicos pronounced him brain-dead. Yeah, a slow night with the sleeping shadows of the blessed in Trump Towers and the slobs at Riker's winding restlessly towards tomorrow. Then she walked into the office, a blonde among blondes and a body among bodies she was not. Awesome at the least, I kicked my feet up on the desk, lit a smoke, uncorked some private stock and said, "You look a little lonely, too, toots. How can I help ya?" (More tomorrow). Duddy.

Dave: The dark hours were becalmed and it was said: The night was perpless. Duddy.

Becalmed perpless nights were rare during my years at the *Daily News,* and, as Duddy's memos illustrate, we covered stories that ranged from sublime to ridiculous. In April 1987 I was urgently dispatched one night to Florida to cover the national crime of the day, a mass murder at a grocery store in Palm Bay, on the coast southeast of Orlando. William B. Cruse, a deluded former librarian, snapped and began shooting people. He killed six, including two police officers, and wounded ten others. After I wrapped up my reporting on that bloody one-day wonder, my bosses told me to swing down to Ft. Lauderdale, where John Gotti, the New York Mafia boss, was said to be on his annual holiday. The *Daily News* mob expert, Jerry Capeci, gave me the name of the hotel where Gotti was staying, so photographer John Roca and I checked in and staked out the place by sitting in the raw bar off the lobby, drinking scotch, and eating crab claws. On the second day I saw Gotti's son, known as Junior, and three other young men enter the lobby and head toward the elevator.

(I recognized young Gotti because he and I had a minor history. In January 1986 Junior had threatened to chop off my head while I was staking out the home of his parents in Howard Beach, Queens, after the elder John Gotti had been implicated in the murder of Paul Castellano, the fellow whose blood was allegedly smeared by Pat Doyle's brogans. When I wrote unflatteringly in the *Daily News* about my tête-à-tête with Junior, his mother sent me a letter in which she wrote, "After reading that bit of trash you passed off as journalism, I'm not surprised that people like Sinatra, Madonna, Diana Ross, etc., 'kick, punch' and 'spit' on you. You are tantamount to vultures that will print anything, no matter how inaccurate, to sell a paper or make brownie points with the boss! . . . An old Indian saying: Don't criticize your neighbor until you have walked a mile in his moccasins! I don't wish the pain and agony in my heart on anyone in this world.")

When I spotted young Gotti at the Florida hotel, I dashed over and managed to squeeze on the elevator with him just before the door closed. Junior didn't recognize me. Therefore, in the service of my newspaper, I was able to eavesdrop on this consequential conversation:

JUNIOR GOTTI:   Push eight, but I think it's going down.
PAL NO. 1:   Nah, it's going up.

The door closed and the elevator began moving.

PAL NO. 2:   It's fuckin' going down.
JUNIOR GOTTI:   I told you it was fuckin' going down.
PAL NO. 3:   He fuckin' told you it was fuckin' goin' down.

I'm not certain that it was entirely for the better, but my colleagues and I at police headquarters spent most of our time on less superfluous endeavors than Gotti family vacations. Mainly, we covered murder.

I worked briefly at the *News* with a reporter named Tom Hanrahan who quit the paper and moved to Maine. The *Bangor Daily News* wrote a profile of Hanrahan not long after he arrived there, and he was quoted in the piece about why he left the New York newspaper: "I didn't want to spend the rest of my life interviewing dead people." Around the newsroom we all laughed about the quote. But gradually I came to understand precisely what Hanrahan meant: on the crime beat your soul slowly withers. The subject matter requires it.

Roughly ten thousand people were shot, stabbed, bludgeoned, beheaded, or otherwise dispatched from life in New York during my time at the *Daily News*. Over time, the peculiar paranoia of Pat Doyle, the old *Daily News*er, began to make more sense, and the pressroom at One Police Plaza seemed ever more like a bunker. I came to believe that New York City was in a terminal spiral and that the police and politicians were too corrupt and inept to do anything about it. My colleagues and I wrote about drug warfare and drive-by shootings. We covered the murders of innocent bystanders and children. We wrote stories as the crime statistics went ever higher. We tried to chronicle the increase in violence at housing projects, where drug trafficking was having the most obvious impact. We covered the slayings of more than a dozen cops, including two young officers who were killed in unrelated shootings a couple of miles apart on one numbing night in October 1988.

We covered the distressing story of the murder of a girl with Down's syndrome on Staten Island who had walked off hand-in-hand with a deranged vagrant who lived in the woods nearby. We wrote stories about Januari Venable, a little girl from East New York, Brooklyn, who dreamed of being an actress, dancer, or doctor but whose dreams were dashed when her single-parent father, a transit cop, was killed by crack dealers.

Patrice O'Shaughnessy and I wrote the initial story about the 1987 beating death of Lisa Steinberg, the six-year-old adopted child of Joel Steinberg, a lawyer, and his abused girlfriend, Hedda Nussbaum. On the morning after the case broke, the front page of the *Daily News* included the headline THE HOUSE OF TERROR/LAWYER AND LOVER HELD IN CHILD ABUSE and a photograph that showed the suspects as they were being booked at the Greenwich Village police precinct. The competition, *Newsday,* had a front page that was dominated by a full-color photograph of little Lisa sitting at a school desk in her classroom. Because the *Daily News* had no photo of the little girl, I had failed as a picture snatcher. A senior editor tore the front page from *Newsday* and taped it to the clock above the *Daily News* city desk in the main office as a flag of my failure. My boss, assistant city editor Bill Boyle, did one of the most valiant things that anyone has ever done on my behalf: he ripped it down.

In the mass of mayhem that we sorted through each day racial crimes were particularly enervating. The death of Michael Griffith at the hands of whites in Howard Beach, Queens, which ultimately ended in three manslaughter convictions, indirectly led to the bizarre story of Tawana Brawley, a black teenager from Newburgh, a town north of New York City, who in 1987 claimed that she had been abducted and raped by white men who smeared her body with feces and scratched KKK onto her skin with barbecue charcoal. Although the story proved to be a fabrication by a confused teen who feared punishment after staying out late one night, the case served as a racial prism in the city. When a Wall Street investment banker was raped, beaten, and left for dead in Central Park in April 1989 by a group of a dozen young black and Hispanic youths, many blacks perceived that the media used a different standard than in the Brawley case, beginning with the fact that the jogger's name was not publicized.

Next came the ghastly murder of Yusuf Hawkins, a black sixteen-year-old who was shot and killed by a white gang in 1989 when he and a few friends rode the subway to Bensonhurst, Brooklyn, to look at a used car that had been advertised in a newspaper classified. Not long after the killing, about 250 people—whites and blacks—marched through Bensonhurst to decry the racism. About one thousand residents of the predominantly white neighborhood gathered on the sidewalks along the march route as a type of counterprotest. As the marchers passed, some residents chanted the name of James Earl Ray, the assassin of the Reverend Martin Luther King Jr. Some chanted "Niggers Go Home," and one young cretin, who seemed to be posing for the media, simply screamed "Niggers!" over and over.

It was obvious to me that the media attention had aroused a few demented individuals, as cameras always will, and the images of those few were then presented to the city, nation, and world through newspapers, radio, and television as being representative. It was a biased sample, a false anecdote. The media played a game of racial arson by presenting these raw images without context. I was bothered and in some ways shamed by the reporting from that march. It was not difficult to make the case that journalists had done more harm than good while reporting the Hawkins case, and I began to wonder what I was contributing to society by documenting the daily mayhem, the worst that humanity has to offer.

A few months after the Hawkins murder, in early 1990, I was in a position to try to influence *Daily News* coverage of another racial bias case in Brooklyn. It was not nearly as serious as the Hawkins case. It began as an argument when a teenager was struck by a bottle carelessly tossed out a window. The two parties involved happened to be of different races, and friends at the scene got riled up and exchanged racial insults until a fight broke out. There were injuries, but none was life threatening.

I made a case with my editor that the story deserved modest treatment—that it was about teenage tempers, not racism. That evening I appeared on WOR radio as the first guest on a live nightly program that previewed the next day's edition of the *Daily News*. Reporters would go on via telephone one at a time and summarize the stories they had worked on that day. The host, Dick Oliver, introduced me and said, "Dave, tell us about this latest bias case in Brooklyn." I gave a thirty-second account, then added that I wasn't certain that the story was the front-page news we were making it out to be. That raised the hackles of Oliver, a former city editor of the *Daily News*.

"Well, do we ignore it?" he asked.

"No," I said, "but I'm not sure that it deserves page one."

"Well, Dave, where would you put it, page fifty-two?" Oliver said.

"Maybe page fifty-two would be better than page one," I responded.

Oliver harrumphed, cut me off, and went on to the next reporter, the next story.

That night at the bar Bill Farrell, a friend of mine who was a reporter for the *News* in Brooklyn, told me that he had heard my exchange with Oliver.

"Dick was a little hard on you, don't you think?"

I shrugged.

Farrell hesitated a moment, then asked, "Hey, Dave, you don't really believe the story belonged on page fifty-two, do you?"

I told him that I did. And as I said it, I understood that it probably was time to get out of daily crime reporting. A few months later I resigned from the *Daily News*.

# chapter 5

# The Crime
# Policy Follies

## CAUTION! POLITICIANS AT WORK

**M**y timing in leaving daily newspapers was auspicious. Not only did I miss a wrenching strike at the *Daily News* by just a few months, but I also managed to avoid covering the sleazy stories in the wondrous streak of the 1990s. And I am shielded from blame for inducing the public's misinformed fear of mayhem because the crime rate was still rising when I left the *News*. I don't mean to say that I wouldn't have been in there pitching the tabloid bales into the maw with everyone else. I might have been at the head of the line. But Providence offered a seat in the loft of sanctimony. So while teaching graduate students at Columbia University to enter a field from which I was growing increasingly alienated, I sat on my perch and observed the degeneration with informed interest.

I observed, for example, on a day in December 1995, a week after Joey Buttafuoco was released from the Long Island jail where he had spent a couple of months for soliciting sex and thereby violating his parole, as WCBS-TV in New York reported that the marriage of Buttafuoco and his wife, Mary Jo, was on the rocks. During the anchor chit-chat after the story was read, the male anchor said to the female anchor, "I knew something was up when she didn't pick him up after he got out of jail last week." The woman smiled broadly and nodded at her colleague's profundity as the bumper music swelled and the broadcast broke to a commercial. It was a metaphoric moment, a freeze-frame of American journalism: anchor happy-talk about our Buttafuocos.

But why not? At that point, all of America knew everything about Joey and Mary Jo, like those loopy out-of-town cousins whose marital foibles are picked over by snoopy relatives. On the day he was released from jail, Buttafuoco was met by the predictable phalanx of journalists from the wire services, local newspapers, tabloid TV shows, and radio and television stations. Reporters shouted the cliché question—"How do you feel?"—and took notes about the latest important moment in his life.

The story was deemed so significant that AP transmitted it on both the New York State and national wires. That evening hundreds of editors at newspapers across North America selected the Buttafuoco story from the scores of possibilities on the news budget. As a result, on the morning of Saturday, December 2, 1995, millions could once again read about the Buttafuocos in their local paper. Even Joey Buttafuoco, who had profited from the comedic serial that his life had become, questioned the sanity of the attention as he left jail. The story was published, among many other places, in the *Houston Chronicle, Atlanta Journal and Constitution, Memphis Commercial Appeal, Dayton Daily News, Los Angeles Times, Sacramento Bee, Palm Beach Post,* and the *San Francisco Examiner.* The story was the first of three items in the state news column of the *Oneonta Daily Star,* a daily newspaper in upstate New York with twenty thousand readers:

### JOEY'S OUT OF JAIL

EAST MEADOW (AP)—Joey Buttafuoco, who lost weight and apparently his taste for the media, waved off a crush of reporters on Friday as he hurriedly left the jail where he had spent 78 days on his second sex-related offense.

"This is baseless and ridiculous," Buttafuoco complained as

he was whisked away in a burgundy Jaguar by his sister, Anne Isabelle.

Buffafuoco, who violated probation by soliciting sex from an undercover cop on Hollywood's Sunset Boulevard, went directly home where his wife, Mary Jo, reportedly was waiting for him.

Buttafuoco, looking pale, slightly grayer and thinner—he reportedly lost 25 pounds—walked out of the Nassau County jail at 10:30 A.M. and generally rebuffed a crowd of reporters and photographers.

But he did answer one question, about how his newfound freedom felt: "It feels good."

Since 1992 the mass media had been attached to Buttafuoco like barnacles. If I had chosen to do so, I could have had informed conversations about Buttafuoco with friends in California, relatives in Nebraska and Florida, and colleagues in Toronto. We all knew too much about Joey, which told me that we knew less than we should have about something else.

Not long after Buttafuoco got out of jail, the Pew Research Center for the People and the Press published an analysis of the public's knowledge of current events, as measured by polls taken from 1989 to 1995. The report concluded that only one in four Americans follows national news closely. Respondents consistently said that they paid less attention to celebrity scandals than serious news. In fact, the Pew report noted that the public "strongly complains" about too much coverage of those stories. For example, just 3 percent of those polled said they followed the break-up of Woody Allen and Mia Farrow "very closely," and 5 percent said they followed scandals among the British royalty very closely. Yet, in a series of questions those same people were most successful in correctly identifying people and events that concerned scandal, entertainment, personality, and crime.

A Pew Center poll found that four in ten Americans had watched at least one of the three made-for-TV movies about Buttafuoco and Amy Fisher. Nearly two in ten watched more than one of the movies. Andrew Kohut, the center's director, said, "Not surprisingly, we found that knowledge about what was happening in Bosnia decreased with the number of Amy Fisher movies watched. Those who viewed none knew more about the Balkan conflict than those who viewed one film, and they, in turn, knew more than those who saw two Fisher movies, etc."

Perhaps the media shouldn't be held accountable when readers and viewers fail current events quizzes. Certainly, those who chose to inform themselves about Bosnia had no great difficulty doing so. We all have our intellectual priorities, and the menu of news and information choices is vast. We create a personalized information diet by subscribing to the *National Review* rather than *People,* listening to Hot 100 instead of National Public Radio while driving to work, watching *Hard Copy* rather than *The Newshour* each evening, and spending our on-line time in The Well rather than the Flirt's Nook.

Yet certain stories and issues manage to bubble to the top of the mass media and popular culture, and others sink like stones. Not surprisingly, stories that are simple and sexy tend to float.

Crime policy has been a sinker. It is not sexy, it can be contradictory, and rarely is it simple, except as presented in political boilerplate, the prevailing manner since 1980, through the Reagan, Bush, and Clinton presidencies, through session upon session of Congress, in state legislatures and city councils from New England to California. "Most politicians can explain their entire anti-crime program in an eight-second soundbite: 'We need more police, more prisons, longer sentences and less parole,'" says Edwin Ellis, a prisoner advocate from Harlem who served twenty-five years for murder. "Any moron can understand that."

The media have been there to record the bromides and count the votes on this month's toughest crime bill ever. But what have they done to hold the politicians accountable, even in the face of evidence that today's solutions did not work yesterday? Not much. Just as crime reporting hasn't evolved much over the years, national crime strategies haven't changed either, despite the high position of lawlessness on the political agenda for most of this century.

Robert Elias, a professor at the University of San Francisco who writes about crime and its victims, says that politicians choose stale, safe strategies that don't work but vaguely respond to the media's simplistic portrayal of crime. He has written:

> Over the years, U.S. crime policy has remained remarkably consistent, with get-tough strategies used to fight periodic "crime wars." Just as consistently, these strategies have failed. Yet policymakers continue to support them, shunning the systematic changes needed to undo the adverse social conditions which generate most crime and most victimization. These policymak-

ers are understandably reluctant to admit the historic failure of
U.S. crime policy, for which they are in no small part responsible. How can they perform this sleight-of-hand? As with most
public policy, Americans learn about government crime policy
largely through the media. The press provides our window on
public problems, on the government's strategies to solve them,
and on how well those strategies succeed (or fail). If Americans
were to read the criminological literature, the failure of our
crime policy would be clear enough. Since most of us don't have
the time or the inclination for such study, we rely upon the mass
media to do it for us. Yet, with few exceptions, the media have
uncritically reproduced official, conservative, "law-and-order"
perspectives with little fundamental analysis of their success or
failure. They have also repeatedly covered and promoted "crime
wars" and "drug wars" which inevitably fail but which are periodically resuscitated (with the media's help) as if these wars had
never been fought—and lost—before. The media fail to hold
policymakers responsible for strategies which predictably don't
work. Indeed, they help make the problem worse; the media's
amnesia, unwitting or not, encourages people to support policies which actually promote the growth of crime.

These policy follies have left the country in a peculiar situation: politicians pursuing strategies of mass incarceration and mandatory sentences that
most experts oppose as wasteful, foolhardy, and racist in effect if not in
intent. The country has been led to believe that imprisonment is an effective
means of fighting crime. "Building more prisons to address crime is like
building more graveyards to address a fatal disease," says Robert Gangi, executive director of the Correctional Association of New York, a prison policy
watchdog group. "In the last twenty years America has made a basic miscal-
culation by looking to the prison system to solve the crime problem. We're
now locked into a march of fatal policy error. We got on the mandatory sentencing train twenty years ago, and now we can't get off, even in the face of
all evidence that it is not working." According to Burton Roberts, a legendary Bronx judge, "It's a matter of the politicians talking tough but acting
stupid." After an exhaustive study of the history of American criminal justice,
the author and legal scholar Lawrence M. Friedman concluded that although

the U.S. system of laws and punishment may have some impact on crime, "It is pretty certain that it is less than most people think; the constant clamor for more prisons, more executions, more police, assumes a potency that is almost surely a delusion." Even those who make a living from incarceration recognize its limitations. "It just doesn't make sense to pump millions and millions into corrections and have no effect on the crime rate," said Morris Thigpen, Alabama's corrections commissioner.

Ninety-two percent of judges who responded to one poll said they oppose mandatory sentences. Supreme Court Justice Anthony Kennedy has called mandatory minimum sentences "imprudent, unwise and often unjust," and Chief Justice William Rehnquist said, "Mandatory minimums . . . are frequently the result of floor amendments to demonstrate emphatically that legislators want to 'get tough on crime.' Just as frequently they do not involve any careful consideration of the effect they might have." The American Bar Association and all twelve regional Federal Judicial Conferences have gone on record to oppose mandatory minimum sentences. The U.S. Sentencing Commission, appointed by Congress in the mid-1980s with an implicit assignment to recommend more mandatory sentences, concluded in its 1993 report that mandatory minimums were costly and largely ineffective. Washington ignored the report.

Simplistic crime policies have left the country with an incarceration rate that is the highest in the civilized world, higher than even prison-happy Russia, and South Africa under apartheid. Canada's incarceration rate is about one-fifth that of the United States's, and Japan's about one-fifteenth.

But the statistics really tell only half the story. Imprisonment in the United States has a profound racial dynamic that the policy debates often overlook. The incarceration rate for black Americans is seven times that of whites. African Americans comprise 12 percent of the U.S. population but 44 percent of the prison population. Conversely, whites comprise 74 percent of the general population but 36 percent of the prison population. Various studies have shown that about one-third of all young black men in the United States are under the supervision of the legal system as inmates, parolees, or probationers, and the figure is even higher in some locales. A 1991 study found that 56 percent of all black men in Baltimore aged eighteen to thirty-five were in prison, on probation or parole, wanted on an arrest warrant, or awaiting court action as a result of an arrest.

The typical white response to such statistics goes something like this: The percentage would decline if blacks would stop committing so much crime. Although few whites admit it, crime and race have been inseparable kitchen-table topics for decades—and perhaps for more than a century. Intuition, bolstered by the mug shots of black faces we see on TV and on the front pages of newspapers, tell us that it is only natural that more blacks than whites are in jail because they are the lawbreakers. But do the facts bear that out?

As everyone knows by now, a large proportion of the minorities in prison are serving time for narcotics violations. In New York in 1994 racial minorities made up 94 percent of the drug offenders in state prisons. Yet drug usage among blacks closely follows their population profile. According to the U.S. Department of Health and Human Services, thirteen percent of all drug users in the United States are black, but blacks make up 39 percent of all those arrested in drug offenses. And although 38 percent of crack users are black and 52 percent white, 88 percent of all those sentenced for crack offenses are black and 4 percent white.

Nationwide, about half of all state prisoners are in on drug crimes. Most are not kingpins, of course; the prisons are full of drug chaff—young men who sell a few hits of LSD to a friend, foreign "mules" hired at slave wages to bring small quantities of narcotics into the country, lowly members of crack distribution rings who sell the tiny plastic vials on housing-project street corners. Two-thirds of all federal prisoners are serving time for narcotics, triple the number in 1980. The Department of Justice acknowledges that 21.2 percent of the total federal prison population and 36.1 percent of all federal drug prisoners are low-level drug offenders with no record of violence.

Although no conclusive statistics are available, many of the more than half-million state prison inmates serving time for drugs were arrested during police sweeps in ghetto neighborhoods, just like those I observed from the police van in Queens in 1988. Those caught in these nets tend to be crack carhops, the unskilled workers at the bottom of the narcotics hierarchy. Many fit the typical profile of the U.S. inmate: poor, underemployed, uneducated. (Studies show that only about one-third of all inmates have completed high school, and nearly half were not working full time when arrested.) When the police arrest one carhop, another is ready to stand in.

They are given small supplies of crack, heroin, or PCP by a superior—think of him as a neighborhood sales coordinator—and are instructed to staff specific corners and service customers who, more often than not, drive up and conduct the quick transaction without leaving the car, as though visiting a root beer stand. The carhops and their customers are sitting ducks for the police—no more challenging than arresting a streetwalker. The carhop arrests pile up quickly and serve as statistical ammunition that police departments, and the politicians to whom they are accountable, are doing something to take back the streets, as the slogan goes.

The vast majority of the drug carhops arrested are minorities because police inevitably mount street-sweep operations in minority neighborhoods or places frequented by minorities, whether in New York, Los Angeles, Chicago, or Houston. America somehow views a crack dealer—stereotypically black—who sells a few handfuls of $2 vials on a corner outside a housing project as a more nefarious link in the narcotics food chain than the recreational drug user—stereotypically white—who treats his bar buddies to a line or two of powder cocaine on Friday night. Thousands of poor young black Americans are serving ten-year prison sentences for drug offenses that seem to be treated as mere youthful indiscretions when committed by whites. It is more complex, and perhaps less politically expedient, for the police to infiltrate the drug-sales networks in suburban basements or the mall bars.

For young black men an arrest no longer is a social stigma. Imprisonment is so prevalent that it has become a cultural ritual that marks the arrival of adulthood. In 1992 the federal government reported that more than half the youths in long-term state juvenile institutions had immediate relatives who had been incarcerated. Another government survey found that 42 percent of black inmates in state prisons had at least one immediate family member who had been incarcerated.

"When the politicians and the public say 'lock 'em up and throw away the key,' they really mean lock up the young African American males and throw away the key," says Jerome Miller, executive director of the National Center for Institutions and Alternatives, a Virginia-based organization that advocates sentencing alternatives. Miller, who has written extensively about race, crime, and imprisonment, says,

> We'll divert the white senator's son into a treatment program when he's arrested for cocaine, but we demand mandatory sentences and jail time for the black kids and their crack. The entire system is racially driven, but no one wants to talk about race, even to the point of acknowledging the racial disparities that

arise out of our crime policies. We send out these SWAT teams on drug sweeps, and they go into the African American neighborhoods and arrest kids willy-nilly and put them through this demeaning experience. Arrests have now become such a rite of passage in the black community. This is how you build your rep—by not showing any emotion but coming out tougher, meaner, more angry. You have just proven yourself; you have become a piece of society's trash.

About five million violent crimes will be committed in the United States this year, and the perpetrator will not be caught in more than half. One-third of all homicides will go unsolved. Victims of minor nonviolent crimes have about a one-in-ten chance that the case will be solved. Tens of thousands of Americans have lost confidence in a criminal justice system that appears unable to prevent lawlessness and inept at solving a crime after it has happened. These people no longer bother to report crime to the authorities.

A majority of the fifty states and scores of cities are under court order to ease prison and jail overcrowding caused by mandatory sentences. They are pushing prisoners out the back gates to make room for those being bused in the front gates. Prosecutors, judges, and public defenders know that they must plea-bargain away nine in ten criminal cases filed yesterday just to keep up with the influx today. Discretion once used by judges in sentencing is now wielded by prosecutors at the other end of the criminal justice arc, when charges are filed. Prosecutors often can determine the sentence that a crime suspect ultimately will serve when they choose to file a charge that carries a mandatory minimum sentence rather than another that does not. In many jurisdictions judges function as clerks, referring to a sentencing ledger filled with mandates passed down by politicians trying to legislate behavior.

At a number of points in this book I have given my view of the media's culpability in the crime dilemma of the United States—that journalism tends to choose sexy crime anecdotes that perpetuate myths over informative, substantive stories that explain crime. By and large, the media also have failed to hold politicians accountable for anticrime grandstanding that often plays off the sexy anecdotes presented on TV and in the newspapers. We are left with a population that knows everything about Amy Fisher but next to nothing about the development of our national criminal justice policies. So do I kill the messenger? I hope not, although he may deserve a stern cuffing in this case. No, an inattentive public and duplicitous politicians are the other two legs of this tripod of misinformation. It seems clear enough that all of us—journalists, the public, lawmakers—would benefit by knowing a bit more about the history of crime and punishment in the United States. The first lesson is how little the nation has learned over the years.

The crime policies prevalent at the century's end are the progeny of a "war on crime" that began thirty years ago, during the Johnson administration. But politicians have bleated about law and order throughout the nation's history. The United States is and always has been a violent place, more so than most democracies and industrialized nations. There is no compelling explanation for this. One theory holds that the violence of the United States has to do with the principles of freedom on which the country was founded—that there is less state control and more individual autonomy here. To understand this idea of "fatal liberty," as it has been called, consider the crime explosion in Russia and many of the former Soviet satellite nations after the collapse of the communist empire. Others believe that the U.S. crime rate is related to the country's great wealth: there is so much to steal here, and crime has always been a bridge connecting those who have and those who want. Still others blame the broad availability of handguns, used in about half of all U.S. homicides each year, as well as in significant percentages of the assaults, robberies, and rapes.

The search for the root cause of crime seems no nearer a conclusion today, and the question of how best to deal with those who break the law is no less befuddling today than it was a century ago. It's not for lack of discussion that the mystery of American crime has gone unsolved. After the Civil War, as prisons were filling with free but idle black men, a number of cities and states held meetings on prison reform, juvenile crime, and overtaxed courts. Fifty years later, after World War I, the perception was growing that the Protestant ethic of self-control was losing ground to an unruly ethnic population that would be the country's ruination. The United States tried to legislate behavior with the ratification of Prohibition in 1919. When it became clear that this strategy would not bring about rectitude, politicians sought expert advice from lawyers, judges, and police executives. Chicago, Kansas City, Baltimore, Cleveland, and Los Angeles established crime commissions. The National Crime Commission, whose members included Franklin D. Roosevelt, was set up in 1925 with a mandate to reduce violent crime through education and legislation. The commission was not effective because most states did not welcome federal intervention in crime, which had always been considered a home-rule issue. The preamble to the Constitution says that federal law enforcement should exist "to insure domestic Tranquility," and the Federal Bureau of Investigation was created in 1908 as part of the U.S. Justice Department, but it had almost no public profile until J. Edgar Hoover became director in 1924. Through his mastery of frenzy-inducing publicity, Hoover transformed journeymen crooks into public enemies. He helped create the lore of the Roaring Twenties with the ballyhooed pursuit of "the Syndicate," purveyors of the triple vices of booze, gambling, and prostitution.

As that decade of debauchery, as chronicled by the *New York Daily News* and the other jazz journals, drew to a close, Herbert Hoover became the first in a long line of politicians to present himself as a law-and-order candidate—and the first American president to deem crime worthy of mention in his inaugural address. He cited a number of dangers to the moral and economic integrity of the country. "The most malign of all these dangers today is disregard and disobedience of law," he said. "Crime is increasing. Confidence in rigid and speedy justice is decreasing."

Hoover responded to the threat with the strategic solution that has served scores of local, state, and federal politicians since: he commissioned a study. He appointed George W. Wickersham, a former U.S. attorney general, as chairman of the National Commission on Law Observance and Enforcement. Two years later, in 1931, the Wickersham Commission published thirteen detailed reports on such matters as crime and its causes, the failures of criminal justice policy, and conditions in prisons. The reports documented corruption, brutality, and widespread inefficiencies. One report described the proliferation of court catch-up days in which overburdened prosecutors and judges offered plea bargains in exchange for scant sentences. In the commission's *Report on the Causes of Crime,* commission member Morris Ploscowe wrote that something at "the very heart of . . . government and social policy in America" was fundamentally wrong. Wickersham made detailed recommendations for reform, including increased funding for law enforcement to upgrade training, salaries, efficiency, and performance. He suggested broad prison reforms, including expansion of the federal system and an overhaul of parole procedures. But the Great Depression intervened, and the Wickersham reports were destined to become dust collectors.

During the late 1950s *juvenile delinquency* made its way into the lexicon as the first baby boomers became teenagers. This created a predictable crime spike that has been repeated each time the nation's population of young men has ballooned since they are responsible for a vast majority of crime. By the time the presidential campaign of 1964 arrived, more boomers were in their prime crime-committing years, and lawlessness was on the national supper agenda. During speeches late that summer Republican nominee Barry Goldwater borrowed Herbert Hoover's law-and-order bromide, adding a cold war twist. Goldwater declared that crime had become a "growing menace," and his early sound-bite rhetoric grabbed headlines and TV time. Even though Goldwater lost resoundingly, Lyndon B. Johnson understood that his opponent's anticrime theme had resonated with an American public that was confused by social upheavals. Within weeks of his inauguration Johnson created the President's Commission on Law Enforcement and Administration of Justice. "Crime is a sore on the face of America," Johnson said. "It is a menace on our streets. . . . It is a corrupter of our youth." On another occasion he said, "I will not be satisfied until every woman and child in this nation can walk any street, enjoy any park, drive on any highway, and live in any community at any time of the day or night without fear of being harmed."

Perceptively enough, Johnson said even before the study had begun that "jobs, education, and hope" were the long-range solutions to the crime problem. Crime cannot be solved by commission appointments, more cops, and stricter sentences, he said. And even then Republicans and Democrats parried over proprietorship of the crime issue. When Johnson asked Thomas E. Dewey, a Republican, to serve as chairman of his commission, the former New York governor declined because it "looked too much like a political issue-stealing job."

Nicholas Katzenbach, a former U.S. attorney general, eventually agreed to lead the commission, which had nineteen members, including lawyers, judges, and police. It had a staff of sixty-three, 175 paid consultants, and hundreds of unpaid advisers. Its three-year study was billed as the most extensive examination of crime and criminal justice ever undertaken. It surveyed ten thousand U.S. families about their crime experiences and questioned two thousand police agencies about innovations. It conducted prison surveys in every state and 250 sample counties, and it examined police-community relations in more than twenty cities. It sponsored the National Symposium on Science and Criminal Justice and another conference on problems of legal staffing. It studied lower courts in six cities and investigated crime syndicates in four others.

In December 1965, as the Katzenbach commission was just beginning its work, the Republican Party offered its own report on crime, hoping to maintain ideological control of the issue. This was two years after President Kennedy was assassinated, one year after the first Vietnam protests at University of California at Berkeley, and just a few months after the 1965 race riots in Detroit and Los Angeles; L.A. alone had thirty-four deaths, four thousand arrests, and $40 million in property damage from the Watts riot. It was not difficult to convince Mr. and Mrs. America, who had watched these dramas unfold on the nightly television news, that a crisis was at hand. The Republican policy paper on crime blamed Democrat-controlled political machines in big cities like Los Angeles for surrendering in the battle against lawlessness. Complacent Democratic politicians had allowed the war protests and race riots to happen by holding police departments on short leashes, the Republicans said. They warned that crime was beginning to leach out of the cities and into the suburban areas where whites by the thousands had moved after World War II. Cities had become "crime-breeding ghettos" full of delinquents who ventured into the suburbs at night to prey upon the new affluence there. "It's us or them," the report said.

Viewed three decades later the race baiting in the Republican rhetoric seems blatant. The changing racial and social dynamics of the United States, combined with the urban riots and war protests, profoundly influenced the crime initiatives and public panic about crime in the 1960s. In speeches during the fall of 1965 J. Edgar Hoover called civil disobedience "a seditious slogan of gross irresponsibility," and he labeled Martin Luther King Jr. "one of the most notorious liars in the country." In a speech to lawyers in Nashville Charles E. Whittaker, a retired justice of the U.S. Supreme Court (1957–1962), said the lawbreaking was "fostered and inflamed by the preachments of self-appointed leaders of minority groups."

From this perspective, the forces of law and order, armed with truncheons and water cannons, stood in their jackboots at the barricades against the invading wave of sneaker-wearing war protesters and race rioters. The riots followed a series of momentous rulings by the Supreme Court under Chief Justice Earl Warren, a progressive Republican and former California governor, that limited the powers of police and prosecutors. In *Miranda v. Arizona* (1966), a rape case, the court deemed that police officers must inform crime suspects that they cannot be compelled to speak and have the right to legal counsel before questioning. A pornography case, *Mapp v. Ohio* (1961), established the so-called exclusionary rule, limiting the ability of prosecutors to use evidence that was obtained unlawfully. In *Gideon v. Wainwright* (1963), which involved a destitute man accused of breaking into a billiard hall in Florida, the Warren Court ruled that anyone charged with a crime has a right to legal counsel at state expense. The rulings broadened the rights of accused criminals, and that served to intensify public anxiety about crime.

At various times during his presidency Johnson tried to reassure the nation through the press and television that the United States would endure the social convulsions. In March 1966 he reported rather triumphantly that while crime still was increasing, the rate of increase had slowed from 13 percent in 1964 to 5 percent in 1965. But that summer the race riots spread to fourteen other cities, including Chicago and New York, and the national press focused attention on the burgeoning crime rate in Washington, D.C., a development that, even then, was called a national disgrace. President Johnson said, "I want to make it clear that I want the best police force in the United States here in the capital of our nation, and I want to make it clear that we are going to have it or some fur is going to fly." (The crime problem there proved to be more recalcitrant than the tough-talking Texan could have imagined; in 1997 the federal government launched yet another attempt to clean up the national capital.)

By the end of 1966 the press, politicians, and public alike were clamoring for release of the Katzenbach commission's report as a sign that the government was doing *something* about the crime problem. The report's release had been delayed several times, and commission members were warning that no one should expect its recommendations to solve the crime problem. Finally, in February 1967 the commission issued its long-awaited report. It began, "There is much crime in America, more than ever is reported, far more than ever is solved, far too much for the health of the nation. Every American knows that. Every American is, in a sense, a victim of crime."

As he announced the findings of his commission, President Johnson made his famous declaration of war on crime. The report made two hundred recommendations, but most were general and many had as much to do with the protection of civil liberties as they did with crime prevention. The commission said the criminal justice system was antiquated and starved for funding, the same conclusion reached by Hoover's Wickersham commission thirty-six years earlier. The report did not delineate costs for its recommendations, and in many areas experts said no solutions existed. The report warned, "If every recommendation of the Crime Commission were implemented tomorrow, it is unlikely that there would be a dramatic reduction in crime rates. There is no device, no technology, no tested program that will make the streets measurably safer in the short term."

It was a powerful admission at the end of a study that many hoped would at long last help resolve the country's crime problem. Katzenbach subsequently spent a great deal of time trying to explain why nothing could be done. In particular, he cautioned against scapegoating: "If there had been no 'Negro revolution,' no civil rights movement, no riots, no war in Vietnam, no political furor about four-letter words, and no change in the law or interpretation by the Supreme Court, we would still have a serious and growing crime problem."

A few days after the report was released, Katzenbach sat for an interview with *Look* magazine. The questions and answers are striking for their pertinence today, beginning with Katzenbach's assertion that "there has perhaps never been a time in our history when crime was a source of such great public concern." The interview covered most of the crime issues still picked over at criminology conferences, including morality, the public's fear of crime, juvenile crime, recidivism, and drug treatment. Thirty years later journalists are asking the same questions and getting the same answers. A sample from the 1967 interview:

Q:     Does the trend signify a breakdown in public morality?

KATZENBACH:     No. I don't think you could say that. The Commission did identify some major factors besides a generally increasing population. One is an increasing number of young people—the population group that commits the greatest amount of crime. Another is increasing urbanization—more and more people crowded into cities, thus adding both frustrations and opportunities for crime that don't exist in rural areas. Poverty causes crime, but so does prosperity. There are more things to steal—more cars, more TV sets. Further, when we introduced credit cards and self-service stores into our society, we created new categories of crime.

Q:     Youths under 18 . . . accounted for half of the 1965
arrests for serious offenses. What do we do about this?

KATZENBACH:     Historically, young people commit a disproportionate
amount of crime, and we have more young people
today. The 15-to-17 age group represents 5.4 percent
of population, but accounts for 12.8 percent of all
arrests. . . . Youngsters of 15 and 16 have the highest
arrest rate in the country. If you consider that nearly
one-quarter of our population is under ten, you can
see we face more trouble ahead. . . .

Q:     The public seems more aware of crime and also more
fearful. Is this an undue fear?

KATZENBACH:     Yes and no. There are, of course, rational reasons for
fear. The crimes that get the most attention are those
most likely to induce fear—armed holdups, beatings,
rape, murder—and I think the common idea is that,
therefore, we should fear the stranger. Actually, most
crimes of violence are committed by friends, associ-
ates and relatives—not by strangers. Most crime is
committed by people who live in slums against
people who also live in slums, not by people coming
out of slums and attacking people in the suburbs;
most crime is not interracial, although when it is, it
may get a lot of attention. Negroes in slums fear
crime more—and with more reason—than any
group. The consequence of not making distinctions
between crimes of violence and crimes against
property is unfortunate. . . .

Q:     What is your reaction to the charges that we coddle
criminals and that the Commission report would coddle criminals all the more?

KATZENBACH:     I can understand the frustrations that produce such
charges. But I think that talking about 'coddling criminals' is as meaningless as talking about 'crime.' The
Commission doesn't recommend either harsher or
softer treatment for anyone. But there is a difference
between a criminal who commits a vicious beating or

rape and a teenager who steals a package out of an unlocked car. . . . Our treatment should recognize such differences. Of course, dangerous people should be kept away from society. But they are a tiny fraction of 'criminals.' We should not be so medically, psychiatrically and professionally bankrupt that we can't do anything effective about all the rest.

What we want are programs tailored to the particular case. We need more supervision, training and treatment within the community. Too often, our jails are finishing schools where a minor offender can become a major criminal in a short time. The Commission's survey of penal institutions showed one-third of them have no form of vocational training whatsoever. Where it did exist, it was often aimed at maintaining the prison facility, not training the people for a job on the outside. More than 90 percent of local corrections personnel are simply guards and administrators. Less than three percent are concerned with rehabilitation.

Q: What chance does the released convict have of going straight?

KATZENBACH: Much too little. . . . At least one-third of released offenders are going to commit crimes again, and the second, third and fourth time is much more likely to be serious. . . .

Q: What does the Commission propose for drug addicts?

KATZENBACH: It favors the existing Federal law and laws of some states such as New York and California, which give options for medical treatment to the drug addict who is not involved in peddling narcotics. We favor increased concentration on the medical aspects of drug addictions, more centers within the community for treatment, more supervision to make sure that addicts who seem cured don't fall again.

Q: How can our courts be improved?

KATZENBACH:    First, through better judges, better prosecutors, better defense counsel. Secondly, by removing from the
criminal process those cases that shouldn't be in it,
like drunkenness. . . . When it comes to sentencing,
if the corrections system is what it ought to be, the
judge will have more options.

Q:    All of this will cost money. Where will it come from?

KATZENBACH:    Higher taxes. The Commission is convinced we can
reduce crime, but there are no magic formulas, no
quick and easy solutions. President Johnson has out-
lined our national strategy against crime. It can
succeed. But we are going to have to pay for walkie-
talkie radios for our police forces, for data-processing
equipment for our courts, for the salaries of many
more probation and parole officers. The average
citizen is also going to have to realize that it takes
another kind of sacrifice. He must be willing to serve
on juries, to be a witness, to report crime. He must
quit cutting corners, stop shrugging his shoulders,
end his indifference. He must accept the full
responsibility of his citizenship.

A few years later Katzenbach and President Johnson would acknowledge
that their report, like the Wickersham report, had no effect on the crime
rate in the United States. Perhaps more important, the commission's work
led indirectly to a crucial change in conceptions about punishment—one
that continues to tinge discussions about incarceration today. In the 1960s,
as computerization proliferated and the space program reached toward the
moon, the country had a lingering sense that crime might have a scientific
solution—an anticrime pill or a form of therapy—that could do for lawlessness what antibiotics had done for contagious disease.

The Katzenbach commission supported funding for anticrime innovations
and scientific and sociological research on law enforcement, courts, and
prisons. Partly as a result of the Katzenbach commission's influence, the
Omnibus Crime Control and Safe Streets Act of 1968 created the Law Enforcement Assistance Administration, which was to channel federal money
to the states to pay for innovative projects. To qualify for the funding states

were required to establish criminal justice planning agencies to distribute the money and monitor the projects. Like most states, New York was eager to get a share of the federal funding, and it was a step ahead in the application process because in 1966 Governor Nelson Rockefeller had appointed just such a planning committee to study the most effective means of prisoner rehabilitation. Rockefeller's prison committee hired a number of expert "ologists"—penologists, criminologists, sociologists—to conduct a comprehensive survey of the prison-research literature, then make recommendations about which "treatments"—counseling, medication, exercise, education, group therapy, occupational training—were most likely to transform lawbreakers into productive members of society. To lead the research team the committee hired a New York City sociology professor named Robert Martinson, who was thereby destined to become the unlikely guru of the use of prisons for punishment and incapacitation rather than rehabilitation.

As they began their study, Martinson and his colleagues set out to give measurable scientific responses to a series of unanswered and perhaps unanswerable questions that underlie all crime research and policy: Is crime a "disease" that can be treated and cured, or is it an inevitable condition that can be only controlled? Does crime have a "cause"? Do certain people break laws without compunction because of genetics or because of sociological influences, such as poverty or mushy moral underpinnings? In other words, are criminals born or made? In either case, can the criminal justice system make a behavioral "correction"? Finally, and most important, can a criminal be reformed and rehabilitated in prison, or are penitence, incapacitation, and punishment the sole purposes of penitentiaries?

The question of how best to punish a lawbreaker surely has existed since the first human pilfered a slab of meat or stoned a rival. The Old Testament decrees, "Who so sheddeth man's blood by man shall his blood be shed." The Roman prescript of thirty-nine lashes, inflicted upon Jesus in a biblical account, has been broadly borrowed over the centuries and leveled against everyone from runaway slaves in Mississippi to adulterous lovers in Massachusetts. Ancient Babylon gave us the law of retaliation—an eye for an eye—that still exists as a rationale for corporal punishment. Although he lived six centuries before Jesus, a magistrate in Athens named Draco is memorialized to this day for the severe (draconian) code of laws that he helped create. The Romans added the concept of fines as a punishment a century later. Modern penology was framed by Cesare Beccaria, whose 1764 book, *Crimes and Pun-*

*ishment*, argued that punishment should be swift and certain, not dependent upon judicial whimsy, and that any punishment that does not deter crime should be abolished. Beccaria also wrote that the punishment should fit the crime; if heads are lopped off for stealing a single lira or a million, a criminal with petty inclinations might as well choose to go for the big payday if he is going to die in either case.

In Beccaria's day, jail and prison sentences began to replace physical punishment as the sanction of choice against criminals. In eighteenth-century America public whippings grew less prevalent, but shame before the community remained a key part of many prison sentences. Local authorities allowed citizens to enter the prisons to watch the criminals at hard labor. In an experiment that brings to mind today's renewed popularity of chain gangs, Pennsylvania in 1776 ordered prisoners to work on public construction projects, often building streets and highways. Citizens and criminals often taunted one another, and the project was scrapped as a failure when the Commonwealth approved a prison reform act in 1790. A prevailing theory of the day held that the dormitory-style prisons common at the time bred even more crime because criminals shared techniques while incarcerated; jails served as crime finishing schools, and convicts emerged from behind bars as more accomplished pickpockets and keyswifts.

Modern prisoner-maintenance philosophy evolved from Philadelphia's Walnut Street jail, the first to feature individual cells. Prisoners were in solitary confinement most of the time, and talking was not allowed. At a state prison in Auburn, New York, inmates worked together during the day but slept in solitary cells at night. At prisons such as Auburn, and Sing Sing, at Ossining, New York, inmates were forced into a tight daily regimen. From morning rouse until lights-out prisoners adhered to a schedule maintained by a series of bells, whistles, and queues. Meal portions were measured to the ounce, and personal possessions were carefully controlled.

Sociologists believed that the ritualized conduct could help correct the behavioral defects of the prisoners by teaching them the discipline they failed to learn early in life. In 1830 and 1831 two young Frenchmen, Gustave de Beaumont and Alexis de Tocqueville, toured the United States while seeking a model for French democracy. They were struck by the prison reforms here, and their 1833 book, *On the Penitentiary System in the United States and Its Applications in France*, still stands as required reading for serious students of crime and punishment. Friedman, the legal historian, wrote,

Beaumont and De Tocqueville strongly believed in the system, as did almost all the prison reformers of the day. The prison was stern but effective medicine. Men turned to crime because of their defective background, their weak wills, their bad society. The prison cured these problems. It provided the missing training, the missing backbone. It was a caricature of the unyielding, disciplined, incorruptible family that the prisoners had never had for themselves.

The notion that prisons can reform behavior would prevail for more than a century, although its popularity did wane and wax over the years; civility and brutality varied from prison to prison and guard to guard, with racial, ethnic, and religious minorities often singled out for abuse.

In 1870 the National Prison Association was formed to address the inhumane treatment of prisoners, particularly the blacks who were being stuffed into cells after the Civil War. The association called for a new round of reforms, including segregation of prisoners by severity of crime, education for prison administrators, and industrial training to prepare prisoners for life on the outside. The association also advocated a separate justice system for juveniles, and at its urging the first "reformatory" for young offenders was opened in 1876 in Elmira, New York. The Elmira Reformatory is an important venue in prison history because it adopted another favorite concept of the association, indeterminate sentencing. A judge who sent a youth to Elmira did not decree a specific sentence. Instead, young convicts fixed their own release date by earning merits and demerits based upon conduct, punctuality, personal bearing, appearance, and success at vocational training. The reformatory's directors functioned as a parole board, periodically reviewing inmates' portfolios to determine whether they had been sufficiently "cured."

A popular myth holds that "liberal" notions such as indeterminate sentencing, rehabilitation, and earned parole became institutionalized during the 1960s. In fact, New York adopted the Elmira Reformatory model for adult offenders as early as 1901. California adopted a broad version of the sentencing policy in 1917, and the practice soon spread across the country. Indeterminate sentences feature a broad range: typically, five years to life for second-degree murder or robbery, six months to life for assault with a deadly weapon, five years to life for the sale of narcotics. As with the youths at Elmira, inmates stood before parole boards periodically to make a case that they had earned release by being sufficiently reformed, cured, and rehabilitated. Indeterminate sentencing and earned parole were the standards for most of the twentieth century. Probation, through which convicted criminals are diverted to intense supervision as a sentencing alternative to jail or prison, also expanded to broad usage. The Elmira reforms led to other innovations with a goal of behavioral "correction": increased vocational training, education, counseling and psychotherapy, group therapy, and medical treatment for drug addicts, alcoholics, sex offenders, and the mentally ill.

Through the mid-1960s most penologists agreed that these modern innovations had made criminal rehabilitation a viable possibility, although they disagreed about which technique or combination of techniques worked best. That was the question that Robert Martinson was commissioned to answer by Governor Rockefeller's Special Committee on Criminal Offenders. Martinson explained:

> The field of penology has produced a voluminous research literature on this subject, but until recently there has been no comprehensive review of this literature and no attempt to bring its findings to bear, in a useful way, on the general question of "What works"? . . . The Committee was organized on the premise that prisons could rehabilitate, that the prisons of New York were not in fact making a serious effort at rehabilitation, and that New York's prisons should be converted from their existing custodial basis to a new rehabilitative one. The problem for the Committee was that there was no available guidance on the question of what had been shown to be the most effective means of rehabilitation. My colleagues and I were hired by the committee to remedy this defect in our knowledge; our job was to undertake a comprehensive survey of what was known about rehabilitation.

Martinson's team meticulously reviewed all known prison research projects conducted in the English language between 1945 and 1967. Team members found 231 studies that met their exacting standards for unbiased social science research. Typically, the studies gauged the behavioral improvement of a group of prisoners that received a particular type of "treatment"—group counseling and occupational therapy, for example—against the improvement of a control group of inmates that did not receive the same treatment. The studies used various methods of measuring an offender's improvement: adjustment to prison life, vocational success, educational achievement, personality and attitude changes, and general adjustment to life outside prison. But the bottom line in penology is the rate of recidivism—the relapse into crime after release from prison—and that, appropriately, was the key behavioral improvement investigated.

In 1970 Martinson presented the Rockefeller committee with a fourteen-hundred-page report that had a jaw-dropping conclusion: "With few and isolated exceptions, the rehabilitative efforts that have been reported so far have had no appreciable effect on recidivism." This was not what the committee wanted—or expected—to hear. It contradicted prison projects that had already begun, in expectation of different findings by Martinson. The committee accepted the study but locked it away, even refusing Martinson's request that he be allowed to publish it on his own. A criminal justice legend promptly grew around Martinson's study. In legal circles it became widely known that politicians had suppressed the report because it debunked the myth of prison rehabilitation. In 1972 a Bronx lawyer with inside information subpoenaed the report as evidence in a criminal case. The document thus entered the public domain, and Martinson finally was able to publish a summary and analysis of his findings in 1974.

He wrote,

> It may be that there is a more radical flaw in our present strategies—that education at its best, or that psychotherapy at its best, cannot overcome, or even appreciably reduce, the powerful tendency for offenders to continue in criminal behavior. Our present treatment programs are based on a theory of crime as a "disease"—that is to say, as something foreign and abnormal in the individual that can presumably be cured. This theory may well be flawed, in that it overlooks—indeed, denies—both the normality of crime in society and the personal normality of a very large proportion of offenders, criminals who are merely responding to the facts and conditions of our society.

The Martinson study, which became widely known among experts as the "Nothing Works" report, was used to advance the prison-as-incapacitation point of view. Yet its conclusions were not that simple. Martinson stressed that although nothing had appeared to work so far in reducing recidivism, that might mean that penologists had not found the proper rehabilitative treatment. He acknowledged that his study might be used to rationalize tougher treatment of criminals. But he warned in the report that draconian sentences can "offend the moral order of a democratic society."

The final line of his report published in *The Public Interest* read, "As we begin to learn the facts, we will be in a better position than we are now to judge to what degree the prison has become an anachronism and can be replaced by a more effective means of social control." In other words, Martinson pondered the futility of imprisonment. This was in character with earlier writing and research he had done. Jerome Miller, the Virginia criminologist, described Martinson, who once served as chairman of the sociology department at City College in Manhattan, as a Troskyite who "advanced the conclusion that we should actually begin closing prisons down."

Unfortunately, Martinson is not available to explain and frame his research. In 1980 he leaped to his death from a window of his ninth-floor apartment in Manhattan. Miller sees Martinson's suicide as a metaphor for what would follow in U.S. corrections.

"In his earlier writings, he was an abolitionist when it came to prisons," Miller says. "He wrote one paper after another that said, basically, 'Prison doesn't work as an effective deterrent against crime, so we might as well open the gates and let them all out until we figure out some better plan.' It seems bitterly ironic that Martinson should now be used as the backbone for these crazy imprisonment strategies. He saw it coming, of course, and he was very upset during the latter portion of his life. He got manic over it."

Between 1967, when Johnson declared war on crime, and 1974, when Martinson's report was made public, the crime rate had continued to escalate, and the country seemed no nearer a solution. Richard Nixon was elected twice on a tough-on-crime platform, and the more conservative Warren Burger replaced Earl Warren as chief justice of the Supreme Court. Lyndon Johnson, in his 1971 autobiography, acknowledged that crime "was a more massive and profound problem than any of us had realized." And in 1972 James Vorenberg, who worked under Katzenbach as executive director of Johnson's crime commission, wrote that the country's crime problem had grown worse, not better, since the report was issued: "Five years later, crime is unquestionably a far worse problem for the country than it was then, and our system of criminal justice—the police, courts, and corrections agencies—seem less capable of coping with it."

After political ideology began to shift in the early 1970s, Martinson's study provided the harbor from which politicians could launch the antirehabilitation flotilla. The "Nothing Works" report was cited by a number of criminologists at Rand Corp., an influential think tank in Santa Monica, California, whose key research patrons included the U.S. government. The theory had an important ally in James Q. Wilson, the professor and criminologist whose 1975 book, *Thinking About Crime*, served as a conservative policy primer on criminal justice. In the book Wilson argued that the notion of prison rehabilitation was unrealistic. He wrote, "It requires not merely optimistic but heroic assumptions about the nature of man to lead one to suppose that a person, finally sentenced after (in most cases) many brushes with the law, and having devoted a good part of his youth and young adulthood to misbehavior of every sort, should, by either the solemnity of prison or the skillfulness of a counselor, come to see the error of his ways and to experience a transformation of his character."

Rand conducted a number of studies in the mid- and late 1970s that cited the Martinson report, and that research helped define criminal justice policy for city, state, and federal legislators and law enforcement agencies. Most important, the national standard for sentencing changed from indeterminate to determinate. After all, if prisons could not "cure" behavioral problems, indeterminate sentences—one year to life, with the prisoner earning release based upon his rehabilitation—seemed senseless. The new flat-time guidelines replaced broad sentences with more specific ranges—one to three years, five to ten years, twenty-five years to life.

Illinois and Maine were the first states to eliminate indeterminate sentencing, and they were followed closely by California, whose legislature in 1976 approved the Uniform Determinate Sentencing Act. An odd coalition of conservative politicians and traditionally liberal organizations supported the measure, including the Prisoners Union and the Northern California chapter of the American Civil Liberties Union. Governor Edmund G. (Jerry) Brown Jr. endorsed it. Conservatives, including many prosecutors and police officers, supported determinate sentencing because they did not believe that judges and parole board members were punishing prisoners adequately. Many liberals viewed indeterminate sentencing as potentially capricious, based upon the whim of parole board members. One billboard case cited by liberals involved John Lynch, a California man who exposed himself to a car-hop at a drive-in restaurant in 1967. He was convicted and, under indeterminate sentencing, remanded to prison for a term of "not less than one year." Five years and four parole rejections later Lynch languished in prison because the parole board had not deemed him cured. Lynch finally was released by court order.

California faced moderate opposition to determinate sentencing, primarily from the criminal defense bar and a few liberal legislators, because the change removed discretion from judges and handed it to politicians. As Rand researchers Albert J. Lipson and Mark A. Peterson reported in 1980:

> They [the opposition] feared that public outrage about atypical, heinous crimes would result in penalties that were too high. . . . It was suggested that the legislature would consider the interests of the majority of their constituents who were concerned with public protection and demanded harsher penalties, rather than the rights of the unpopular minority directly affected by their actions. Furthermore, the legislature was seen as having little time or expertise to develop a rational sentencing system that would require continuing adjustments and fine tuning.

The Lipson-Peterson report quoted an anonymous California state senator who described that dynamic:

> Public attitudes have gotten tougher over the last five years I have been in the Senate, and the legislature has responded to the get-tough view. The people are tired of violent crime and want the legislature to "do something" about it. The legislature doesn't know what to do to solve the crime problem and is frustrated with unsuccessful efforts at rehabilitation. The only thing we can do immediately is raise penalties. Some tough bills get votes now that they would not have gotten several years ago.

Another unnamed legislative interviewee added, "Politically it's never bad to increase penalties. With assumption of sentencing responsibility, it's hard for the legislature to resist pressure to raise sentences. There is nothing to counteract the penalty spiral."

True to that prediction, California legislators could hardly contain their fervor for longer sentences. They enacted the state's sentencing reform law in 1976, but it did not take effect until July 1, 1977. In the intervening months, even before the new sanctions were instituted, the legislature amended the law to stiffen a number of penalties: the maximum sentence for rape was increased from five to eight years, for arson from four to six, for first-degree burglary from four to six, for vehicle theft from three to four.

The California Legislature in the late 1970s approved a number of other measures that were important clarions of the new criminal justice era. It eliminated the state parole authority's powers of "safety valve" prisoner release to deal with prison overcrowding emergencies; it reduced funding for probation, and it renamed its parole agency. The California Community Release Board became known as the California Board of Prison Terms. In 1976 the state legislature began to dabble heavily in another new policy concept: mandatory sentences. Although determinate sentencing dictated the range of imprisonment for a particular offense if prison were the punishment of choice, it allowed judges the options of probation or a suspended sentence in lieu of prison. This was unacceptable to politicians who believed that judges tended to be too soft on criminals. Mandatory sentencing laws require prison sentences of a specific duration for those convicted of certain crimes.

In the 1970s most mandatory sentences targeted narcotics. In 1973, the year that Congress created the Drug Enforcement Administration, New York enacted a series of mandatory minimums under what became known as the Rockefeller drug laws. State legislators in Massachusetts, Connecticut, and Missouri enacted their own mandatory minimums. Congress also clambered aboard the mandatory sentencing train. During the 94th Congress, in 1975 and 1976, members introduced nearly three dozen Senate bills and House resolutions calling for mandatory minimum sentences.

The concept was not new to U.S. criminal justice. Mandatory sentences had existed for piracy and murder on federal property for nearly two hundred years, for example. In 1956 Congress provided mandatory minimum sentences under the Boggs Act at the urging of FBI director J. Edgar Hoover, as part of federal efforts to control narcotics during the *Reefer Madness* era. But Congress repealed those laws in 1970 under the Comprehensive Drug Abuse Prevention and Control Act. George Bush, then a congressman from Texas, explained his support for the repeal legislation: "Contrary to what one might imagine, however, this bill will result in better justice and more appropriate sentences. . . . Federal judges are almost unanimously opposed to mandatory minimums, because they remove a great deal of the court's discretion. . . . As a result (of the repeal), we will undoubtedly have more equitable action by the courts, with actually more convictions where they are called for, and fewer disproportionate sentences."

Five years later the inequity of mandatory sentences apparently had developed new political popularity. Mandatory sentences allow politicians to assert direct control over judges because those mandates always supersede any federal or state sentencing guidelines by which a judge normally is bound. And when politicians get their hands in it, the criminal justice system is reduced to political puppet play. Today, state codes mandate sentences for most crimes involving narcotics, violence, and repeat offenders. In essence, a judge must refer to two sentencing ledgers: one listing mandatory minimum sentences by infraction, the other listing the guidelines to be used only if there is no mandatory minimum. If the infraction in question is listed in the mandatory sentencing ledger, the judge has no choice but to hand down that sentence. If there is no mandated minimum, the judge refers to the guidelines ledger. The guidelines often begin with sentences that are longer than the mandatory minimums, but they allow reductions based upon extenuating circumstances—no criminal history, family considerations, occupation, degree of culpability, remorse.

In a red-flag report commissioned by the U.S. Department of Justice, Rand researchers Joan Petersilia and Peter W. Greenwood wrote in 1977,

> There is mounting public distress over not only the high rate of violent crimes but also the rise in property crimes such as burglary. Encouraged by the mass media, the public has begun to blame the leniency of the courts for the high level of crime. Many citizens believe that a "get-tough" policy in the courtroom would (1) help protect them against serious criminals by imprisoning such person for longer periods, and (2) deter other persons from crime because of the harsher sentences they would expect to receive if caught. This notion not only exists in the popular realm but is also being advanced by respected law enforcement personnel. Mandatory prison sentences are emerging as a major issue of national debate. . . . These new

sentencing reforms imply greater system costs. . . . Advocates of new mandatory sentencing schemes have generally ignored the likely extra burden on the correctional system. Specifically, policymakers need to know which type of offender and what length of sentence are likely to produce the largest reduction in crime, and the impact that such mandatory penalties will have on the prison population. The research reported here attempted to do both. The results suggest that mandatory sentences can reduce crime as a result of incapacitation effects, but the increase in prison population entailed by such policies may be unacceptably large.

The prediction of a boom in the prison population soon proved accurate in California. The number of inmates, which had been stable for twenty years, increased 12 percent between 1977, when flat-time sentencing took effect, and 1978. Prison commitments per 100,000 population increased from 32.4 in 1977 to 39.2 in 1978, the highest rate in the state's history.

The prescient study by Petersilia and Greenwood also predicted models of violent crime reduction versus prison population growth. The researchers said that a sentencing policy that focused on recidivists would have the least effect on crime while increasing prison populations the most. A three-year mandatory term for any felony conviction, for example, would lead to a 22 percent reduction in the crime rate while increasing the prison population by 225 percent.

In fact, California's numbers are even more stark. Since 1980 the state's prison population has increased nearly sevenfold, from 22,500 to about 140,000 in 1997, while the state corrections budget has increased more than tenfold. The payoff was a 13 percent reduction in crime from 1980 to 1991. Yet this statistic, from a study entitled "Why Does Crime Pay?" by the National Center for Policy Analysis in Dallas, has been cited repeatedly by advocates for more prisons as proof that incapacitation works.

There are other statistics, however. While one-third of all black men in their twenties are under criminal supervision in California, the rate is less than 6 percent for whites in the same age group. In 1990 about sixty-eight thousand black men in their twenties were imprisoned in the state. That same year fewer than fifteen thousand black men in their twenties were attending four-year colleges in California. As a result of a three-strikes law, which is being applied more often in California than elsewhere, the prison population is expected to reach about 210,000 by the turn of the century. The state prison budget, 2 percent of the state budget in 1980, is expected to consume 16 percent of the state's financial resources at the peak of prison population. The question, of course, is how much are taxpayers willing to pay to feel safe?

The same remonstrations that led to these punishment reforms in California began rumbling on the federal level in 1975. Conservative politicians wanted stiffer sentences, and liberals, including Massachusetts senator Edward Kennedy, had long lobbied for reform of a federal system of justice that varied broadly among the ninety-five districts, often based upon the seemingly arbitrary decisions of a judge. When Ronald Reagan was elected in 1980, he seized the opportunity and built a bipartisan coalition for federal sentencing reform. Reagan had been an interested observer during the period of criminal justice reform in California. As governor from 1966 to 1974, he sang Goldwater's law-and-order tune, but many of his crime-related proposals were stymied in political parrying with the Democrat-controlled State Assembly. In 1984 the U.S. Senate approved the Comprehensive Crime Control Act by a one-vote margin; the House vote was 316–91. Among its provisions, the act abolished parole in the federal prison system and established the U.S. Sentencing Commission, a seven-member agency in the judicial branch of government.

The idea was to devise a more rational, uniform set of criminal sentences. Paul H. Robinson, one of the original commissioners, wrote,

> Rather than simply continuing past practices, the newly created United States Sentencing Commission was directed to devise and articulate a sentencing policy . . . to direct the decisions necessary for guidelines that would further the statutorily defined purposes of sentencing—the imposition of just punishment, the deterrence of potential offenders, the incapacitation of dangerous offenders, and, where possible, rehabilitation. The ultimate goal was a rational sentencing system and a system that would be perceived as rational.

After two years of work the commission presented Congress with eight hundred pages of sentencing guidelines in the spring of 1987. It assigned a standardized sentence to each crime—typically expressed in a range of months, such as seventy to eighty-seven months—that a judge could increase or reduce based upon aggravating or mitigating circumstances, such as brutality of the crime or degree of remorse. The new guidelines essentially disallowed consideration of details of personal background, including employment history and community standing, which judges traditionally had used as factors in sentencing. Parole was not an option, although prisoners could earn a 15 percent early-release credit—fifty-four days per year served—by behaving.

When the guidelines were sent to Congress on April 13, 1987, Commissioner Robinson took the unusual step of sending along a formal dissenting view. He argued that the guidelines were far from rational and coherent because they failed to systematically rank offenses by degree of seriousness. He also protested that the commission had failed to predict the financial effect of the guidelines on prison populations and courts. "These guidelines may well produce more irrationality and more unwarranted disparity than exists today," he wrote.

It is not possible to know whether the guidelines, in their pure form, would have been effective over a long term because Congress immediately got its political mitts on them. Politicians began amending the sentencing act, which took effect November 1, 1987, to include mandatory sentences. The act decreed that any mandatory sentence introduced by congressional amendment would override the determinate sentences required under the guidelines. Just as they do on the state level, mandatory sentences remove from a federal judge's discretion the ability to suspend a sentence or punish with probation, based upon mitigating circumstances. In many cases prosecutors determine the sentence—contingent upon a guilty verdict, of course—when they choose to file one charge over another. "I, as a sitting lifetime judge appointed by the president and confirmed by the Senate, have less authority now than 30 years ago, when I was an assistant U.S. attorney," said Terry J. Hatter Jr., a federal judge in California.

That authority has diminished each year since 1987 as Congress has amended the sentencing guidelines more than five hundred times, often to add new mandatory minimums. The guidelines are so befuddling, even to judges and prosecutors, that a legal primer entitled "Most Frequently Asked Questions About the Sentencing Guidelines" had ballooned to 162 questions and 53 pages by 1994, when the seventh edition was published.

If human lives and tax money were not at stake, the promulgation of mandatory sentences would be amusing. Each high-profile crime is met with a spate of new mandatory sentences, often both in state legislatures and Congress. Tragic cases like the murder of Polly Klaas, the girl abducted from her California home during a sleep-over in 1993, are reduced to political theater. Politicians have made it particularly illegal to kill someone in a post office, to shoot children with an automatic weapon on a playground, and commit murder on a maritime platform or by sabotaging a railroad train, as though such crimes were not already unlawful. These laws grow out of expedience and strategic positioning, not rational thought. The perfect federal mandatory minimum sentencing amendment would double the sentence of anyone caught breaking any law in the home district of any federal politician.

The removal of judicial discretion has profoundly changed the U.S. system of justice. A judge no longer has the legal leeway to make informed judgments. Mandatory sentences send everyone through the same judicial meat grinder. Youthful indiscretion no longer is an excuse for breaking a law. Prisons are filled with sundry suckers and schmucks—some innocent, some not so innocent—serving a mandatory 8.5 years for a drug violation. In federal drug cases, a scale and ledger mete out justice: five years for one gram of LSD, ten years for ten grams; five years for ten marijuana plants, ten years for one thousand; five years for five grams of crack, ten years for fifty grams; five years for five hundred grams of powder cocaine, ten years for five kilos; five years for one hundred grams of heroin; five years for ten grams of methamphetamine or PCP.

Unless a son, daughter, nephew, or grandson happens to be a recipient of one of these sentences, the numbers are not likely to discommode legislators. Each vote on a crime bill, each increase in the prison population, can help build a politician's tough-on-crime dossier. The consultants tell politicians that when they oppose any anticrime proposal—to imprison parking violators, let's say—they must understand that they leave themselves open to a thirty-second attack ad in their next reelection campaign. No politician wants to get Willie Horton-ed like Michael Dukakis was.

Just as the Rand report had predicted in 1980, politicians began to legislate by emotion and anecdote when they took direct responsibility for prison terms. They also took responsibility for the criminal justice system when they usurped control of sentences as the country's primary response to crime. By any rational measure this criminal justice policy has been a costly folly. The United States stands alone among Western countries in its futile and expensive attempt to use prison to treat drug users. But many politicians have become imprisoned by their rhetoric. Even today, some help perpetrate the myth that the country's criminal justice system is somehow soft on criminals. The United States has more crime and more people behind bars than any other civilized nation on earth, and the politicized sentencing policies of the past fifteen years will continue to increase prison populations by as much as 10 percent a year well into the new millennium. Florida, for example, estimates that its prison population will grow from 68,000 in 1995 to 150,000 by 2006. The annual cost of maintaining prisoners will triple during that period, from $1.2 billion to $3.4 billion.

Far from trying to calm the crime anxiety of the population, many key political leaders continue to perform like Chicken Little when it comes to crime, inciting the public with warnings that the worst is yet to come. Bill McCollum, the Florida congressman who heads the House Republican Leadership Task Force on Crime, is a prime practitioner. McCollum was a leader during the legislative "truth-in-sentencing" rampage of the mid-1990s, citing statistics from a Justice Department survey that said violent offenders in thirty-six states serve only about one-third of their sentence.

"The only way to keep these dangerous individuals off the streets is to build more prisons, get the states to change their laws to require violent repeat offenders to serve at least 85% of their sentences, and have minimum mandatory sentences," McCollum wrote in May 1994. He advocated elimination of bail in favor of mandatory pretrial detention and challenges to court decrees that have limited prison populations. McCollum concluded: "The public doesn't want their tax dollars poured down the drain. They want reform. They want the bad guys locked up and the keys thrown away."

McCollum's colleague in the House, Representative David A. Levy, a New York Republican, wrote,

> Today, more communities are living in fear of violent crime. While the U.S. hasn't reached the point of anarchy, criminals seem more willing than ever to risk prosecution. The reason is that, even if they are caught, they are unlikely to be punished severely. In short, despite what we were told in school, crime does pay. . . . Criminals threaten our lives, property, and sense

of security. Legislation must be passed to punish criminals severely. We no longer can permit the lawless to rule the lawful.

And then there is Newt Gingrich, our futuristic House Speaker, whose vision for postmodern criminal justice includes public executions. Here is the Associated Press report:

### GINGRICH SUGGESTS TOUGH DRUG MEASURE

ATHENS, GA., AUG. 26 (AP)—Speaker Newt Gingrich said on Friday that he would ask Congress to enact legislation imposing the death penalty on drug smugglers, and he suggested that mass executions of people convicted under such a law might prove an effective deterrent.

Mr. Gingrich, speaking to about 400 people at a money-raising event for Representative Charlie Norwood, Republican of Georgia, said, "The first time we execute 27 or 30 or 35 people at one time, and they go around Colombia and France and Thailand and Mexico, and they say, 'Hi, would you like to carry some drugs into the U.S.?', the price of carrying drugs will have gone up dramatically."

Mr. Gingrich said his proposal, which he said he would make in a bill to be filed next month, would impose a mandatory death penalty on people convicted of bringing illegal drugs into the United States.

"If you import a commercial quantity of illegal drugs," he said, "it is because you have made the personal decision that you are prepared to get rich by destroying our children. I have made the decision that I love our children enough that we will kill you if you do this."

Mr. Gingrich, expanding on his remarks today, said that he would limit appeals of a death sentence for smuggling to 18 months from conviction.

Mr. Gingrich told about 1,500 people at a youth football and cheerleading jamboree in Canton, 34 miles north of Atlanta: "They'd have one chance to appeal. They wouldn't have 10 years of playing games with the system. We should say to them, 'When you make the decision that you're going to get rich at the expense of our children, you are signing your own death warrant.'"

Mr. Gingrich did not say whether he would execute people convicted of bringing in small quantities of drugs for personal use or what types of drugs would be subject to his proposed statute.

In 1978 the film *Midnight Express*, based on a true story, sent a shiver up the spine of anyone who had ever smoked a joint (the majority of the adult U.S. population, by some estimates). It recounted the experiences of William Hayes, who was busted in 1970 at the Istanbul airport while in the phenomenally stupid act of attempting to smuggle two kilos of hashish back to the United States. The film was striking for several reasons: the draconian sentence, the primitive conditions at the notorious Sagimilcar fortress prisons. Mostly, though, the film effectively portrayed the heart-rending waste of a human life until Hayes managed an unlikely escape. If the screenwriter, Oliver Stone, remade the film today, he could set it at any number of U.S. prisons because Hayes would receive a sentence here that many view as no less draconian—as long as life in prison. And if Gingrich has his way, Stone could end the film with a dramatic flourish: the public execution of Hayes and thirty-four others.

With the encouragement of leadership like that offered by Gingrich, the country has edged closer toward Turkish-style justice, toward a Singapore solution to crime. Americans seem to demand contrition from criminals. We want shame and humiliation. We want them to hurt like we hurt, cower like we cower. We want to take away their television sets, pool tables, barbells, occupational training, education. (The latest popular anticrime slogan advocates "No-Frills Prisons.") It seems to me that we are creating idle angry inmates who will leave prison more hostile and incorrigible than they went in. Prisoners feel they have nothing to gain by behaving because they are destined to serve 85 percent of their mandated minimum sentence no matter what. They have no hope. One manifestation is the inmate ritual of hurling feces at guards (the cons call it *defecation education*), which has become so prevalent that many states have passed laws deeming it a special form of assault.

The 1994 federal crime bill cut off Pell grant funding for the twenty-seven thousand inmates who attended college classes in prison each year. The use of Pell funding for prisoners sent the wrong "message" to citizens, the politicians said, even though no law-abiding person was denied funding because money had gone to an inmate; even though the inmate funding amounted to just $35 million of the $6 billion in Pell money distributed each year; even though education has been proved to reduce recidivism. (A Texas study found that the 60 percent recidivism rate was reduced to 5.6 percent for those who earned a bachelor's degree, and New York's recidivism rate of 45 percent was cut nearly in half among those who earned college diplomas in prison.)

In January 1996 more than a third of the members of the California Assembly voted in favor of a proposal that would have subjected graffitists to paddling. It would have allowed judges to order parents to whack their children up to ten times in court as punishment for writing graffiti. Another failed proposal by the same legislator, Mickey Conroy, would have brought back spanking in schools. He said his proposals had "overwhelming support" from the public. "I am only attempting to put another tool in the judge's hands," Conroy said. A New Hampshire legislator in 1996 introduced a proposal that would have authorized public bare-bottom spanking.

Alabama in May 1995 became the first of a number of states to reinstitute chain gangs. Some inmates break limestone rocks with ten-pound sledgehammers; others pick up trash on highways. An assistant warden in Alabama said chain gangs counteract "the perception that prison life was too easy." Those selected for chain-gang duty are not incorrigibly violent; they are burglars, druggies, check kiters, parole violators. Florida and Arizona followed Alabama's lead, and a number of other states considered proposals. "After working 12 hours for 30 to 90 days, shackled to four other prisoners, an inmate is going to think twice about committing another crime," said Brett Granlund, a Republican assemblyman who introduced the California legislation.

During the same week that Granlund introduced his chain-gang bill, a letter to the editor appeared in the small daily newspaper near my home in upstate New York. It articulated well the national ethos on punishment. The letter was written by a woman in response to an earlier letter from a county jail inmate who complained about conditions and treatment there:

INMATES SHOULD STOP COMPLAINING

IN HIS RECENT LETTER to the Star on Jan. 11, Mr. Michael Hunt complains about jail treatment, as his inmate friend Johnnie Young has done. Mr. Hunt, these police brutality stories are starting to wear a little thin. You and Mr. Young are in jail because you didn't want to live within society's guidelines of proper human behavior. You both chose to make up your own rules.

You both are extremely fortunate because our modern society, rather than punish criminals, now seems to try to rationalize and make excuses for improper behavior. It is unbelievable how tolerant we have become toward crime. We are now told that the poor and underprivileged choose a life of crime because of society's mistreatment, such as your complaints. If you send someone to jail, it's not supposed to be a pleasant walk in the park. It's supposed to be hard. That's why we call it punishment, Mr. Hunt.

We are putting our police on the defensive today. We keep warning them what not to do. They are becoming increasingly afraid of false charges, so many cops will try to play it safe and do nothing. We are shackling our police with all these restraints, just to protect the rights of you and Mr. Young. Police see their efforts thwarted at every turn and become more frustrated because the system returns the criminal to the street to commit more crimes.

If you and Mr. Young are so mistreated, why are you being allowed so much free time to air your complaints to the local newspapers? Maybe if you both had learned in the past to acquire some personal responsibility, you wouldn't be in the situation you find yourselves.

The writer's angst and anger are understandable primal reactions against crime. The public is confused and frightened, and crime has proved to be a crafty enemy.

Thirty years after President Johnson vowed to "take back the streets" of Washington, D.C., it hasn't happened. Journalists have recorded and reported this slogan hundreds of times since the dawn of the Reagan era; it is recited by everyone from lowly city council members to presidents. Yet today our capital city still has a reputation as the homicide capital of the United States—and, by extension, the world. The Republican Party made "take back the streets" an item in its "Contract with America." The GOP and the Democratic Party managed a rare moment of concord when they named the 1994 federal crime bill the Taking Back the Streets Act. President Clinton then expropriated the bromide in his State of the Union Address in 1996; the taking back of the streets was the fourth of his seven challenges for America. It is the official slogan of the war on crime.

In 1980 John J. Degnan, New Jersey's attorney general, used the phrase to help frame his portrait of the crime dilemma:

> The dimension of the problem facing New Jersey and the nation in the area of street crime is, at the outset of this decade, monumental, and it will take a monumental rethinking and alteration of law enforcement and local government relationships to handle it. The problem lies in the paralysis of fear that grips each of us when we must make a conscious decision over whether to go out at night or whether to let our children walk the few blocks to a friend's house. The problem lies in the ambivalence we have exhibited until now in making the choice to take back our streets, our neighborhoods and our cities from the criminal and his element.

A few months later the police in Hollywood, California, used the phrase to describe their efforts to rid Hollywood Boulevard of a gang after two murders there in a month. Cops flooded the boulevard, emptying their traffic citation books. "We are going to take back the streets from the gang members," Sgt. Bob Rebhan promised. "We are putting pressure on them. We want the gang members to know that Hollywood is not a place for them to commit crimes." A short time after the task force disbanded for the night, two people were shot on the boulevard.

In February 1984 New York City police began Operation Pressure Point, a ballyhooed enforcement initiative billed as "an all-out effort to take back the streets" from heroin traffickers on the Lower East Side of Manhattan. This was a can't-miss story, because journalists enjoy military-style code names almost as much as they like snappy slogans. They published and broadcast hundreds of thousands of words about Operation Pressure Point, whose primary strategy was mass arrest—thirteen hundred in one eighteen-day period, for example. Most stories amounted to congratulatory odes. Few pointed out that the police were trying to catch quicksilver—that the drug-dealing was bound to squirt into some other neighborhood. Throughout the mid-1980s Mayor Edward Koch and New York police authorities cited Operation Pressure Point as a model of a successful law enforcement strategy against the drug menace.

Los Angeles borrowed the strategy, right down to the use of a code name, with its Operation Retake the Streets in 1985. An account in the *Los Angeles Times* cited seven hundred arrests "with the help of drug-sniffing dogs and officers on horseback." It described the operation as

> the latest in a series of police blitzes on the Rampart area, where dealers peddle marijuana, heroin and cocaine on sidewalks and street corners in daring daylight sales. The area, stretching between downtown and Hollywood, is heavily populated with immigrants from all over the world, and police say more than half of the dealers and users arrested are illegal aliens, mostly from Mexico, Central and South America. The Police Department has hit the area with several task forces in the past year, but most of those efforts have been three-day undercover operations. Police have been discouraged to see the dealers return to their street posts within days. . . . "We've had task forces before," said Commander Jim Chambers. "We'd put people in jail and they'd be getting out. We believe if we stay there and keep our presence there, we'll take back the streets."

Two years into Operation Pressure Point, the *MacNeil-Lehrer NewsHour* on PBS convened a panel of police executives to talk about the war on drugs and the efficacy of drug sweeps like those in New York and Los Angeles. Captain Patrick Carroll of the New York City Police Department, who was in charge of Pressure Point, described the process: "It was like securing ground in a battle. We'd send our undercover officers in to make narcotic buys and so on, and after they had finished then we'd flood the area with uniformed patrol. You'd take an area and you'd hold that ground. And we did that block by block in the Pressure Point target area, and slowly but surely we gained control of the streets that way."

Anthony Bouza, an outspoken former NYPD commander who was at the time police chief in Minneapolis, was asked for his reaction to Pressure Point and the drug war in general:

I think it's kind of a joke. Who are they kidding? . . . They're playing a shell game with the people, pushing the thing around from one place to another. The nation is awash in drugs; we're losing everywhere, and to hear police officials talk about taking control of the problem is a real absurdity. I think it would be more befitting a humor show than one dealing in reality. We have—on one hand we have a tremendous supply; the prices are not going up; the pushers are being displaced and moved about. We have a huge demand, and as long as there's going to be a demand, somebody's going to come in with a supply. The reality is that the seizures are getting bigger and bigger; we are awash in drugs, awash in alcohol. Nobody wants to talk about the real problems relating to poverty, joblessness, illiteracy, unemployment, single-parent families. That's all too boring. Everybody wants to go out there with a flame thrower, and they're just chasing their tails. To me it's an absurdity, it's a joke. We're losing the war on drugs.

Bouza didn't know it at the time, but perhaps the best joke of all was that while the New York City police, reputed for their street smarts, were consumed with chasing heroin dealers around lower Manhattan in an effort to take back the streets, crack arrived in the city. Hardly a cop noticed until it was too late, as crime increased to unimagined levels by the late 1980s. Operation Pressure Point, then, serves as an apt fable for the failures of crime policies. Not only have we failed to take back the streets with these alleged get-tough strategies, but we have given away the sidewalks, the highways, and the dirt roads as well.

Now that the country has fully explored the mass-arrest, mass-imprisonment strategy, the new conventional wisdom among crime policy experts is that such strategies are futile, based upon the simple equation that I cited earlier: roughly thirty million felony crimes are committed in the United States each year, but only about one-tenth are "solved" by arrest. Therefore, even if we locked up for life all three million of the perpetrators caught, the crime rate would decline by only 10 percent because the perpetrators in twenty-seven million other crimes are at large. In 1992, 450 politicians and criminal justice experts, including wardens, prosecutors, and police chiefs, signed a position paper that criticized lock-'em-up strategies and urged politicians to be honest with the public in acknowledging that imprisonment has little bearing on the crime rate. One signatory was Joan Petersilia, the criminologist with the Rand Corp. who wrote several influential crime policy studies during the 1970s and 1980s.

In a book of crime policy analysis published the same year that she signed the position paper, Petersilia wrote,

> It is vital that political leaders and criminal justice professionals publicly acknowledge that justice agencies play a relatively limited role in crime control. Failure to do so means that the debate becomes misdirected. We spend inordinate amounts of time and energy debating how best to punish and how punitive various states and nations are in comparison to one another, even though the evidence suggests that punishment may be of limited relevance for crime control. . . . Moreover, those who focus on the criminal justice system are offering the public a false hope, the hope that if the criminal justice system just did its job more competently—and criminals were punished more often and harsher—the public would be safe from most crime. But if 34 million crimes are being committed in this country, and 31 million are never detected, the only way to truly reduce crime is to find some way to stop some of the crime from being committed in the first place.

At last, many experts in the field have begun to boldly criticize dishonest politicians and police officials who perpetrate kindergarten criminology. Peter W. Greenwood, Petersilia's colleague at Rand, wrote,

> The American people are ill-served by public officials who lack the courage to tell some plain truths about crime control. Sweeping, harshly punitive laws, like California's "three-strikes" law and drug enforcement policies that favor long prison terms rather than treatment for users, pick the taxpayer's pocket and do not guarantee safe streets. Most responsible politicians understand this and want to do the right thing, but they also recognize that appearing soft on criminals at the time of deep public fear of violent crime is a passport to political oblivion. It's the old story:

Everybody wants to go to heaven but nobody wants to die. Something must be done, of course, to stem rising levels of lawlessness and violence in our society, but lashing out with ever more Draconian laws is not the answer. We must curb our outrage (lest we do harm to the Constitution and bankrupt ourselves in the process) and approach the problem with a coolheaded determination to put our money on programs that work—or at least work better and more cost-effectively. Among the most promising are treatment programs for hard-core drug users and stiff prison sentences for felons the *first* time they commit a violent crime, rather than waiting until the second or third time. We must also disabuse ourselves of some illusions. Crime and drug use are not problems that will go away or yield to some ultimate solution. They are as much a part of modern life as disease. . . . Moreover, drugs and violent crime are not separate problems; as a consequence, policies that deal with one and not the other will fail.

In the fall of 1996 I caught up with Greenwood at a conference. I told him that I had read much of his crime research, and I complimented him on the commentary cited here. Greenwood, like Petersilia, has been a leading criminologist for more than twenty years. Didn't it bother him, I asked, that so much of his work had been ignored over the years by politicians in favor of expedient solutions? He smiled and said, "Hey, it's part of the business." That was that, and he moved on to another conversation. I was surprised by the flippancy of his remark, and I later recounted the brief conversation to another prominent criminologist, who shook his head at the story. "Greenwood was lying, probably trying to be polite. The politicians drive us crazy—all of us."

Among criminologists the idea that behavior can be "corrected" has made a comeback. Robert Ross, a Canadian sociologist, has created a seventy-hour counseling course designed to help lawbreakers develop the sensibilities that allow them to make moral decisions. Called *moral reconation therapy* (MRT), this treatment is gaining popularity, largely because the notion that a lack of moral underpinnings may cause certain people to turn to crime has been sanctioned by the writing of conservatives such as James Q. Wilson and William J. Bennett. To some critics MRT evokes the antiviolence treatment in Stanley Kubrick's 1972 film, *A Clockwork Orange*. The morality therapy idea is based upon the sociological theory that, in modern society, behavior to a large extent is based upon the formative messages people receive from the mass media, not from family, church, and community. The therapy attempts to repair the damage done by the violent images predominant in the media.

While the sociologists try to sort that out, the National Council on Crime and Delinquency, a San Francisco–based research organization founded in 1907, has advocated a freeze on corrections spending at all levels of government and abolition of mandatory prison sentences for anyone convicted of nonviolent narcotics violations. The organization says that harsh prison sentences should be reserved for violent felons, repeat offenders who pose a substantial threat to the public safety, and others whose crimes amount to serious violations of the public trust. Except in cases of incorrigible individuals, inmates should once again be allowed to earn early release through work, education, and other self-improvement programs in order to give them some degree of hope and the motivation to redeem themselves, the group says. There also is growing advocacy for a policy change to stop arrests for prostitution and drug use, which some characterize as crimes of personal choice. Modern American criminal justice history has clear precedent for fundamental change in enforcement ideology. Thirty-five years ago more than one-third of all arrests in the United States were for public drunkenness, and the percentage went much higher in some cities. Christopher E. Stone, president of the Vera Institute of Justice, a New York think tank, says his organization's research revealed that drinking violations accounted for about two-thirds of the arrests in New York City in 1961. The comprehensive crime report commissioned by President Johnson noted that three alcoholics had accounted for more than one thousand arrests in Washington, D.C. A shift in enforcement philosophy in the late 1960s, encouraged by Johnson's report, reduced drunkenness arrests to a fraction of their former level. Criminologists of the day had convinced politicians and law enforcement authorities that this was not a wise use of money and resources, and policy was changed.

Will politicians follow the lead of criminologists to a more honest discussion of crime and rational crime policy? The 1996 presidential election made it difficult to be sanguine about the prospects. Both Bill Clinton and Bob Dole trotted out the old soft-on-crime shtick during the few days that the "crime issue" flopped onto the national news agenda. Dole said an increase in the use of drugs by teenagers that had occurred during the Clinton presidency was "nothing short of a national disgrace." In a marvelous example of sloganeering, he said of Clinton, "They raised the white flag in the war on drugs. . . . They turned 'Just Say No' into 'Just Say Nothing.'" Clinton countered that Dole had voted to take money from the president's Safe and Drug-Free Schools program and had voted against the 1994 crime bill, which included stiffer penalties for drug dealers.

This was a prototypical example of the partisan crime policy debate: nyah-nyah politics at its most banal. Playing their appointed role, journalists showed up to record the sound bites and collect the images as Clinton and Dole appeared at dueling photo ops surrounded by supportive police officials. Briefly, crime became a "talking point" on the hustings as Dole played Popeye to Clinton's Bluto. After a couple of days of muscle flexing, a standoff was declared, and the crime issue was allowed to climb back up into the attic, like a crazy uncle. Those of us who were paying attention sighed deeply.

# chapter 6

# Telling the Truth
# Less Poorly

In the fall of 1996, a couple of weeks before the presidential election, I joined forty-five journalists who cover criminal justice and twenty criminologists, judges, and lawyers from across the country for a three-day conference on crime reporting at a retreat center in Glen Cove, New York. It was an uncommon event. There are associations of religion writers, education writers, science writers, baseball writers, business writers, and women sportswriters, to name but a few, and they gather periodically to audit the condition of their specialty. But even though each of the fifteen hundred daily newspapers and many of the TV stations in the United States have at least one full-time crime reporter, those who cover the crime beat have no professional association—another indication of its lowly status. The conference may have been the largest gathering ever of people interested in the topic of criminal justice journalism. And, as best I could tell, it was the biggest assemblage of crime reporters on Long Island since Amy Fisher's arraignment.

During our first evening together we were treated to a talk by Norval Morris, the University of Chicago law professor, who offered a stinging rebuke to both journalists and politicians for their handling of crime. He said public perceptions of crime are far removed from reality because the media and politicians propagate stereotypical myths by emphasizing the most aberrational or sexy anecdotes. No other country attempts to use imprisonment as its leading defense against drug use and crime, he said, and as a result the United States has five times the imprisonment rate of any other in the Group of Seven leading industrialized nations.

Morris is no journalist, but he offered a dead-on assessment of why crime news is poorly covered: it is cheap and easy to produce, and the beat is dominated by untrained reporters who bite too quickly when politicians and police officials offer the populist, superficial, lock-'em-up point of view.

"But remember," Morris concluded, "that the most corrupting lie is the truth poorly told." He paused dramatically as his gaze swept slowly from one side of the conference room to the other, catching the eyes of a number of us. Together, we shifted uncomfortably in our seats. A man behind me leaned forward and nudged my shoulder. "This is it," he said. "This is the *whole problem*."

And so it was. In just twenty minutes Morris had spelled out the *whole problem* of crime policy and crime reporting, and not a soul in the room raised a hand to disagree. That is because we all knew that he is right, everyone in that room, everyone in the business of journalism. Take a predisposition toward simplicity and anecdote, add unsophisticated reporting, a degenerating peer culture, an overworked news staff, the rapture of sex and celebrities, and—poof!—you've got today's crime journalism.

The elders of the profession have been talking about this trend for some years now, to no apparent avail. At a media forum in 1995 Bernard Kalb, a media critic and a former journalist with CBS, NBC, and the *New York Times*, said,

> If you believe, as we all do, that the media is the sentinel of democracy, then the sentinel, for the most part, is AWOL. . . . A public that is misinformed, underinformed, ill informed is not a country whose citizens are using democracy. If you're prepared to entrust democracy to politicians, then you can live with the

kind of programs that you're getting today. But if you believe that democracy requires nourishment, requires real journalistic vitamins rather than a lot of empty calories, then the emptiness, to a large extent, of television news, the preoccupation, the tilt toward "blah-blah" rather than substance, has, in my view, very, very dangerous consequences.

Hedrick Smith, a documentary film producer and a longtime *New York Times* reporter, said, "In our hearts, I think many of us wonder whether the old-fashioned virtues of shoe-leather reporting have given way to the modern three RS of ratings, rumors and rot. . . . To spend more money on the life of Amy Fisher and Lorena Bobbitt than on health care or on education, how far have we come since Edward R. Murrow once hailed television as the greatest classroom in the world?"

Eugene L. Roberts Jr., a respected editor at the *Philadelphia Inquirer* and *New York Times,* said, "Many newspapers seem to be in a race to see which can be the most shortsighted and superficial." According to Walter Cronkite, retired *CBS News* anchor, "Right now what we're seeing is the ascendancy of incredible schlock, incredibly bad television, incredibly irresponsible television. And as usual the bad is driving out the good. It's getting the ratings and therefore the ratings-conscious industry is grabbing hold of this stuff." Carl Bernstein, half of the Pulitzer Prize–winning Watergate team for the *Washington Post*, commented:

> We are moving in the direction of being porn publishers or the equivalent of it. . . . Over the last 20 years we have been abdicating our primary function—the best obtainable version of the truth—and allowed our agenda and priorities to become bastardized and dominated by the triumph of idiot culture. . . . The gravest threat to the truth today may well be from within our own professions because the consequences of a society misinformed and disinformed by the grotesque values of Murdoch culture are truly perilous.

Media critics have tracked some of these tendencies in books and articles. Dozens of conferences, symposia, and other mea culpa sessions have brought journalists together during the 1990s to address tabloidization. Reader-viewer forums and public opinion polls send a message that the media's customers are fed up with the diet they are being served. Yes, those same readers and viewers do bear significant responsibility for consuming garbage. But to argue that issue seems tangential. Look at it this way: the sleazy story is the prostitute, the reader-viewer the john, and the media the pimp. Now which is most culpable, which has the least integrity?

The level of public esteem for journalists has sunk to the netherworld occupied by politicians. More important, reporters and editors are listless, and many are worried about the mores passed along to young journalists during the tabloid era.

We shouldn't be surprised if the rules of journalism are changing for younger members of the profession. Those of us in our forties and fifties grew up watching Cronkite deliver the news on TV. Many young journalists grew up watching newslike performances by Steve Dunleavy, Connie Chung, and Maury Povich. This has been an era in which a continuum of topic and tone has linked the morning paper, daytime talk shows, evening news, true-life crime programs, sitcoms, and late-night talk shows. We may be able to differentiate between the *Daily Tribune, Eyewitness News, Rolanda, and The Tonight Show,* but how well can we gauge the veracity of the information we glean from the various sources if each takes up the same topic? Collectively, is it not a single spewing font?

Veteran reporters and editors say they perceive a difference in young journalists today, and it is characterized by a heightened tabloid sensibility. Even Deborah Norville, a host of the tabloid television program *Inside Edition,* has said that she is concerned about declining standards and a lax attitude toward accuracy among young reporters on her show. Another journalist I spoke with cites "the Sam Donaldson Syndrome." She explains, "These kids somehow get the idea that journalists are supposed to be loud, brash, and demanding. They don't understand that, in the real world, no one gets information that way." Several other reporters note that they entered journalism in the 1970s, during the post-Watergate wave. The model for reporters then was a lone wolf who collected information quietly, even secretively. "I see more of a pack mentality now," says a California newspaper reporter, "and everyone wants to shout questions, like everything is an OJ press conference."

Twenty years ago I would blanch at the film cliché of a media pack with boom microphones and starched hair yelling silly questions as an official arrived at one venue or another. Then it seemed false. Today it's all too accurate. And I used to scoff at the old saw that journalists did one thing or another "to sell newspapers." Like most reporters, I believed that my duty was to inform. "To sell newspapers" struck me as a sophomoric criticism; the truth was much more complicated, I believed. Now I'm not so sure.

I asked Scott Higham of the *Baltimore Sun* whether the fundamental rules of journalism have changed as a result of the tabloid influence of paying sources, reenacting events, hyperaggressive behavior, and a focus on sleaze. Higham, a thoughtful journalist who has covered criminal justice beats at several newspapers, witnessed the international frenzy of the Kathy Willets Florida Nympho story while he was a reporter for the *Miami Herald*. He says,

> The rules haven't changed for me. For those of us who have been in the business for a while, we're doing our jobs the way we always have. But I think the rules are changing for younger people who see that kind of journalism and think that it's the standard, and that's the scary thing. You see these reporters who use any tactic and technique to get a piece of information, no matter what it might do to their reputation. These people have to be taught what they're doing to themselves, and what they're doing to their profession.

Jerome Miller, the Virginia criminologist who has dealt with reporters on crime policy issues for many years, says he too has identified a change in journalists since the mid- to late 1980s, as reporters have increasingly lived up to their characterization by the famed muckraker I. F. Stone as "stenographers with amnesia." Miller says,

> I've seen a sea change in the media in crime policy issues just in the past decade. More and more, the journalists I speak to seem to pop in and pop out of the stories for one day. None of them seem to know the issues. They move in and show that they can recite the slogans and give superficial coverage to the big case of the day, then they leave. The next time a big story breaks, a new face will show up with a microphone or notebook, and we start all over again. You just don't get the depth that you should get on the issue. No one seems to care about history, depth, and context.

So there seems to be a quorum, and the vote is nearly unanimous that journalism is ill. With such singularity of opinion, why hasn't recovery begun in earnest?

The reasons are several, beginning with competitive pressures and a newsroom culture that foments inertia, uniformity, and a we-know-best arrogance. No matter how high minded the plan for future coverage might be after hand-wringing over the last sleazy crime story, the pressure to pile on after a new one breaks simply overwhelms newspapers and television news broadcasts if the competition is covering the story. News still is defined as whatever the competition is covering. A reporter who worked the story about the Olympic Park bombing in the summer of 1996 for the *Atlanta Journal and Constitution,* the first newspaper to identify Richard Jewell as a suspect, said that criticism of his paper for its coverage of the story amounted to "sour grapes" by competitors who got scooped. Many journalists cling to a macho self-image that they have some sort of mandate to be reviled and obnoxious. For example, Leslie Stahl, a correspondent for CBS's *60 Minutes,* said, "We are going to be loathed and despised for one reason or another no matter what we do. There's the goal; that's our job." This seems to be a confused rendering of the sensible aphorism that a journalist's goal is respect, not admiration.

Jerry Nachman, the television news executive and former editor of the *New York Post,* was asked during a journalism conference whether O. J. Simpson could get a fair trial, considering all the media attention lavished on the case. He responded that ensuring a fair trial for Simpson or anyone else was not the media's responsibility. "We work a different side of the street," he said. That theme resurfaced when the *Trentonian,* a down-market tabloid daily newspaper in New Jersey, was criticized for irresponsibility after it referred to a murder suspect as a "monster," "maggot," and "squirt boy" in its pretrial coverage of the case. A judge said the rabid coverage forced him to move the trial to another county. Asked later whether he felt remorse for prompting the expensive change of venue, the paper's publisher, H. L. Schwartz III, growled, "The judge has to look out for the guy's rights, but we don't."

This might sound like Neanderthal journalism, but the sentiment is more familiar than I would like to admit. Like most journalists, I believed that no one outside the business could be a legitimate critic because outsiders cannot understand our function. During my time as police bureau chief at the *Daily News,* I was interviewed by a Barnard College professor who was researching why crime news does not contain more sociological context. She cited a story I had written about a drug bust, and she asked me whether I had considered including information about what factors prompt people to use drugs. That struck me as absurd, and I told her that my boss would suggest that I seek counseling if I filed such a story. I rejected her criticism based upon both content and source, the latter because I believed that she was a bow tie–wearing egghead and therefore insufficiently ink stained. Now here I am, not so many years later, suggesting that the egghead had a point.

I had used two of the three de rigueur defensive reactions of journalists: wrong criticism, wrong critic. The third is censorship. A few years ago David Bartlett, then the president of the Radio-Television News Directors Association, was asked to address the idea that TV news has significant room for content improvement. As I have noted, an inferiority complex leads broadcast journalists to be particularly thin skinned about criticism. Bartlett managed to use all three defenses. He wrote,

> For better or worse, local television news quite accurately reflects the needs and interests of the viewing public. Yet critics persist in charging that television is shallow, sensational and inaccurate. Anyone who wants to depend on the newspaper as a primary source of information is free to do so. But hearing newspaper critics beat up on local television news reminds me of a dinosaur condemning a mammal for acting silly. Television has always been a better mirror than a spotlight. It reflects reality far more effectively than it creates it. The public would be better served if politicians and special interest groups spent more time dealing with the reality that television news reports and less time trying to coerce television journalists into sweeping uncomfortable realities under a rug of censorship.

Bartlett wielded a fourth popular media maxim: We simply report the news as we see it. This denial of the media's immense influence on public perceptions of crime and other issues is unsettling, but Bartlett is not alone. For example, when President Bush suggested that journalists might play a role in the crime issue, he was belittled. Here was *Newsweek*'s version:

## CLARK KENT, PLEASE CALL YOUR OFFICE

GEORGE BUSH, a lifetime member of the National Rifle Association, made it clear in the presidential campaign that he was firmly opposed to tough gun-control laws, as is, of course, the NRA. The organization spent $1.5 million on ads attacking Bush's opponent, Michael Dukakis, for his pro-gun control positions. Last week Bush, a hunter, made it clear that he remains resolute in his opposition, despite a rising outcry against a plague of assault weapons. This month, a Senate Judiciary subcommittee opened hearings on the weapons; police officers from around the country urged Congress to ban both automatic and semiautomatic rifles commonly used in drugs wars. "The police of America are pleading with you," Los Angeles police chief Daryl Gates told the committee.

In an Oval Office session with reporters, Bush said he supports laws banning AK-47s but is against outlawing semiautomatics. "I would strongly go after the criminals who use these guns," he said. "I'm not going to suggest that a semiautomated hunting rifle be banned." And, he was asked, can he, as the "No. 1 resident," do anything about the situation in Washington, the murder capital of the country? "Well, we need the help of the press to do something about it," he said. The editors of the *Daily Planet* had better transfer Clark Kent to the Washington bureau.

Perhaps this false modesty from an institution so powerful is one reason that journalists are held in such low esteem. It is not becoming. It may have been youthful delusion, but it seemed that when I entered the field, it was the best party-chat occupation imaginable: meet someone new, say you are a journalist, and the reaction almost always was one of keen interest: "Oh, that's interesting. Tell me about it." Today when I tell people that I am a journalist (or, worse yet, a journalism professor at an Ivy League school) the reaction is more likely, "Oh, so you're part of the problem. So you're part of the liberal monolith. You're responsible for the garbage in my newspaper and on my TV." Media criticism is a booming field. Anyone you stop on the street can give a ten-minute extemporaneous speech (twenty minutes if it's a Rush Limbaugh fan) about the media's superficiality, sensationalism, and bias.

For several years I made a point of collecting impressions of the media from nonjournalists that I met. Beginning in 1994 nearly everyone mentioned the O. J. Simpson coverage as a form of personal watershed in their relationship with the news. A doctor in Cooperstown, New York, says, "We've tried to subscribe to several papers in the area, but every one of them is so superficial that we're starved for substance. We've looked around for an alternative, but I'm not sure that a good one exists." An executive with a nonprofit foundation in New York City says she has given up on the mainstream media, preferring specialty magazines that address her particular interests. "I avert my eyes to newspapers and television news," she says. "To me, it's like pornography. I know it exists, but I also know that it's for someone else, not for me." A homemaker in the Midwest says that she views the media as "a necessary evil." A guitar maker in Texas says that the daily news has become irrelevant to his life. A salesman in Minnesota says he doesn't have the time or inclination to pay attention to the news.

I don't mean to be like Limbaugh in indicting the media collectively. The best of journalism is as good as it has ever been because many journalists manage to rise above the tabloid onslaught. As *Newsday* gorged itself on Buttafuoco stories, for example, its columnist Jim Dwyer wrote a number of sane, measured, acute criticisms of criminal justice policy and drug laws. The housing-project reporting in Chicago by Alex Kotlowitz of the *Wall Street Journal* clearly showed the effect of crime on the socioeconomic group and race most deeply effected; it compares favorably to reporting by the famed muckraker Jacob Riis one hundred years ago.

In 1996 Alfred Lubrano and Rita Giordano produced similarly deep, important stories about life in housing projects for the *Philadelphia Inquirer.* Sam Vincent Meddis has done an admirable job of covering crime and drug policy in *USA Today.* John Woestendiek and his newspaper, the *Philadelphia Inquirer,* produced a number of important investigations about violence, crime, and the criminal justice system. The *Washington Post* published a series, nominated for a Pulitzer Prize in 1992, that explored the causes and consequences of gun violence, and another *Post* project dissected U.S. sentencing guidelines. David Freed of the *Los Angeles Times* was nominated for a Pulitzer in 1991 for his series on the effects of the burgeoning crime rate on that city's criminal justice system. A Pulitzer finalist for the *L.A. Times,* published in December 1996, should be required reading for every crime reporter and editor in the country. Reporters Frederic N. Tulsky and Ted Rohrlich conducted a computer-assisted analysis of the 9,442 homicides in Los Angeles County from 1990 through 1994, and their findings were stunning. Only half the homicides were "solved" by arrest, and just one-third led to convictions on charges of murder or manslaughter. Using careful quantification, Tulsky and Rohrlich concluded that killers of whites were more likely to be punished than killers of blacks or Latinos; the slayings of blacks and Latinos were less likely to be solved; the killings of whites were more likely to be publicized by the media; and high-profile killers were more likely to be treated severely by prosecutors.

In 1994 the *Chicago Tribune* published a yearlong series about killings of children in that city. That same year the *Miami Herald* produced an impressive package of crime policy stories. (The series had the unfortunate title "Crime and No Punishment," with *No* colored blood red in the reprint of the series that I read.) Tom Hallman Jr. of the *Oregonian* in Portland has written rich stories about crime and the underclass. WTVS in Detroit won the prestigious duPont Award in 1995 for its special series entitled "The Last Hit: Children and Violence."

Specialty legal publications have tracked the effect of mandatory sentences on the judicial system well enough. Among general interest publications, *The Atlantic Monthly* and *Harper's* stand out for printing thoughtful, substantive studies about crime and crime policy, including the *Atlantic's* two-part story by Eric Schlosser in 1994 that dissected marijuana laws. *Common Cause Magazine, The Progressive, The Humanist, The New Yorker, The New Republic,* and *The National Review* all have published important stories about crime and narcotics.

Deserving of special note is the work of David C. Anderson, a journalist who for the past fifteen years has been one of the country's most acute observers of crime and criminal justice. Anderson, an author and a former staff member at the *New York Times,* writes about crime with a rare clarity and depth. In 1981 Ronald Reagan delivered an important policy speech on crime in which he used inflammatory statistics to warn the public of the burgeoning menace of lawlessness. Anderson wrote a brief response on the editorial page of the *Times.* It read in part,

> Nobody knows how bad the crime rate really is, or how much it changes from year to year. Which raises a question about politicians. Crime, or more precisely, the fear of crime, is unde-

niably a powerful public issue; it's also one of the least understood. Public officials have a duty to explain as well as to allay
the problem. Merely quoting the FBI statistics will only contrib-
ute to misunderstanding. Their casual use may indicate an interest in mining a rich lode of public frustration for easy political
profit, rather than a true sense of the problem. At times, the
most appealing course for any politician is to freely admit his,
and our, ignorance.

The country might have saved a few billion dollars had Anderson's common sense been heeded. Unfortunately, the media's admirable body of work
on crime was overwhelmed by the political rhetoric and by the preponder-
ance of trashy coverage.

But as the turn of the century approaches, an antitabloid backlash has begun to take root in some areas of the mass media. (This was inevitable, Paul
Klite of Rocky Mountain Media Watch says, because "the excess is inherently unsustainable. We had bottomed out.") Tabloid TV has responded to pressure by advertisers to clean up. Rupert Murdoch did his part by pulling the
plug on *A Current Affair.* The remaining tabloid TV shows, including *Inside Edition* and *Hard Copy,* have made public declarations that they no longer air the
most disgusting fare.

Daytime talks shows—a key player in the tabloid era—have had more
conversions than a Baptist tent revival. Some shows were dumped outright,
including those of Charles Perez, Carnie Wilson, Richard Bey, and Gabrielle
Carteris. Danny Bonaduce, who vowed during his first show to uphold a high
standard and who aired his first show on cross-dressers two weeks later, also
lost his cordless microphone. Talk-show host Mark Walberg, whose program
was "reformatted" by its producer, New World Entertainment, might have
been speaking for all his colleagues when he said he was "not feeling very
good about myself." Geraldo Rivera had another makeover, as well. "The days
of screaming and confrontation are over," said Marty Berman, president of
Rivera's production company, Investigative News Group. He issued a "Talk
Show Bill of Rights" that promised to ban studio violence, accentuate the positive side of human nature, and to "keep in mind the fact the kids might be
watching the show." This certainly qualifies as a conversion of biblical proportion because the image of Rivera with white tape criss-crossed over his
broken nose after catching one in the puss during an in-studio dust-up (one

of his highest-rated shows ever) would serve as an apt tombstone illustration for the tabloid era.

There are holdouts to the old way, of course. During the February 1997 sweeps period (when viewership numbers are used to set advertising rates), Jerry Springer's topics included two shows about stripping, one about prostitution, one about cross-dressing, and one that featured a couple who worked in adult films, while Sally Jessy Raphael took on teen prostitutes, homemade sex videos, and nude dancing, among other blue subjects. Berman has moved into a peculiar perch in the loft of sanctimony. He now spends time tsk-tsking his sleazy colleagues for their failure to find the one and true way toward substance, which must mean Rivera's ratings are not so good. Berman said, "The fact is, they never changed. To me, it's shocking—shocking—that the stations have not responded harshly. . . . With all the criticism and all that has been written, some shows appeared to have thumbed their noses and say, 'We don't care.'"

The tabloid trip would be complete if the mainstream media now follow Rivera and the rest of the trash TV pack back up the hill. It won't happen effortlessly. "The descent to hell is easy," as Virgil wrote in the *Aeneid,* "but to reclimb the slope, escape to the upper air, this is labor." Nonetheless, there are signs that substance may be coming back into vogue in newspapers, magazines, and, more incrementally, on local TV.

One example was an astute cover story by *U.S. News & World Report* in late September 1996, the week after President Clinton and Bob Dole posed for endorsements by police organizations and briefly parried over which deserved to wear the chief's cap as toughest on crime. It was the first issue of the magazine's new editor, James Fallows, whose 1996 book *Breaking the News* had sharply criticized his profession. The story package appeared to serve notice that he was prepared to walk the walk, as they say in Washington. The cover featured the headline POPGUN POLITICS and showed Clinton and Dole dressed as cops. The subheadline inside the magazine read, IF IT SOUNDS GOOD, SAY IT. AT THE MOMENT, CRIME IS KING IN THE PRESIDENTIAL RACE, AND ALL CANDIDATES PAY HOMAGE—EXCEPT TO THE TRUTH.

The story was written by Ted Gest, a well-informed veteran of the criminal justice beat. He provided an erudite take on crime that addressed a number of the prevailing myths:

Over the decades crime rates have sometimes risen and fallen with no more apparent logic than shifts in the weather pattern. The recent downturn is convenient for Clinton's re-election prospects, but experts have little faith that the improvement will last very long. . . . Although ambitious politicians and fevered news reports often suggest that all Americans live in fear, violent crime occurs most often in clusters, in drug-plagued central cities.

At long last a number of newspapers in the mid-1990s took up the vital point that blacks and those who live in poverty, not soccer moms or angry white males out in the affluent suburbs, have legitimate reasons to fear crime. The *Charlotte Observer* embarked upon its version of a violence project, entitled TAKING BACK OUR NEIGHBORHOODS, in 1994, as murder reached a new high in that North Carolina city and as two police officers were killed by an ex-convict. The project, done in conjunction with a local TV station and two radio stations, provided readers with a breakdown of crime rates by neighborhoods. The statistics established that affluent neighborhoods were best served by the police yet had the least amount of crime.

The *Observer* series made clear that the problem of violence is an issue of socioeconomics and race. It reported that 77 percent of the victims of violence were black, most violence was intraracial, and more than half of all violence occurred in a handful of minority and low-income neighborhoods. It also pointed out that police were particularly ineffective in solving violent crimes there, making arrests in only 15 percent of the incidents, less than half the citywide rate. The paper offered a special forum for residents of those neighborhoods to ask questions of the authorities. Many questions were plaintive pleas: Why aren't there more police here if this is where the crime is? Most crime happens at night, so why are most cops on duty during the day? Why don't the police stop drug dealing and prostitution at places where they know it occurs?

During the course of the eighteen-month project, the *Observer* continued to publish daily stories about violence—murders, carjackings, robberies. But it also published story packages that described in detail the crime problem in each of ten neighborhoods. The stories offered statistical quantification, comments from residents, and reactions from politicians and police officials. The paper cosponsored nine town meetings about crime, its causes, and its effects. At the meetings it became clear that many residents of poor neighborhoods wanted desperately to organize to get better police services but had no idea how to do so. The *Observer* became a nexus between the neighborhoods and the one thousand volunteers who stepped forward to offer help with everything from teen pregnancy counseling to neighborhood watches. The paper published suggestions for solutions from many different voices. It also gave a refreshingly frank assessment: crime is a black-hole problem, and no simple fixes are forthcoming. The *Observer* now adds contextual statistics to its routine anecdotal crime stories more often than most papers.

A related point here must be broached. Mention of the *Charlotte Observer* raises the issue of civic journalism, a type of trendy advocacy reporting that has become a tinderbox topic in the business. Opponents say civic journalism too often amounts to boosterism and can be used as a cudgel to promote one point of view in an issue with many sides. These opponents say that advocacy belongs on the editorial page, not the front page. Proponents say civic journalism is a new label for a venerable notion: leadership. Civic journalists help set an agenda to make their community a better place, then hold leaders accountable to that agenda.

The *Observer,* part of the twenty-eight-newspaper Knight-Ridder chain, is a leader in the civic journalism movement, and the violence project probably qualified as an example. I don't know if that matters. I do know that it was smart, informative, and honest criminal justice journalism—honest right down to the rather surprising wrap-up story. The project was a huge investment of space and resources—scores of stories and thousands of column inches produced by six reporters, ten photographers, and a number of editors. It would be easy to laud the effort if it had turned out that crime declined in those Charlotte neighborhoods while the *Observer* was so earnestly informing its readers about the problem. But the final piece, published on December 3, 1995, reported that although violent crime had declined 19 percent in Seversville, one particularly bad neighborhood, the crime rate had *increased* 4 percent countywide and by as much as 30 percent in other neighborhoods that had been part of the paper's focus. The paper did not soft peddle that fact. "For two years," the story by Liz Chandler and Gary L. Wright said, "Charlotte has waged a fresh attack on the crime and poverty ravaging the central city. But no one can claim victory."

Jim Walser, an *Observer* editor who handled many of the stories, says he and his colleagues probably would have preferred a decline in crime, but they were nonetheless satisfied that the public was better informed about the complexities of criminal justice as a result of the series. "Crime was an increasing problem here, and we decided that by publishing the daily accounts of mayhem that occurred in certain neighborhoods we weren't really telling the full story about crime to our readers," he says. "Our point was to put it out there for everyone to see, and we did that. . . . We tried to go a step beyond what most crime reporters are able to do because of time constraints and other factors."

Charlotte's crime problem also played a somewhat ironic role in an innovation in local TV news coverage. During the early 1990s local TV stations began to grow more and more overtly tabloid. Many adopted bold graphics and new sets that copied tab TV shows like *A Current Affair* and *Inside Edition*. Some even used the heavy-breathing techniques used by "reality" police shows such as Fox's *Cops*—jumpy camera shots, grainy black and white video, slow motion, dramatic music. In early 1996 KVUE, the ABC affiliate in Austin, Texas, decided to set itself apart from the mayhem-infused story line-up of KEYE, a tabloid-tinged competitor, by reconsidering its coverage of crime in a project promoted as "KVUE Listens to You on Crime." The station announced to its viewers that crime stories would no longer be aired unless they met at least one of five conditions: Does action need to be taken? Is there an immediate threat to safety? Are children threatened? Does the crime have significant community impact? Is there a crime-prevention angle?

The architects of the plan were Cathy McFeaters, the news director, and Carole Kneeland, the vice president for news. McFeaters, a ten-year TV news veteran, had worked in the early 1990s at WSOC, the ABC affiliate in Charlotte, which later would become one of the *Observer*'s broadcast partners in the violence series. Charlotte is a metered market, meaning that ratings are measured daily, so the pressure to finish first is intense, not only during an extended ratings period but for each newscast. As a result, WSOC and other Charlotte stations tended to be top heavy with titillating body-bag journalism. WSOC has turned up in the Top Ten mayhem ratings of the Rocky Mountain News Watch.

McFeaters says she grew so disgusted with the mindless blood lust of WSOC that she decided to leave journalism. Fortuity interceded, and she ended up in Austin, where she found a kindred spirit in Kneeland. Both women emphasize that KVUE's crime coverage has nothing in common with the gimmicky "family friendly" method practiced by WCCO in Minneapolis, among others. "We still cover crime," Kneeland says. "We just don't do the body-bag thing. We still send crews on crime stories, just like everyone else. We get the video, we interview the authorities and the witnesses and all that. And then when the crew gets back in, we all sit down and say, 'OK, now where are we going with this story?'"

A legitimate gripe might be that the KVUE model amounts to hand holding that condescends to viewers. It seems to me, though, that the project is an admirable attempt to do *something* to improve the quality of crime coverage on local TV, which is overdue for a full-body makeover. KVUE has done away with morgue shots and meaningless warehouse fires, and it doesn't do the mindless stand-ups at long-gone-cold crime scenes and the goofy helicopter stories. That seems like a good start. And by developing guidelines that go against the conventions, the station is forsaking the ubiquitous consultants from Iowa who have created such conformity in broadcasting.

Everyone in television news is aware of these criticisms, and changes are afoot, particularly in smaller cities. In the summer of 1997, more than a dozen TV news directors told me they are covering crime differently. Like KVUE, WNYT in Albany, New York, no longer airs bodybag shots, and mindless stakeouts are all but banned. WCPO in Cincinnati is airing longer pieces about significant topics, foregoing routine wrecks and fires. At KEZI in Eugene, Oregon, news director Rick Jacobs has posted crime-reporting rules, including an edict that grieving people should never be accosted by a camera. All the news directors say their crime stories focus on solutions.

Maybe this is hand-holding. But it has become clear that the public does not do a good job of deciphering crime anecdotes into realistic trends. Besides, one person's hand-holding is another's context.

In the fall of 1990 Beth Reinhard, one of my students at the Columbia University Graduate School of Journalism, profiled Anna Quindlen, the former *New York Times* reporter and columnist. Reinhard wrote that Quindlen had a "here's-the-deal style" that set her work apart. The phrase resonated with me. Reinhard meant that Quindlen has a knack for leading readers through a bramble of information to a clear path on the other side. She does it not with billowing polemics but with simple facts augmented by essential details—the story behind the story—that other journalists might have neglected to mention. Quindlen's best work takes readers by the hand and says, Come with me. Let me explain this to you.

During the late 1980s, as drug-driven violence rose to new peaks in New York City, my colleagues, my competitors, and I wrote hundreds of anecdotal stories about murders. Inevitably, those that got the most attention were the aberrations—the murder of a doctor or a grandmother, someone who wasn't supposed to die in that manner. I'm not sure that my paper or any other ever got to the heart of what was happening in New York.

The fundamental truth about the crack scourge was hidden in the routine homicides, the Unblees—unidentified black males—who turned up each morning in vacant lots in Jamaica, Queens, and East New York, Brooklyn. Cops gave those cases short shrift, and so did the media. It turns out that the murder rate among white people stayed about the same during the crack epidemic as it had been for decades, but the rate of minority murders soared. We missed that story because we were busy chasing the exceptions.

Clearly, we need more here's-the-deal reporting about crime and less coverage of sleazy crime and false anecdotes. To begin with, perhaps the nation should agree that, with a population of 260 million, a certain number of gruesome events will happen somewhere every day, and the rest of us don't need to see it on TV or on the front page of our local newspapers.

That is not to say that routine violence shouldn't be covered. This, in fact, is one unfortunate backlash trend at many newspapers in larger cities. Several crime reporters tell me that editors have become so sensitive to focus-group complaints about bad news that they choose the politically correct path of ignoring many routine violent crimes—those that don't involve a citizen of high standing or an important local venue. The routine violence is precisely what *should* be covered closely, not because it is interesting necessarily but because it is representative and therefore important. Ultimately, the murder of a streetwalker might be more consequential than the murder of a female college student, even though news convention says the hooker gets ignored while the student goes on the front page.

Whether they work in print or broadcast, reporters can take stories from the blotter and go a step further to translate and frame. If the crime is part of a pattern, share that information with readers or viewers. But if a crime is atypical, that too must be reported—and prominently. Editors and news directors must scrutinize their decisions to report one crime story and not another. Is the decision to play up the story based on socioeconomics or race? Why should people care about the story? Does it leave news consumers with a false impression, or does it raise a question about safety that is not answered? Can another story clarify that impression or answer the question? The reading and viewing public can help by contacting a newspaper or TV station that airs an offensive, misleading, confusing, or superfluous story to register a protest in a brief temperate manner. Most newspapers now publish telephone numbers and e-mail addresses for key editors.

For their part, reporters and editors would do well to wean themselves from the police department agenda and spend more time examining strategies and holding the authorities responsible for those that fail. Criminal justice experts say that a lack of timely critical scrutiny by the mainstream press is largely responsible for the predominance of simplistic crime policies. Of course, this will require a more sophisticated style of crime coverage. In 1996 Mark Rollenhagen, a courts reporter at the *Cleveland Plain Dealer,* began compiling a national directory of crime reporters so that a journalist working on a story that bleeds over into another city can quickly find a contact who might be able to offer advice to the out-of-towner. Within the first couple of months Rollenhagen heard from about two hundred reporters, from tiny dailies to the most prestigious national papers. An association that builds on Rollenhagen's idea could help further professionalize the beat by offering tips, training, and resources that would allow reporters to better understand the complex system that they are covering. Young reporters could learn the steps in policy decisions or gain access to authorities on crime prevention and statistical analysis. This could help even unseasoned reporters to get beyond the hollow rhetoric that has driven crime policy for so many years.

Every newspaper that has a full-time police reporter and a courts reporter probably should have another full-time reporter to cover criminal justice policy. Failing that, editors should see to it that police and courts reporters are freed from the daily drudgery so they can spend as much of their time on more substantive policy stories as they do on murder and mayhem.

These changes could help present crime news responsibly, not as necrophilia, and lead readers and viewers to a deeper understanding of the nation's enduring crime dilemma. Lori Dorfman, codirector of the Berkeley Media Studies Group in California, has been an advocate for including several essential details in every crime story: Did the victim and perpetrator know one another? Was alcohol involved? Where was the weapon obtained? Was the victim insured? Others have advocated establishing a "death page," where stories about everything from murders to fatal accidents to weather catastrophes to obituaries could be collected and presented in a manner that would be less sensational.

I'm not sure that a change in packaging is the answer. Content is the key, and the media could make one sweeping change today by eliminating or minimizing the use of sleazy crime stories that have so dominated the news and swamped the stories of substance. The media have begun to temper their sky-is-falling tone about violence and crime, and now they can help promote a rational national discussion by emphasizing fundamental truths about the problem: that demographics probably have a greater effect upon crime than any police strategy ever will; that, in the long run, the solutions to crime will be "jobs, education, and hope," as Lyndon Johnson put it in 1965; that crime has a most profound effect upon low-income city residents and those who live on the margins of society; that law enforcement strategies have singled out racial minorities for the harshest treatment; that the criminal justice system has become cankered by mandatory sentences; and that our politicians cannot be trusted to make rational decisions about issues so thoroughly sullied by vote grabbing.

After ten years of shuffling along as followers, newspapers and serious TV news broadcasts should stride forward and retake their traditional position as news agenda setters. Tabloid television and the supermarket rags will get along fine without them. Jerry Nachman, the former *New York Post* editor who understands the tabloid dynamic as well as anyone in the country, said,

> I think there's a solution. I'm frequently asked to be on "Nightline" to defend so-called tabloid behavior, and invariably it's because "Nightline" wants to do the Buttafuoco story or the Leona Helmsley or the Trump story, and rather than the producer saying let's do the story, they do a story on how the tabloids do it. . . . Here's the solution: Don't do those stories. Leave them for the popular press. You guys just cover the Bosnias and we won't have this problem.

In other words, the high-collar media should button back up. No rational reason exists for excessive coverage of sleaze and sensationalism by the serious press because for some time the most responsible U.S. newspapers also have had the highest circulations. The facts say that quality sells. Some news organizations have now developed internal guidelines spelling out that they will not be compelled to run a sleazy story simply because a competitor was willing to go first. Guidelines are fine but only if they are used. When a supermarket tabloid revealed in the fall of 1996 that Dick Morris, the Clinton consultant, had a long-running relationship with a prostitute, few in the media could resist piling on. At the very least, peeping-tom stories that involve purchased information must be clearly labeled to let readers and viewers know how much was paid and by whom so they have context with which to gauge the stories' veracity.

Will tabloidization kill journalism as we know it? Probably not. Crime, sex, and celebrity have occupied prominent positions in the press for centuries, from the ribald penny press era, through the yellow epoch of Pulitzer, to the Roaring Twenties. The Republic survived *Confidential* magazine in the 1950s, and it probably will survive the Rupert Murdoch influence. But the sleaze impulse has left a scar on the media. People are more media savvy today, and journalists may not understand the ramifications of the scorn the public feels for them. They have lost their grip on respect, trust, and confidence, their most valuable occupational commodities. Journalists may know that they are viewed as manipulative enemies by the public, but they seem not to understand what that means.

The financial judgment against ABC in the Food Lion civil fraud case in 1997 was a pretty good clue. When journalists argue about the public's right to know, they think of Watergate and the Pentagon Papers. But when nonjournalists hear that phrase, they think of Princess Diana, Amy Fisher, and O. J. Simpson. As these two versions of the media reality grow increasingly perpendicular, we are likely to see more verdicts against journalists. A number of polls have shown that more and more Americans are willing to curb the media's rights to report certain details in some cases. At some point, if journalists are not willing to show self-restraint, they might find it imposed upon them.

It also is likely that their performance on past frenzy stories will subject journalists to more "handling" by gatekeepers and spokespersons. In the past journalists typically had special access and up-close vantage points at news events, in part to foster goodwill and curry favor. Today, many journalists complain, they are being bull-penned in remote locations and denied direct access to key figures in breaking stories. From police departments to corporate boardrooms, decision makers seem to be asking, Who needs friends like these? Another worrisome trend concerns the applicant pool of young journalists, whose quality already is being questioned by some editors. Will the best and the brightest of young people continue to choose a profession that has grown to be so reviled? I haven't met any summa cum laude used-car salesmen.

It seems a good time to convene a journalism summit to deal with these issues and others, including the competitive pressures and peer culture in the news business. Perhaps it is time to resurrect the National News Council, an organization that sought to improve standards of journalism in the 1960s and 1970s until it failed for a lack of support—journalists don't like to be told how to run their business. Although it had no real sanction powers like, say, the boards that oversee doctors and lawyers, the council served as a valuable monitor and conscience for the profession during its brief lifetime. If a national group is not viable, regional or state groups might be. A news council is functioning effectively in the state of Minnesota. A typical—and often acute—gripe about the media is that they are accountable to no one. New councils can provide some degree of accountability. At the very least, all members of the media must hold themselves accountable for their decisions, from the moguls like Murdoch, to publishers and news executives who allowed content and standards to decline, to the editors who selected or assigned offensive stories, to the reporters who wrote them, and even to those in the business who were not directly involved. Many journalists say they have been ashamed by their organization's tabloid-style handling of one story or another. Most of the time, they acknowledge, they fail to take a stand.

How different it all might have played out over the past ten years if more of us had done so—if more of us had been willing to stand up in the newsroom and ask, as Paul Reynolds, the former Maine newspaperman, put it, "Why are we doing this? What the hell has happened to journalism?"

## Introduction

1 **"Sorry to bother you"**: This dialogue and much of that in chapter 4 are approximations based upon my recollections, not written notes.

7 **Crime content in the news**: These estimates are confirmed by many sources, including the *Tyndall Report,* published six times a year by Andrew Tyndall of ADT Research, New York, N.Y.; Rocky Mountain Media Watch, "A Day in the Life of Local TV News in America," Denver, January 11, 1995; and more scholarly studies, including Doris Graber's *Crime News and the Public* (New York: Praeger, 1980), and by a review of published analyses of newspaper crime coverage by Harry L. Marsh, "A Comparative Analysis of Crime Coverage in Newspapers in the United States and Other Countries from 1960–1989: A Review of the Literature," *Journal of Criminal Justice* 19 (1991). Marsh concluded,

(1) The vast majority of newspaper crime coverage pertains to violent or sensational crimes. (2) The high percentage of violent crimes reported in the newspapers are not representative of the percentages reflected in official crime data. (3) The over-emphasis of violent crimes and failure to adequately address personal risk and prevention techniques often lead to exaggerated fears of victimization in certain segments of society. (4) Newspaper coverage tends to support police views and values about crime and criminals and is generally favorable to the police image and their relationship with the public.

8 **"Low, cheap tabloids"**: Roy Edward Lotz, *Crime and the American Press* (New York: Praeger, 1991), 117.

## 1. Dancing with Trash in America the Violent

15 **"Dance with trash"**: Bernard Kalb, panelist, "America Through the TV Looking Glass," Alfred I. duPont Forum, Columbia University, New York, January 26, 1995.

16 **Annual cost of prisoner maintenance**: Bureau of Justice Statistics, U.S. Department of Justice, *Sourcebook of Criminal Justice Statistics (1995)* (Washington, D.C.: U.S. Department of Justice, 1996).

16 **Prison population projections**: For comprehensive analysis of the effects of the inmate population explosion in the future see Steven R. Donziger, ed., *The Real War on Crime: The Report of the National Criminal Justice Commission* (New York: HarperPerennial, 1996), and James B. Steinberg, David W. Lyon, and Mary E. Vaiana, eds., *Urban America: Policy Choices for Los Angeles and the Nation* (Santa Monica, Calif.: Rand, 1992).

17 **"Mandatory minimums are"**: Wendy Kaminer, *It's All the Rage: Crime and Culture* (Reading, Mass.: Addison-Wesley, 1995), 218–19.

17 **"Little to do with"**: J. Jennings Moss, "Democrats Mug Bush; Crime Bill Shot Down," *Washington Times,* June 21, 1991.

17 **"This could be"**: Adam Clymer, "Crime Bill Approved 61–38, But Senate Is Going Home Without Acting on Health," *New York Times,* August 26, 1994.

17 **"We are going"**: Kaminer, *It's All the Rage,* 197.

19 **Polls on alternatives to incarceration**: Edna McConnell Clark Foundation, "Seeking Justice: Crime and Punishment in America," New York, 1995.

19 **"Wacko"**: Michael Kramer, "The Political Interest: Tough. But Smart?" *Time,* February 7, 1994.

19 **"Promises what we know"**: "Three-Strikes Zips Out of Assembly," *California Journal Weekly,* February 7, 1994.

20 **Willie Horton**: For a thorough account of the Horton case see David C. Anderson, *Crime and the Politics of Hysteria: How the Willie Horton Story Changed American Justice* (New York: Times Books, 1995).

20 **"Mistakes like Willie Horton"**: Norval Morris, featured speaker, Covering Crime Conference, sponsored by the Vera Institute of Justice and the *Columbia Journalism Review*, Glen Cove, New York, October 24, 1996.

21 **Crime coverage by network TV**: "1993—The Year in Review," *Media Monitor* 8 (January–February 1994), newsletter of the Center for Media and Public Affairs, Washington, D.C.

22 **"Americans are scared"**: Michael J. Mandel and Paul Magnusson, "The Economics of Crime," *BusinessWeek*, December 13, 1993.

22 **"Something precious is gone"**: Jerry Adler, "Growing Up Scared: How Our Kids Are Robbed of Their Childhood," *Newsweek*, January 10, 1994.

22 *U.S. News* **cover story**: Ted Gest, "The Truth About Violent Crime: What You Really Have to Fear," *U.S. News & World Report*, January 17, 1994.

22 *Time* **on crime**: Richard Lacayo, "Lock 'Em Up and Throw Away the Key: Outrage over Crime Has America Talking Tough," *Time*, February 7, 1994.

23 **Times Mirror poll**: Times Mirror Center for the People and the Press, "Economic Recovery Has Little Impact on American Mood," Washington, D.C., March 1994.

26 **"That newscast sounds"**: Paul Klite, interview by author, March 1996.

27 **Local TV news survey**: Rocky Mountain Media Watch, "Pavlov's TV Dogs: A Snapshot of Local TV News in America," Denver, September 20, 1995. The survey covered 58 cities. The sample included 28 stations in large cities, 44 in medium-sized cities, and 28 in small cities. Videotapes of the newscasts were evaluated by Rocky Mountain News Watch in Denver.

28 **"What we witness"**: Ibid.

28 **Second mayhem-rating survey**: Rocky Mountain Media Watch, "A Day in the Life of Local TV News in America," Denver, January 11, 1995. The survey included fifty stations in twenty-nine cities.

29 **"It's hard to think"**: Brad Edmonton, "Crime Crazy," *American Demographics*, May 1994.

## 2. Rupert, Amy, and OJ

33 **"Slam into the wall"**: Anna Quindlen, "Talking About the Media Circus," *New York Times Sunday Magazine,* June 26, 1994.

33 *Newsday's* **Fisher story**: Phil Mintz, "Amy's Jail Pal Claims Romance," *Newsday,* April 5, 1993.

36 **Dennis Potter's "Rupert" disease**: Ken Auletta, "Who's Afraid of Rupert Murdoch," *Frontline,* Public Broadcasting Service, November 7, 1995.

37 **Murdoch on *Melrose Place***: Ken Auletta, "The Pirate," *New Yorker,* November 13, 1995.

38 **"That will make news"**: Maury Povich with Ken Gross, *Current Affairs: A Life on the Edge* (New York: Putnam, 1991), 51.

38 **"I was, in fact"**: Ibid., 100, 109.

39 **"'A Current Affair' is"**: John Corry, "'A Current Affair,' Tabloid Journalism," *New York Times,* August 20, 1986.

39 **"All my life"**: Povich, *Current Affairs,* 124.

41 **"There are two things"**: Steve Daley, "'Capone's Vaults' a Mind to Producers Only," *Chicago Tribune,* April 24, 1986.

42 **Interview with Andrea Reynolds**: Esther Pessin, "Von Bulow Lover Refuses to Turn Over Book," United Press International, August 20, 1986.

42 **"Bible belle Jessica Hahn"**: Esther Pessin, "Hahn: I Was a Virgin," United Press International, September 28, 1987.

43 **Payments for information**: The tabloid television shows are reluctant to reveal the precise amounts paid for interviews. The amounts cited here and elsewhere in the book are based upon reports in the media and, in some cases, information from reporters and producers who worked on the stories.

44 **"He was wonderful"**: James Brady, "Now Stand By, America: Here Comes Steve Dunleavy," *Crain's New York Business,* July 31, 1988.

44 **Lipsyte and Dunleavy quotations**: Tony Schwartz, "Mr. Blood-and-Guts," *Newsweek,* October 17, 1977.

45 **"How do you tell"**: Dennis Hevesi, "Murdoch II: As Good as the Original?" *New York Times,* March 28, 1993.

46 **"Simply, I think"**: Steve Dunleavy, *Reliable Sources, CNN,* June 26, 1993.

46 **"It ended up"**: Charles Feldman, *CNN News,* June 11, 1992.

46 **Dunleavy's great stories**: "Dunleavy, the Colorful Character," *USA Today,* December 9, 1991.

46 **Murdoch's great story**: Auletta, "The Pirate."

46 **"We wanted to own"**: Bill Carter, "Now It Can Be Told: Tabloid tv Is Booming," *New York Times,* December 23, 1991.

48 **"She bit and kicked"**: Larry Tye, "For a Figure in Rape Inquiry, A Week of Fights, Racy Photos," *Boston Globe,* April 25, 1991.

48 ***New York Times* names Smith accuser**: Fox Butterfield with Mary B. W. Tabor, "Woman in Florida Rape Inquiry Fought Adversity and South Acceptance," *New York Times*, April 17, 1991.

50 **"There would have been"**: Charles Walston, "Tabloid tv Has Changed the Rules," *Atlanta Constitution,* November 17, 1991.

50 *Independent's* **Nympho headline**: David Adams, "Solid Gold Waitress Unravels South Florida's Moral Fibre," *Independent* (London), September 15, 1991.

51 **"It's (sex) my"**: Joanne Kenen, "'Nympho' Hooker Case Turns into Huge Legal Tangle," Reuters, September 13, 1991.

54 **"What you've got"**: Rick Bragg, "Sex, Sleaze, Cash: The Willets Story," *St. Petersburg Times,* September 22, 1991.

55 **"Ever-twisting nympho"**: Ned Zeman, "Fort Lauderdale Is Talking," *Newsweek,* September 23, 1991.

55 **"After agreeing"**: Scott Higham, Knight-Ridder News Service, "Sex Videotape Case Ends in Guilty Pleas," *Houston Chronicle,* December 14, 1991.

57 **"I guess it had"**: Scott Higham, interview with author, March 1996.

57 **"They gave good"**: John Corporon, senior vice president for news, WPIX, appearing on *Reliable Sources, CNN,* June 26, 1993.

57 **Paying sources**: Louise Mengelkoch, "When Checkbook Journalism Does God's Work," *Columbia Journalism Review* (November 1994).

57 **"Edging toward respectability"**: Andrea Sachs, "Mud and the Mainstream," *Columbia Journalism Review* (May–June 1995).

58 **"We haven't changed"**: Ibid.

58 **"Five years ago"**: Mary Nemeth, "Hot off the Presses," *Maclean's,* January 24, 1994.

58 **"The forest coming"**: Howard Rosenberg, "How TV News Spiraled into 'Tabloidgate,'" *Los Angeles Times,* February 14, 1994.

58 **"You let the tabloids"**: David Lamb, "Into the Realm of Tabloids," *Los Angeles Times,* February 13, 1992.

58 **Royal scandal story**: William E. Schmidt, "Extra! Princess in Phone Shock!" *New York Times,* August 28, 1994.

59 *Washington Post* **story**: Paula Span and Laurie Goodstein, "The Bright and Slimy Star," *Washington Post,* January 28, 1992.

60 **"For the second time"**: Chuck Raasch, Jeffrey Stinson, and John Hanchette, "Clinton Denies Anew Allegations of Marital Infidelity," Gannett News Service, January 23, 1992.

60 **"We didn't give"**: Lamb, "Into the Realm of Tabloids."

60 **"That's an accurate"**: Paul Reynolds, interview with author, April 1996.

62 **"One reporter watches"**: David Margolick, "A Peek Under the Tent of the West Palm Beach Media Circus," *New York Times,* December 15, 1991.

62 **"The carnival sideshows"**: Public Broadcasting Service, "Tabloid Truth," *Frontline,* February 15, 1995.

63 **"The competition for ratings"**: Bill O'Reilly, "We Pay for News; We Have To," *New York Times,* February 26, 1994.

63 **"You can't just"**: Mike Tharp and Betsy Streisand, "Tabloid TV's Blood Lust," *U.S. News &World Report,* July 25, 1994.

64 **"I did it!"**: David Margolick, "Deputy Tells of Emotions of Simpson," *New York Times,* December 15, 1994, and "Simpson Judge Sets Date for Pretrial Hearing on DNA and Rules on Jail Outburst," *New York Times,* December 20, 1994.

64 **"It was an unattributed"**: Howard Kurtz, "Truth or Tabloid Trash? New York Times Quotes Enquirer on OJ Story," *Washington Post,* December 21, 1994.

64 **"For Steve Dunleavy"**: Ray Richmond, "Start of Simpson Trial Galvanizes TV Tabloids; Case's Celebrity Elements Blur Lines Between Trash Talk, Mainstream News," *San Francisco Examiner,* September 25, 1994.

64 **The Simpson civics lesson**: One fine example of civics lesson journalism came on November 8, 1995, when a number of U.S. newspapers appropriated a jewel of investigative reporting about O. J. Simpson from the tabloid TV show *American Journal.* The *New York Daily News* published the story under the headline OJ STUNK UP THE JOINT, GUARD SEZ. It began, "'Odor in the court!' O. J. Simpson became so depressed at one point during his double murder trial that he stopped bathing for a week, a jail guard says."

64 **"The closely watched"**: Warren Richey, "Black Mark for FBI Lab May Taint Bomb Trials," *American Christian Science Monitor,* February 3, 1997.

65 **"The O. J. Simpson"**: Reynolds interview.

66 **"It's like a carnival"**: Larry Reibstein, "The Battle of the TV News Magazine Shows," *Newsweek,* April 11, 1994.

66 **"Overwhelming viewer demand"**: Josef Adalian, "Fox: 'Chase' Is On," *New York Post,* February 5, 1997.

## 3. Seven Little Sins, So Many Stories

71 **"Newsmongers"**: Joe Saltzman, "Tabloid Hysteria," *USA Today, the Magazine of the Society for the Advancement of Education,* May 1994.

71 **" 'Tis the Misfortune"**: Ibid.

72 **"Full freighted with"**: *Boston News-Letter,* August 28, 1721.

72 **James Franklin's *Courant***: An account of Franklin and his paper can be found in Jeffrey A. Smith, *Printers and Press Freedom: The Ideology of Early American Journalism* (New York: Oxford University Press, 1988).

73 **"The reader is placed"**: Steven Jaffe, "Unmasking the City: The Rise of the Urban Newspaper Reporter in New York City, 1800–1850," doctoral dissertation, History Department, Harvard University, 1989.

73 **"We deem it"**: Ibid.

74 **"Those indecent police reports"**: Ibid.

74 **"John McMan"**: Ibid.

75 **"Fellows who are"**: Ibid.

75 **Ellen Jewett murder**: Journalism historians have feasted heartily on the carcass of the Jewett coverage. For one thorough account see Andie Tucher, *Froth and Scum: Truth, Beauty, Goodness, and the Ax Murder in American's First Mass Medium* (Chapel Hill: University of North Carolina Press, 1994). See also Jaffe, "Unmasking the City." There is some question about the correct rendering of the names of the murder victim and the madam: Helen or Ellen, Rosanna or Rosina.

76 **"The perfect figure"**: Richard Kluger, *The Paper: The Life and Death of the New York Herald Tribune* (New York: Knopf, 1986), 36.

76 **"Instead of relating"**: *New York Herald,* April 30, 1836.

77 **"Mankind, even such"**: Jaffe, "Unmasking the City."

77 **"A good police reporter"**: Ibid.

78 **"What the triod"**: George Goodrich Foster, *Fifteen Minutes Around New York* (New York: Dewitt and Davenport, 1854), 24.

78 **"What are the fifty newspapers"**: Charles Dickens, *American Notes and Pictures from Italy* (1842; London: Oxford University Press, 1957), 88.

79 **"There is not a newspaper editor"**: Simon Michael Bessie, *Jazz Journalism: The Story of Tabloid Newspapers* (New York: Russell & Russell, 1938), 41.

80 **"The entire World newspaper"**: Joseph Pulitzer, *New York World,* May 11, 1883.

80 **Pulitzer memoranda**: Edwin Emery, *The Press and America: An Interpretive History of the Mass Media* (Englewood Cliffs, N.J.: Prentice-Hall, 1972), 311–12.

81 **"A yellow journal"**: *New York Post,* quoted in Emery, *Press and America*, 373.

82 **"What we're after"**: Arthur McEwen, *Collier's,* February 18, 1891.

82 **"A shrieking, gaudy"**: Emery, *The Press and America*, 350.

82 **"The louder the yellow press"**: Bessie, *Jazz Journalism*, 58.

83 **"Suppose it's Halley's"**: McEwen, *Collier's.*

84 **"Blood on the roadsides"**: Emery, *Press and America*, 365.

84 *Journal*'s **banner headline**: "The Whole Country Thrills with War Fever," *New York Journal,* February 18, 1898.

84 **"It wasn't much"**: John D. Hicks, *A Short History of American Democracy* (Boston: Houghton Mifflin, 1943), 605.

84 **"The most spectacular"**: Irvin S. Cobb, *Exit Laughing* (1942), cited in Lawrence M. Friedman, *Crime and Punishment in American History* (New York: Basic Books, 1993), 397.

85 **"Its vulgarizing influence"**: George W. Alger, *Moral Overstrain* (Cambridge, Mass.: Riverside, 1906), 10.

85 **"WHO DEGRADED THE PAPER?"**: W. J. Granberg, *The World of Joseph Pulitzer* (London: Abelard-Schuman, 1965), 158–59.

86 **Keith Murdoch and Lord Northcliffe**: A number of British press histories describe these relationships. See, for example, S. J. Taylor, *The Great Outsiders, Northcliffe, Rothermere, and the Daily Mail* (London: Weidenfeld and Nicolson, 1996), and Reginald Pound, *Northcliffe* (New York: Praeger, 1960).

87 *Daily News* **mission statement**: "Who We Are," *New York Daily News,* June 26, 1919.

88 **"Lady Luck so absorbed"**: Bessie, *Jazz Journalism*, 97.

88 **Quotes about the** *Daily News:* Ibid., 213.

90 **"Don't fail to read"**: *New York Daily Graphic,* January 11, 1928.

90 **Snyder electric chair photo**: *New York Daily News,* January 14, 1928.

91 **"Most were brief"**: Emilia Nadel McGucken, "Crime News Reporting in the *New York Times,* 1900 to 1950: A Content Analysis," doctoral dissertation, University of Akron, May 1987.

## 4. Anything Particularly Cruel

94 **"I had no training"**: Ilene Prusher, interview with author, March 1995.

95 **"I'm looking for anything"**: Melvin Mencher, *News Reporting and Writing* (Madison, Wisc.: Brown & Benchmark, 1997), 249.

96 **Crime news in the media**: The broadcast figure comes from surveys by Rocky Mountain Media Watch, a Denver-based advocacy organization. The newspaper figure comes from a number of published studies and books, including Doris Graber, *Crime News and the Public* (New York: Praeger, 1980), and Roy Edward Lotz, *Crime and the American Press* (New York: Praeger, 1991).

97 **"Most of the music"**: Richard Kluger, *The Paper: The Life and Death of the New York Herald Tribune* (New York: Knopf, 1986), 242.

97 **"I can tell you"**: Ray Ring, *Arizona Kiss* (New York: Little, Brown, 1991).

97 **"News is the inexact"**: Gerald W. Garner, *The Police Meet the Press*, (Springfield, Ill.: Charles C. Thomas, 1984), 19.

98 **Newspaper coverage of violence**: Harry L. Marsh, "A Comparative Analysis of Crime Coverage in Newspapers in the United States and Other Countries from 1960–1989: A Review of the Literature," *Journal of Criminal Justice* 19 (1991): 73. Here Marsh cites his doctoral dissertation, "Crime and the Press: Does Newspaper Coverage Support Myths About Crime and Law Enforcement?" Sam Houston State University, Huntsville, Texas.

99 **"The more newspapers print"**: Linda Heath, "Impact of Newspaper Crime Reports on Fear of Crime," *Journal of Personality and Social Psychology* 47 (2) (1984).

100 **Jennifer Levin stories**: "Girl's Slaying Suspect: Sex Play 'Got Rough,'"

*New York Daily News,* August 28, 1986, and "How Jennifer Courted Death," *New York Daily News,* August 29, 1986.

100 **"Making love" Levin story**: Murray Weiss, "Caught 'Em in the Act," *New York Daily News,* September 2, 1986. I played a small role in the Levin coverage. Anthea Disney, a *Daily News* editor from Great Britain who later would move to key positions in the Rupert Murdoch media empire, assigned me to spend a Friday evening drinking and posing as a preppy at the Manhattan bar where Levin and Chambers had been before the slaying. It wasn't much of a story; the place was empty except for a few other people who looked suspiciously like reporters posing as preppies.

100 **"Suggesting reasons"**: Ellen Levin, "Twice Wounded," *Media Studies Journal* (Winter 1992), 47. For a detailed account of the press coverage of the Levin slaying see also Helen Benedict, *Virgin or Vamp: How the Press Covers Sex Crimes* (New York: Oxford University Press, 1992).

104 **"Crime news is mutually"**: Mark Fishman, "Police News: Constructing an Image of Crime," *Urban Life* 9 (January 1981): 371–94.

104 **"I think that many"**: Tom Hallman Jr., interview with author, October 1996.

105 **"Every now and then"**: Lincoln Steffens, *The Autobiography of Lincoln Steffens* (New York: Harcourt, Brace, 1931), 285.

106 **"It is doubtful"**: Mark Fishman, "Crime Waves as Ideology," *Social Problems* 25 (June 1978): 531–43.

107 **"Know-nothing approach"**: Lotz, *Crime and the American Press*, 63, 68–69.

108 **Prison inmate report**: The study was conducted over twelve years by a "think tank" of inmates at Green Haven Correctional Facility in Stormsville, New York. The New York City neighborhoods are Bedford-Stuyvesant, Brownsville, and East New York, all in Brooklyn; Harlem and the Lower East Side in Manhattan; the South Bronx, and South Jamaica, Queens.

108 **Drug, nonviolent felon percentages**: The statistics cited were compiled by the Correctional Association of New York based upon information from the New York State Department of Correctional Services.

109 **"Vowing to drive"**: Heidi Evans, "New War on Drugs," *New York Daily News,* March 2, 1988.

110 **State drug sentences**: New York State Department of Correctional Services.

118 **Famous *Daily News* headline**: "Ford to City: Drop Dead," *New York Daily News,* October 30, 1975.

118 **"Toots and Caspar"**: Simon Michael Bessie, *Jazz Journalism: The Story of Tabloid Newspapers* (New York: Russell & Russell, 1938), 15.

119 **"Who're you"**: This and other dialogue in this chapter are approximations based upon my recollections, not written notes.

120 **"Dumping" notes to another reporter**: This was a common practice at the *Daily News* that might bear a bit of explanation. It was one of the last newspapers in the United States to widely employ the old-fashioned system of "legmen" who worked out on the streets and a "rewrite desk," a bank of writers who sat before keyboards in the main office.

126 **"Like a frozen piece"**: Joseph McNamara, "Crime Was His Passion," *New York Daily News*, November 6, 1987.

131 **"I didn't want"**: Tom Weber, "Crime Reporter Leaves Seamy City for Maine Living," *Bangor Daily News*, February 6, 1987.


## 5. The Crime Policy Follies

137 **Current events analysis**: Pew Research Center for the People and the Press, "Times Mirror News Interest Index: 1989–1995," Washington, D.C., December 1995. (The Times Mirror Center for the People and the Press became the Pew Research Center on January 1, 1996.)

137 **"Not surprisingly"**: Ibid.

138 **"Most politicians can"**: Edwin Ellis, interview with the author, October 1995. See also James S. Kunen, "Annals of Justice: Teaching Prisoners a Lesson," *New Yorker*, July 10, 1995.

138 **"Over the years"**: Robert Elias, "Official Stories: Media Coverage of American Crime Policy," *Humanist* 54 (January–February 1994).

139 **"Building more prisons"**: Robert Gangi, interview with author, February 1993.

139 **"It's a matter of the politicians"**: Burton Roberts, interview with author, March 1997.

140 **"It is pretty certain"**: Lawrence M. Friedman, *Crime and Punishment in American History* (New York: Basic Books, 1993), 15.

140 **"It just doesn't"**: Quoted in Edna McConnell Clark Foundation, "Americans Behind Bars," New York, 1992.

140 **Judges on mandatory sentences**: The Gallup Poll, commissioned by the American Bar Association and conducted in the summer of 1993, included responses from 350 state and 49 federal judges.

140 **Kennedy and Rehnquist quotations**: Cited in David B. Koepel, "Prison Blues: How America's Foolish Sentencing Policies Endanger Public Safety," Cato Institute, Washington, D.C., May 17, 1994.

140 **Costly, ineffective sentencing policy**: U.S. Sentencing Commission, "Drugs and Violence," Washington, D.C., 1993.

140 **International incarceration rates**: William DiMascio, "Seeking Justice," Edna McConnell Clark Foundation, New York, 1995.

140 **Racial incarceration disparities**: Bureau of Justice Statistics, U.S. Department of Justice, "Prisoners in 1994," Washington, D.C., 1995. The rate of incarceration was nearly 1,500 per 100,000 residents for blacks and about 200 per 100,000 for whites.

140 **Black men in Baltimore**: Jerome Miller, "Hobbling a Generation: Young African-American Males in the Criminal Justice System of America's Cities; Baltimore, Maryland," National Center on Institutions and Alternatives, Alexandria, Va., 1992.

141 **New York drug offenders**: New York State Department of Correctional Services.

141 **Black drug use, arrests**: U.S. Department of Health and Human Services, "Preliminary Estimates from the 1993 Household Survey on Drug Abuse," Washington, D.C., July 1994.

141 **Crack use, arrests**: U.S. Sentencing Commission, 1995.

141 **Percentage of low-level drug offenders**: Bureau of Justice Statistics, U.S. Department of Justice, "Prisoners in 1994," Washington, D.C., 1995.

141 **Studies on inmate education, employment**: See, for example, Richard Tewsbury, "Literacy Programming for Jail Inmates: Reflections and Recommendations from One Program," *Prison Journal* (December 1994).

142 **Juveniles with relatives incarcerated**: Bureau of Justice Statistics, Office of Justice Programs, U.S. Department of Justice, *National Update* 1 (4) (April 1992): 7.

142 **Black state inmates with a family member incarcerated**: Bureau of Justice Statistics, Office of Justice Programs, U.S. Department of Justice, "Survey of State Prison Inmates, 1991," Washington, D.C., March 1993, p. 9.

142 **"We'll divert the white"**: Jerome Miller, interview with author, March 1996.

144 **America's violent history**: For comprehensive accounts of violence in the United States, see Lawrence M. Friedman, *Crime and Punishment in American History* (New York: Basic Books, 1993), and Fox Butterfield, *All God's Children: The Bosket Family and the American Tradition of Violence* (New York: Avon, 1995).

144 **Use of handguns by criminals**: Franklin E. Zimring, "Gun Control," undated report for the National Institute of Justice, U.S. Department of Justice; Bureau of Justice Statistics, U.S. Department of Justice, "Crime in the United States, 1993," Washington, D.C., December 1994, p. 18; and Bureau of Justice Statistics, Office of Justice Programs, U.S. Department of Justice, "Survey of State Prison Inmates, 1991," Washington, D.C., March 1993, pp. 18–19.

144 **American criminal justice history**: Historical background comes from a number of sources, including Friedman, *Crime and Punishment*, and Thomas E. Cronin, Tania Z. Cronin, Michael E. Milakovich, *U.S. v. Crime in the Streets* (Bloomington: Indiana University Press, 1981).

145 **"The most malign"**: Cronin, Cronin, and Milakovich, *U.S. v. Crime*, 28.

145 **"The very heart of"**: Friedman, *Crime and Punishment*, 274.

146 **"Crime is a sore"**: Ibid.

146 **"I will not be"**: Cronin, Cronin, and Milakovich, *U.S. v. Crime*, 29.

146 **"Looked too much"**: Cronin, Cronin, and Milakovich, *U.S. v. Crime*, 29.

147 **"Crime-breeding ghettos"**: Ibid., 36

147 **Hoover, Whittaker quotations**: Ibid., 35, 33.

148 **"I want to make"**: Ibid., 32.

149 **"If every recommendation"**: President's Commission on Law Enforcement and Administration of Justice, *The Challenge of Crime in a Free Society* (Washington, D.C.: U.S. Government Printing Office; New York: Avon, 1968). (The report was published a year after its release.)

149 **"If there had been"**: Cronin, Cronin, and Milakovich, *U.S. v. Crime*, 26.

149 *Look* **interview excerpt**: Warren Rogers, "The Chairman of the National Crime Commission Answers Some Tough Questions About Crime," *Look,* March 7, 1967.

153 **History of punishment**: Information about the history of punishment comes from a number of sources, including John A. Garraty and Peter Gay, eds., *The Columbia History of the World* (New York: Harper & Row, 1981); and Friedman, *Crime and Punishment*.

153 **"Who so sheddeth"**: Gen. 9:6.

154 **"Beaumont and De Tocqueville"**: Friedman, *Crime and Punishment*, 80.

156 **"The field of penology"**: Robert Martinson, "What Works? Questions and Answers About Prison Reform," *Public Interest* 35 (Spring 1974).

157 **"With few and isolated exceptions"**: Ibid.

157 **Martinson report**: The article from *The Public Interest* was published in longer form as a book entitled *The Effectiveness of Correctional Treatment* (New York: Praeger, 1975), coauthored by Douglas S. Lipton and Judith Wilks.

157 **"It may be that"**: Martinson, "What Works?"

158 **"Offend the moral order"**: Ibid.

158 **Martinson suicide**: One of Martinson's coauthors on the study, Wilks, also met a tragic end. She had a mental breakdown, turned to living on the streets in New York City, and disappeared during the 1980s. The third coauthor, Lipton, works as a criminologist in New York.

158 **"In his earlier writings"**: Miller interview. See also Rick Szykowny, "No

Justice, No Peace: An Interview with Jerome Miller," *Humanist* (January–February 1994).

158 **"Was a more massive"**: Lyndon B. Johnson, *The Vantage Point* (New York: Holt, Rinehart and Winston, 1971), 355.

158 **"Five years later"**: James Vorenberg, "The War on Crime: The First Five Years," *Atlantic Monthly,* May 1972, pp. 63–69.

159 **"It requires not merely optimistic"**: James Q. Wilson, *Thinking About Crime* (New York: Basic Books, 1975), 170.

160 **John Lynch case**: Friedman recounts the case in *Crime and Punishment*, 306–307.

160 **"They [the opposition] feared"**: Albert J. Lipson and Mark A. Peterson, "California Justice Under Determinate Sentencing: A Review and Agenda for Research," Rand Corp., Santa Monica, California, June 1980.

160 **"Public attitudes"**: Ibid.

160 **"Politically it's never bad"**: Ibid.

161 **Sentencing legislation in the 94th Congress**: Joan Petersilia and Peter W. Greenwood, "Mandatory Prison Sentences: Their Projected Effects on Crime and Prison Populations," Rand Corp., Santa Monica, California, 1977.

161 **"Contrary to what one might imagine"**: *Congressional Record,* September 23, 1970.

162 **"There is mounting public distress"**: Petersilia and Greenwood, "Mandatory Prison Sentences."

163 **California prison populations**: Lipson and Peterson, "California Justice."

163 **Often-cited study about crime reduction**: Morgan O. Reynolds, "Why Does Crime Pay?" National Center for Policy Analysis, policy backgrounder no. 123, Dallas, December 8, 1992.

163 **Young black men in prison, college**: Andrea Ford, "Prison Life, Parole Touch High Level of Young Blacks," *Los Angeles Times,* November 2, 1990.

164 **California prison projections**: For a full account of past and future trends in California, see Joan Petersilia, "Crime and Punishment in California: Full Cells, Empty Pockets, and Questionable Benefits," chap. 7 in James B. Steinberg, David W. Lyon, and Mary E. Vaiana, eds., *Urban America: Policy Choices for Los Angeles and the Nation* (Santa Monica, Calif.: Rand, 1992).

164 **"Rather than simply continuing"**: Paul Robinson, "Dissenting View of Commissioner Paul H. Robinson on the Promulgation of Sentencing Guidelines by the United States Sentencing Commission," U.S. Government Printing Office, Washington, D.C., May 1, 1987.

165 **Early-release credit**: The legislative mandate that convicts must serve 85 percent of their sentence before achieving parole eligibility became known by polit-

ical slogan as "truth in sentencing." It was an extremely popular tough-on-crime bromide during the mid-1990s and was widely adapted by federal and state legislators.

165 **"These guidelines may well"**: Robinson, "Dissenting View."

165 **"I, as a sitting lifetime judge"**: Neil Steinberg, "The Law of Unintended
Consequences," *Rolling Stone,* May 5, 1994.

166 **Drug offenders in prison**: In an interview with the *Connecticut Law Tribune* ("Barr: Clinton Administration Soft on Crime; Former Attorney General Hits
Administration for Root-Causes Rhetoric, Going AWOL on Drug War," August 23,
1993), William Barr, the U.S. attorney general under George Bush, had his own take
on drug sentences:

> The notion that there are sympathetic people out there who become
> hapless victims of the criminal justice system and are locked away in
> federal prison beyond the time they deserve is simply a myth. The peo-
> ple who have been given mandatory minimums generally deserve
> them—richly. This country has spent a decade trying to get across two
> essential messages: First, that we have a tough federal criminal-justice
> system—if you do the crime, you'll do the time. Second, that par-
> ticipating in drug trafficking is morally reprehensible. Backpedaling on
> mandatory minimums subverts these messages at just the wrong time.

167 **Florida prison population, budget projections**: Don Boyett, "Tough
Prison Laws Will Cost Big Bucks," *Orlando Sentinel,* January 18, 1996.

167 **"The only way"**: Bill McCollum, "Needed: A Federal-State Partnership for
Regional Prisons," *USA Today, the Magazine of the Society for the Advancement of Education,* May 1994.

167 **"Today, more communities"**: David A. Levy, "Violent Criminals Must
Stay in Prison," *USA Today, the Magazine of the Society for the Advancement of Education,*
May 1994.

168 **Gingrich drug execution idea**: Associated Press, "Gingrich Suggests
Tough Drug Measure," *New York Times,* August 26, 1995. The Gingrich idea might be
viewed as one way to help the United States return to its traditional values, because
public executions were the rule through the first half of the nineteenth century.
Some local jurisdictions charged admission and issued tickets. In 1827 an oversub-
scribed viewing stand collapsed at an execution in Cooperstown, New York, and two
people—beyond the intended—were killed. That same year an estimated thirty
thousand people turned out for the hanging of Jesse Strang, a farmhand who murdered a prominent businessman, in Albany, New York, according to Friedman in
*Crime and Punishment.*

170 **Education and recidivism**: Edna McConnell Clark Foundation, "Seeking Justice: Crime and Punishment in America," New York, 1995.

170 **"Overwhelming support"**: Reuters, "Calif. Assembly Rejects Graffiti Paddling Bill," January 31, 1996.

170 **"The perception that prison life"**: Brent Staples, "The Chain Gang Show," *New York Times Sunday Magazine,* September 17, 1995.

170 **"After working 12 hours"**: Reuters, "California Legislator Proposes Chain Gangs," January 16, 1996.

170 **"In his recent letter"**: Karen Semelson, "Inmates Should Stop Complaining," letter to the editor, *Daily Star* (Oneonta, N.Y.), January 19, 1996.

172 **"The dimension of the problem"**: Joseph F. Sullivan, "P.B.A. Hails Degnan's Urban-Crime Plan," *New York Times,* December 7, 1980.

172 **"We are going to take back the streets"**: United Press International, "L.A. Gangs Still Control the Streets," July 12, 1981.

173 **"The latest in a series"**: Susan Seager, United Press International, "Police Announce Retake the Streets Anti-Drug Push," *Los Angeles Times,* June 27, 1985.

173 **Comments by Carroll and Bouza**: Public Broadcasting Service, *The MacNeil-Lehrer NewsHour,* April 22, 1986.

175 **"It is vital"**: Joan Petersilia, *Urban America: Policy Choices for Los Angeles and the Nation*, ed. James B. Steinberg, David W. Lyon, and Mary E. Vaiana (Santa Monica, Calif: Rand, 1992), 199.

175 **"The American people are ill-served"**: Peter W. Greenwood, "Some Plain Truths About Curbing Crime," *Rand Research Review* (spring 1995).

177 **Alcohol arrests in New York**: Christopher E. Stone, interview with author, February 1997.

178 **"Nothing short of a national disgrace"**: Bob Dole, speech at Palos Park, Illinois, August 25, 1996, as transcribed by Federal News Service.

## 6. Telling the Truth Less Poorly

180 **Comparison of U.S. incarceration rate**: The Group of Seven countries are Canada, France, Germany, Italy, Japan, England, and the United States.

180 **"If you believe"**: Bernard Kalb, panelist, "America Through the TV Looking Glass," Alfred I. duPont Forum, Columbia University, New York City, January 26, 1995.

181 **"In our hearts"**: Hedrick Smith, panelist, "Declining Standards in News: Is It All Television's Fault?" Alfred I. duPont Forum, Columbia University, New York City, January 27, 1994.

181 **"Many newspapers seem"**: Eugene L. Roberts Jr., speech to the National Press Club, Washington, D.C., November 5, 1993.

181 **"Right now what we're seeing"**: Walter Cronkite, panelist, National Association of College Broadcasters Conference, Brown University, Providence, Rhode Island, November 19, 1988.

181 **"We are moving"**: Carl Bernstein, speech to Southern Newspaper Publishers Association, as reported in George Garneau, "Trash Journalism," *Editor & Publisher* (October 29, 1994).

183 **"The rules haven't changed"**: Scott Higham, interview with author, March 1996.

183 **"I've seen a sea change"**: Jerome Miller, interview with author, March 1996.

184 **Quorum on journalism's problems**: One exception is Allen Neuharth, retired chairman of Gannett, the large U.S. newspaper chain that owns *USA Today* and more than one hundred other papers. During the duPont conference on news standards at Columbia University in 1994, Neuharth argued against the premise of the gathering. He said, "Overstating the case and drawing intellectually dishonest conclusions are bad. . . . Let us not convict the news media before the evidence has been gathered, let alone evaluated."

184 **"Sour grapes"**: Alicia Shepard, "Going to Extremes," *American Journalism Review* (October 1996).

184 **"We are going to be loathed"**: Anna Quindlen, "Talking About the Media Circus," *New York Times Sunday Magazine,* June 26, 1994.

184 **"We work a different side"**: Jerry Nachman, panelist, "Why Everyone Hates the Media," annual conference of the American Society of Magazine Editors, New York, April 11, 1995.

184 **"The judge has to look out"**: Chip Rowe, "Off the Record," *American Journalism Review* (January–February 1996).

185 **"For better or worse"**: David Bartlett, "Bad News: Viewers Like It," *American Journalism Review* (September 1993).

185 *Newsweek* **story about Bush and crime**: "Clark Kent, Please Call Your Office," *Newsweek,* February 27, 1989, Periscope: National Affairs.

188 **"Nobody knows how bad"**: David C. Anderson, "How Bad Is Crime? No One Knows," *New York Times,* October 5, 1981.

189 **"The excess is inherently unsustainable"**: Paul Klite, interview with author, March 1997.

189 **"Not feeling very good"**: Josef Adalian, "The Changing Face of Talk," *New York Post,* January 4, 1996.

189 **"Keep in mind"**: Ibid.

190 **"The fact is"**: Richard Huff, "'Sleazy Does It' Still Daytime's Motto," *New York Daily News,* February 27, 1997.

190 **"Over the decades"**: Ted Gest, "Popgun Politics," *U.S. News &World Report,* September 30, 1996.

192 **"For two years"**: Liz Chandler and Gary L. Wright, "Hope Amid Despair," *Charlotte Observer,* December 3, 1995.

193 **"Crime was an increasing problem"**: Jim Walser, interview with author, February 1997.

194 **"We still cover crime"**: Cathy McFeaters, interview with author, October 1996.

197 **"I think there's a solution"**: Quindlen, "Talking About the Media Circus."